# THE ROLE AND FUTURE OF DIGITAL ECONOMY AGREEMENTS IN DEVELOPING ASIA AND THE PACIFIC

Edited by Pramila Crivelli and Rolando Avendano

MAY 2025

ASIAN DEVELOPMENT BANK

ADB

6 ADB Avenue, Mandaluyong City, 1550 Metro Manila, Philippines
Tel +63 2 8632 4444; Fax +63 2 8636 2444
www.adb.org



ISBN 978-92-9277-293-2 (print); 978-92-9277-294-9 (PDF); 978-92-9277-295-6 (ebook)
Publication Stock No. TCS250153-2
DOI: http://dx.doi.org/10.22617/TCS250153-2



Notes:
In this publication, "$" refers to United States dollars.
ADB recognizes "China" as the People's Republic of China; "Hong Kong" as Hong Kong, China; "Korea" as the Republic of Korea; "United Kingdom of Great Britain and Northern Ireland" as the United Kingdom; "United States of America" and "America" as the United States; and "Vietnam" as Viet Nam.

Cover design by Michael Cortes.

# Contents

# Tables, Figures, and Boxes

**Tables**



**Figures**

**Boxes**

# Foreword

In an era when digital transformation accelerates at an unprecedented rate, digital economy agreements (DEAs) have gained vital importance for Asia and the Pacific. The rapid development of information and communication technologies has reshaped the global economy, altering trade dynamics and encouraging new approaches to regulatory frameworks. This edited volume reflects the commitment of the Asian Development Bank (ADB) to supporting its members in navigating these transformative changes and contributing to a more inclusive and resilient digital economy and trade.

This volume is both a product of and a contribution to ADB's broader efforts to advance digital trade and regulatory cooperation in the region. It draws insights from two complementary technical assistance projects. The first, *Unpacking the Implementation "Black Box,"* delves into the practical challenges of identifying institutional gaps, mapping regulatory processes and putting into practice digital regulations. The second, *Measuring the Impact of Digital Regulatory Cooperation,* explores methodologies and metrics to assess the effectiveness of digital trade rules and their practical outcomes. This volume consolidates early findings to lay a foundation for future research and dialogue on digital trade and regulations.

The volume is structured to provide an accessible, in-depth view of digital regulatory cooperation, examining topics that range from the foundations of DEAs to more advanced regulatory issues. It serves as a guide for understanding the institutional frameworks, policy needs, and operational processes involved in the adoption of digital regulations. While it provides valuable groundwork, this volume is not an end point. Instead, it marks a key milestone of a broader effort to bridge the gap between the formal language of DEAs and their practical application. It also highlights the need to align digital trade rules with regulations in other areas. More specifically, the chapters cover five core topics: regional trends in digital regulations, Digital Economy Performance Agreement (DEPA) provisions, digital standards, cross-border payments and Central Bank Digital Currencies (CBDCs), and digital taxation. By addressing these challenges, the volume aims to equip policymakers, industry leaders, and other stakeholders with the tools to navigate the demands and challenges of digital trade agreements effectively.

The diversity in economic and digital development across Asia and the Pacific underscores the importance of adaptable and inclusive approaches to digital trade. Leading adopters of DEAs offer valuable lessons, while emerging economies provide insights into the challenges of implementation. This volume highlights these diverse perspectives, offering initial solutions and guidance to harmonize digital rules and strengthen cooperation across borders.

Looking ahead, we strongly believe in the immense economic potential of unified approaches to digital trade and regulatory cooperation. This volume, alongside ADB's ongoing projects, aims to foster informed policymaking and support inclusive growth in the digital age. By balancing depth and breadth in the issues it explores, and through the different angles it takes, the volume seeks to engage a wide spectrum of audiences. We hope this work contributes to a shared understanding of digital regulatory cooperation and its practical challenges and opportunities, serving as a vital resource for building a more cohesive and sustainable digital economy in Asia and the Pacific.

**Bruce Gosper**
Vice-President for Administration
and Corporate Management
Asian Development Bank

# Acknowledgments

The editorial team would like to thank all contributors to this book volume: Stephanie Honey (Honey Consulting), Henry Gao (National University of Singapore), Martin Chorzempa (Peterson Institute of International Economics), Jooyoung Kwak (Yonsei University), Heejin Lee (Yonsei University), Julien Chaisse (City University of Hong Kong), Rolando Avendano (ADB), Pramila Crivelli (ADB) and Edgar Hovhannisyan (ADB).

This volume was prepared with support from the Regional Cooperation and Integration Division of the Economic Research and Development Impact Department of the Asian Development Bank (ADB) under the overall supervision of Jong Woo Kang, Director, Regional Cooperation and Integration Division. The concept of the edited volume benefited from inputs from Jong Woo Kang (ADB), and Cyn-Young Park, Executive Director, South East Asian Central Banks (SEACEN) Research and Training Centre. The editors are also thankful for the initial discussions and suggestions provided by Bernard Hoekman (European University Institute [EUI]), Martina Ferracane (EUI), Janos Ferencz (Organisation for Economic Co-operation and Development [OECD]), Javier Lopez-Gonzalez (OECD), Rupa Chanda (United Nations Economic and Social Commission for Asia and the Pacific), Kijin Kim (ADB), and the participants of key workshops and events, including the Central Asia Regional Economic Cooperation Program (CAREC) Digital Trade Forum 2024, the EUI–OECD–United Nations Economic Commission for Latin America and the Caribbean (ECLAC) Conference on Building a Competitive Regulatory Environment 2023, and events conducted as part of the preparation and dissemination of the "Aid For Trade in Asia and the Pacific Report" and the "Asian Economic Integration Report" 2022.

The volume was supported by ADB's technical assistance project, Digital Regulatory Cooperation: Unpacking the Implementation "Black Box" – A Mapping of Regulatory Practices, Degrees of Implementation and Practical Gaps (Technical Assistance 10032), financed by the Republic of Korea e-Asia and Knowledge Partnership Fund. Paulo Rodelio Halili oversaw the production of the volume. James Unwin edited the manuscript, and Michael Cortes typeset and produced the layout, and created the cover design. Monina Gamboa proofread the report, while Levi Lusterio did the page proof checking. Amiel Bryan Esperanza provided administrative and secretarial support. The editorial team, likewise, acknowledges the printing and publishing support by the Printing Services Unit of ADB's Corporate Services Department and the publishing team of the Department of Communications and Knowledge Management.

# Authors

**Pramila Crivelli** is an economist at the Regional Cooperation and Integration Division, Economic Research and Development Impact Department of the Asian Development Bank (ADB).

**Rolando Avendano** is an economist at the Regional Cooperation and Integration Division, Economic Research and Cooperation Department of ADB.

**Edgar Hovhannisyan** is an international consultant and economic research analyst at the Regional Cooperation and Integration Division, Economic Research and Cooperation Department of ADB.

**Stephanie Honey** is the Managing Director of Honey Consulting and a former trade negotiator with expertise in international trade, digital and services trade, and regional economic integration. She advises governments, international organizations, and the private sector.

**Henry Gao** is a professor of law at the Singapore Management University specializing in digital trade and e-commerce. He also serves as a senior fellow at the Centre for International Governance Innovation.

**Jooyoung Kwak** is a professor of international business at Yonsei University School of Business. Her research focuses on nontariff barriers, digital trade, and sustainable development.

**Heejin Lee** is a professor at the Graduate School of International Studies, Yonsei University. He specializes in ICT for Development, digital standardization, and innovation in developing countries.

**Martin Chorzempa** is a senior fellow at the Peterson Institute for International Economics, focusing on financial technology and digital currencies. He is the author of *The Cashless Revolution: China's Reinvention of Money*.

**Julien Chaisse** is a professor of law at the City University of Hong Kong. He specializes in international economic law, cyberlaw, and dispute resolution and serves as editor for leading academic journals.

# Abbreviations

| | |
|---|---|
| ADB | Asian Development Bank |
| AI | artificial intelligence |
| AML/CFT | anti-money laundering/combating the financing of terrorism |
| ASDEA | Australia–Singapore Digital Economy Agreement |
| ASEAN | Association of Southeast Asian Nations |
| BEPS | base erosion and profit shifting |
| BIS | Bank for International Settlements |
| CBDC | Central Bank Digital Currency |
| CBPR | Cross-Border Privacy Rules |
| CEN | European Committee for Standardization |
| CENELE | European Committee for Electrotechnical Standardization |
| CEPA | Comprehensive Economic Partnership Agreement |
| PRC | People's Republic of China |
| CHIPS | Clearing House Interbank Payment System |
| CPTPP | Comprehensive and Progressive Agreement for Trans-Pacific Partnership |
| CSA-IoT | Cloud Security Alliance-Internet of Things |
| DEA | digital economy agreement |
| DEPA | Digital Economy Partnership Agreement |
| DST | digital service tax |
| DSTRI | Digital Services Trade Restrictiveness Index |
| EFTA | European Free Trade Area |
| EPA | economic partnership agreement |
| ETSI | European Telecommunications Standards Institute |
| EU | European Union |
| FATF | Financial Action Task Force |

| | |
|---|---|
| FPS | faster payment system |
| FSB | Financial Stability Board |
| FTA | free trade agreement |
| G20 | Group of Twenty |
| GATS | General Agreement on Trade in Services |
| GATT | General Agreement on Tariffs and Trade |
| GDP | gross domestic product |
| GDPR | General Data Protection Regulation |
| GloBE | Global Anti-Base Erosion |
| ICT | information and communication technology |
| IEC | International Electrotechnical Commission |
| IIA | International Investment Agreement |
| IMF | International Monetary Fund |
| IoT | Internet of Things |
| ISO | International Organization for Standardization |
| ITU | International Telecommunication Union |
| JSI | Joint Statement Initiative |
| KSDPA | Korea–Singapore Digital Partnership Agreement |
| KYC | Know Your Customer |
| Lao PDR | Lao People's Democratic Republic |
| LDC | least developed country |
| MAS | Monetary Authority of Singapore |
| MFA | multifactor authentication |
| MLETR | Model Law on Electronic Transferable Records |
| MNE | multinational enterprise |
| MSMEs | micro, small, and medium-sized enterprises |
| NGO | nongovernment organization |
| OECD | Organisation for Economic Co-operation and Development |
| RCEP | Regional Comprehensive Economic Partnership |
| RegTech | regulatory technology |
| RTA | regional trade agreement |
| RTGS | real-time gross settlement |
| SMEs | small and medium-sized enterprises |
| SWIFT | Society for Worldwide Interbank Financial Telecommunications |
| TAPED | Trade Agreements Provisions on Electronic Commerce and Data |
| TPP | Trans-Pacific Partnership |
| TPSEP | Trans-Pacific Strategic Economic Partnership Agreement |
| TUAC | Trade Union Advisory Committee |

| | |
|---|---|
| UNCITRAL | United Nations Commission on International Trade Law |
| UNCTAD | United Nations Conference on Trade and Development |
| UNDP | United Nations Development Programme |
| UPI | Unified Payments Interface |
| US | United States |
| USJDTA | US–Japan Digital Trade Agreement |
| USMCA | United States–Mexico–Canada Agreement |
| VAT | value-added tax |
| W3C | World Wide Web Consortium |
| WTO | World Trade Organization |

# Introduction

The coronavirus disease (COVID-19) pandemic was a massive shock to global logistics systems and supply chains. It severely impacted most traditional forms of international trade, and some were halted under the elevated uncertainty and restrictive government measures. In response, digital forms of trade in goods and services came to the rescue (Figure I.1). Going digital in many cases raised survival chances and brought a buffer for adjustment to the rest of the economy. Recognizing the huge potential of digital trade for Asia and the Pacific, and aiming to facilitate a smooth adjustment process, the Asian Development Bank (ADB) dedicated several reports to digital trade, digital services trade and aid for trade.[1] These put special emphasis on the role of digitalization for services trade in the Asia and Pacific region. Most of this research was produced in the aftermath of the pandemic when most countries in the region were still wrestling with the aftershocks of the initial turmoil.

A few years forward, rapid development of information and communication technology (ICT) does not seem to be showing signs of slowing. Recent breakthroughs in generative artificial intelligence (AI) and related fields calmly remind us that once in a while the pace of technological advance will surprise, regardless of how fast we try to adjust our expectations. And whereas we, as a society, are slow to internalize important discussions on the implications of these advancements, economic life cycles of services and goods react much faster. In the constant search for economic returns, economic actors instantly spot and absorb the opportunities. A wide

[1] Asian Development Bank (ADB). 2022a. *Asian Economic Integration Report 2022: Advancing Digital Services Trade in Asia and the Pacific*; ADB. 2022b. *Aid for Trade in Asia and the Pacific: Leveraging Trade and Digital Agreements for Sustainable Development*; ADB. 2022c. *Unlocking the Potential of Digital Services Trade in Asia and the Pacific*; ADB. 2023. Building an Information-Sharing Mechanism to Boost Regulatory Frameworks on Cross-Border Data Flows. *T20 Policy Briefs*. May 2023.

**Figure I.1: Trade in Goods, Services, and Digital Services in Asia and the Pacific**
(2005 = 100)

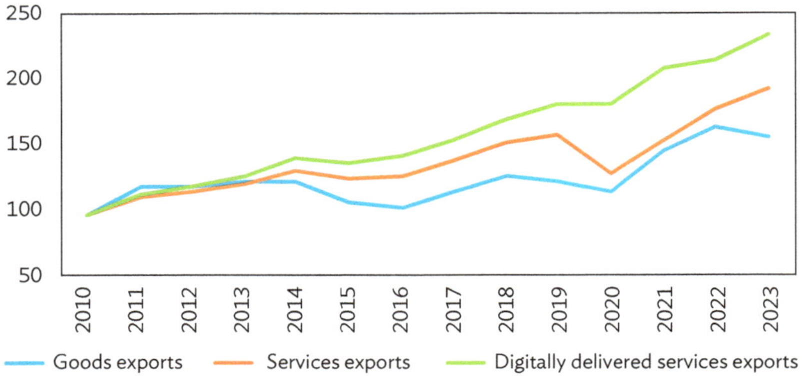


Source: Asian Development Bank calculations using World Trade Organization-United Nations Conference on Trade (accessed November 2024).

spectrum of tech-enabled solutions, packaged under the term digitalization and more broadly Industry 4.0, are now central to the global economy through different channels—a process with historic roots and boosted by the pandemic. Post-pandemic, reality has only further strengthened the irreversible shift toward more digitalized life and economic relations. Trends in digital transformation can be tracked through multiple measures and indicators, such as increased connectivity access, bandwidth usage, digital skills, and ICT integration in business processes (Figure I.2).

These advancements affect digital trade from both the demand and supply sides. For example, increasing access to the internet, with 67% of the global population connected in 2023 (International Communication Union 2024), has secured a consumer base for digital solutions such as e-commerce, mobile fund transfers, e-healthcare, e-finance, and online education. On the other hand, integration of advanced digital technologies into manufacturing and supply chains is reshaping how goods and services are produced and delivered globally. Technologies such as AI, the Internet of Things (IoT), advanced robotics, cloud computing, and blockchain drastically boost productivity and efficiency, allow for digital management, production, and delivery of a wide range of services and goods that are creating economic opportunities not seen before.

**Figure I.2: Number of Internet Users**
(billions)

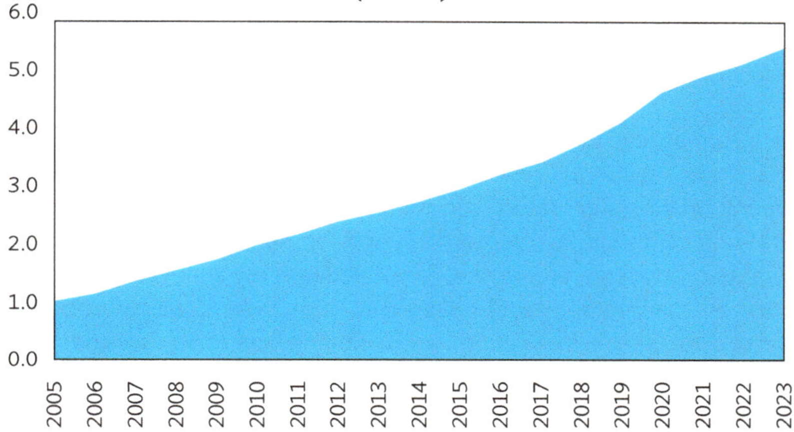


Source: International Telecommunication Union (ITU) (accessed 6 September 2024).

As the impact of digitalization continues, more research is being done to explore their effects and the regulatory challenges they bring. Different studies have looked at various aspects of this changing landscape, offering useful insights into how digital technologies, trade, and regulation interact.

For instance, restrictions on digital services not only impact the services sector, but extend to manufacturing exports.[2] Indeed, more stringent digital policies can create barriers to cross-border trade in both goods and services.

These findings underscore the need for more balanced regulatory frameworks that allow innovation without compromising security or privacy. Evidence suggests that stricter data localization and transfer policies can deter digital exports,[3] increase operational costs and reduce innovation.[4] The current landscape of digital trade regulations also underscores how overlapping standards can complicate cross-border digital activity, and the importance of more convergent initiatives, such as the Joint Statement Initiative (JSI)

2 Yang, F., Y. Wang, and U. Whang. 2024. Trade restrictions on digital services and the impact on manufacturing exports. *The Journal of International Trade and Economic Development.* 33(4). pp. 523–550.

3 Gupta, S., P. Ghosh, and V. Sridhar. 2022. Impact of data trade restrictions on IT services export: A cross-country analysis. *Telecommunications Policy.* 46(9). 102403; and Van der Marel, E. and M.F. Ferracane. 2021. Do data policy restrictions inhibit trade in services? *Review of World Economics.* 157(4). pp. 727–776.

4 Cory, N. and L. Dascoli. 2021. *How barriers to cross-border data flows are spreading globally, what they cost, and how to address them.* Information Technology and Innovation Foundation.

at the World Trade Organization (WTO).[5] It is, therefore, important to continue mapping the regulatory landscape, identifying commonalities in cross-border data transfer regulations, and emerging areas of convergence. This offers a potential pathway toward more predictable and transparent data transfer rules that can support global trade.

These studies give only a glimpse of the growing body of research on how digital trade, regulatory issues, data restrictions, security, and international cooperation are interrelated, and the opportunities and challenges digital trade is facing today. A common finding is emerging: while advancements in digital technology create new possibilities for global trade, regulatory barriers—especially those related to data—can pose significant obstacles. Harmonizing these regulations and finding common ground across jurisdictions is increasingly important as the digital economy grows and evolves.

The current edited volume is a natural continuation of ADB's efforts to contribute to the research and search for solutions to these challenges. The primary aim is to facilitate focused discussion around the status and future of digital trade and emerging regulatory challenges, globally and within Asia and the Pacific.

However, several trends define today's economic context. Geopolitical tensions, strengthening deglobalization signals, and a gradual reversal toward more self-sufficiency complicate the path to an efficient regulatory cooperation. The pandemic and Russia's war in Ukraine were key turning points, where countries realized that existing supply chains were overly cost-optimized and started to prioritize resilience in sourcing, improved responsiveness to demand, a focus on national security, and even risk environmental concerns in favor of shortening some parts of supply chains. Add shadow trade wars between major powerhouses exercising the agility of gray zones in the WTO and other transnational trade agreements, and we can easily describe the current state of affairs as a golden opportunity wrapped in thorns. Collectively achieving regulatory coherence for the digital trade has never been so rewarding, yet it is as hard as ever to do so, given the fragmented nature of regulatory space in the world. Even focusing only on Asia and the Pacific, we can still observe a high degree of heterogeneity across different countries' approaches to digital regulatory frameworks (Figure I.3).

[5] Casalini, F., J.L. González, and T. Nemoto. 2021. Mapping commonalities in regulatory approaches to cross-border data transfers.

**Figure I.3: Digital Services Trade Restrictiveness Index Heterogeneity Index for Asia and the Pacific, 2022**

| | Partner | | | | | | | | | | | | | | | | | | |
|---|---|---|---|---|---|---|---|---|---|---|---|---|---|---|---|---|---|---|---|
| **Reporter** | AUS | JPN | ROK | NZL | BRN | KHM | PRC | IND | IDN | KAZ | LAO | MYS | NPL | PAK | PHL | SGP | THA | VUT | VNM |
| AUS | | 0.02 | 0.22 | 0.08 | 0.29 | 0.34 | 0.37 | 0.32 | 0.29 | 0.47 | 0.40 | 0.11 | 0.22 | 0.35 | 0.11 | 0.26 | 0.08 | 0.18 | 0.25 |
| JPN | 0.02 | | 0.24 | 0.10 | 0.31 | 0.37 | 0.39 | 0.34 | 0.26 | 0.45 | 0.42 | 0.13 | 0.24 | 0.37 | 0.13 | 0.28 | 0.10 | 0.16 | 0.27 |
| ROK | 0.22 | 0.24 | | 0.14 | 0.18 | 0.41 | 0.30 | 0.22 | 0.30 | 0.45 | 0.34 | 0.25 | 0.20 | 0.25 | 0.20 | 0.32 | 0.14 | 0.25 | 0.19 |
| NZL | 0.08 | 0.10 | 0.14 | | 0.29 | 0.42 | 0.37 | 0.24 | 0.29 | 0.47 | 0.40 | 0.11 | 0.30 | 0.35 | 0.11 | 0.26 | 0.08 | 0.26 | 0.17 |
| BRN | 0.29 | 0.31 | 0.18 | 0.29 | | 0.30 | 0.29 | 0.20 | 0.36 | 0.42 | 0.49 | 0.27 | 0.27 | 0.26 | 0.23 | 0.46 | 0.25 | 0.32 | 0.25 |
| KHM | 0.34 | 0.37 | 0.41 | 0.42 | 0.30 | | 0.30 | 0.43 | 0.38 | 0.28 | 0.34 | 0.36 | 0.25 | 0.24 | 0.36 | 0.28 | 0.34 | 0.37 | 0.34 |
| PRC | 0.37 | 0.39 | 0.30 | 0.37 | 0.29 | 0.30 | | 0.28 | 0.17 | 0.38 | 0.40 | 0.38 | 0.31 | 0.23 | 0.43 | 0.39 | 0.45 | 0.31 | 0.32 |
| IND | 0.32 | 0.34 | 0.22 | 0.24 | 0.20 | 0.43 | 0.28 | | 0.33 | 0.43 | 0.44 | 0.35 | 0.35 | 0.31 | 0.35 | 0.39 | 0.29 | 0.43 | 0.29 |
| IDN | 0.29 | 0.26 | 0.30 | 0.29 | 0.36 | 0.38 | 0.17 | 0.33 | | 0.34 | 0.40 | 0.35 | 0.27 | 0.23 | 0.30 | 0.26 | 0.32 | 0.27 | 0.36 |
| KAZ | 0.47 | 0.45 | 0.45 | 0.47 | 0.42 | 0.28 | 0.38 | 0.43 | 0.34 | | 0.23 | 0.48 | 0.45 | 0.32 | 0.48 | 0.29 | 0.47 | 0.45 | 0.42 |
| LAO | 0.40 | 0.42 | 0.34 | 0.40 | 0.49 | 0.34 | 0.40 | 0.44 | 0.40 | 0.23 | | 0.46 | 0.30 | 0.30 | 0.50 | 0.26 | 0.44 | 0.34 | 0.41 |
| MYS | 0.11 | 0.13 | 0.25 | 0.11 | 0.27 | 0.36 | 0.38 | 0.35 | 0.35 | 0.48 | 0.46 | | 0.28 | 0.32 | 0.09 | 0.37 | 0.11 | 0.29 | 0.18 |
| NPL | 0.22 | 0.24 | 0.20 | 0.30 | 0.27 | 0.25 | 0.31 | 0.35 | 0.27 | 0.45 | 0.30 | 0.28 | | 0.13 | 0.28 | 0.28 | 0.22 | 0.17 | 0.35 |
| PAK | 0.35 | 0.37 | 0.25 | 0.35 | 0.26 | 0.24 | 0.23 | 0.31 | 0.23 | 0.32 | 0.30 | 0.32 | 0.13 | | 0.37 | 0.29 | 0.35 | 0.29 | 0.22 |
| PHL | 0.11 | 0.13 | 0.20 | 0.11 | 0.23 | 0.36 | 0.43 | 0.35 | 0.30 | 0.48 | 0.50 | 0.09 | 0.28 | 0.37 | | 0.32 | 0.06 | 0.29 | 0.23 |
| SGP | 0.26 | 0.28 | 0.32 | 0.26 | 0.46 | 0.28 | 0.39 | 0.39 | 0.26 | 0.29 | 0.26 | 0.37 | 0.28 | 0.29 | 0.32 | | 0.26 | 0.37 | 0.30 |
| THA | 0.08 | 0.10 | 0.14 | 0.08 | 0.25 | 0.34 | 0.45 | 0.29 | 0.32 | 0.47 | 0.44 | 0.11 | 0.22 | 0.35 | 0.06 | 0.26 | | 0.26 | 0.21 |
| VUT | 0.18 | 0.16 | 0.25 | 0.26 | 0.32 | 0.37 | 0.31 | 0.43 | 0.27 | 0.45 | 0.34 | 0.29 | 0.17 | 0.29 | 0.29 | 0.37 | 0.26 | | 0.35 |
| VNM | 0.25 | 0.27 | 0.19 | 0.17 | 0.25 | 0.34 | 0.32 | 0.29 | 0.36 | 0.42 | 0.41 | 0.18 | 0.35 | 0.22 | 0.23 | 0.30 | 0.21 | 0.35 | |

Source: Author's calculations based on Organisation for Economic Co-operation and Development Digital Services Trade Restrictiveness Index.

Countries in Asia and the Pacific play a key role in digital services trade with around 23% total contribution to the total turnover in 2023, underscoring the region's importance in the digital economy. Countries like the People's Republic of China (PRC), India, Japan, the Republic of Korea, and Singapore have emerged as digital trade powerhouses, driving technological progress and innovation. Some are particularly active in digital trade agreements. The Sankey diagram (Figure I.4) highlights their significant role in agreements like the Digital Economy Partnership Agreement (DEPA), the Regional Comprehensive Economic Partnership (RCEP), and the Comprehensive and Progressive Agreement for Trans-Pacific Partnership (CPTPP). The surge in these types of agreements after the pandemic underscores their growing importance in the international trade landscape. These agreements not only facilitate smoother cross-border digital transactions, but also promote regulatory coherence and technological advancement.

The region's dominance in digital trade is fueled by strong domestic ICT sectors, dynamic e-commerce markets and platforms, and significant investments in digital infrastructure development. For instance, robust digital platforms and high-tech domestic market make the PRC a key importer and stakeholder in data flows and storage, while India and Indonesia are known for their burgeoning ICT sectors and e-commerce industries.

**Figure I.4: Timeline of Digital Trade Agreements and Free Trade Agreements with Digital Provisions**

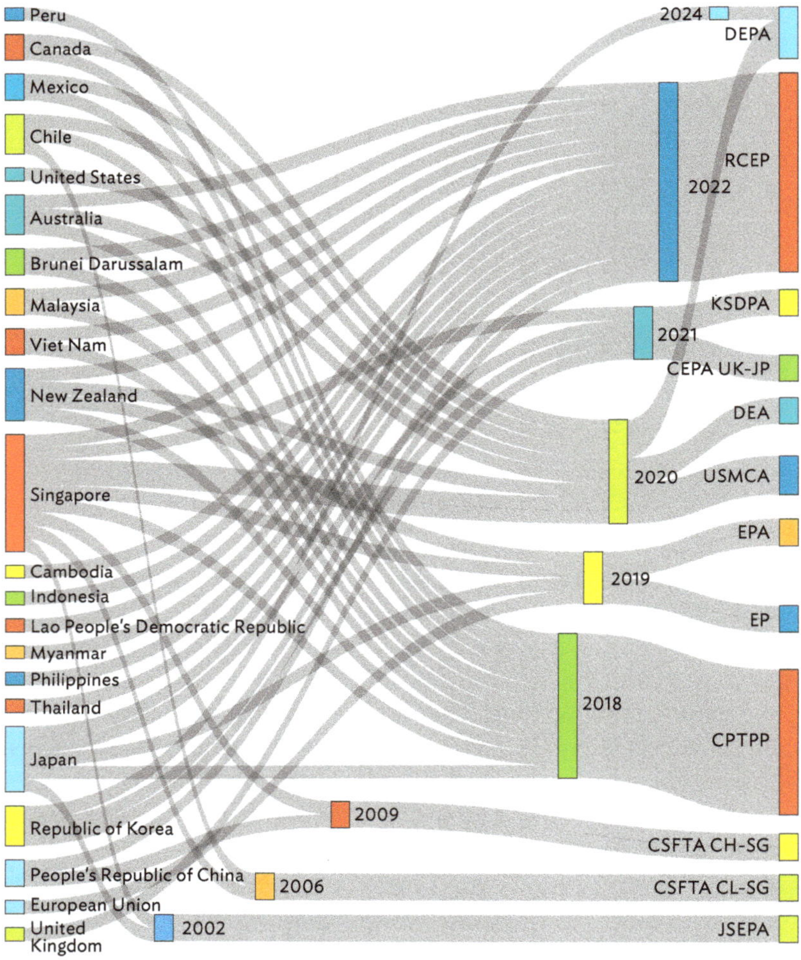


CEPA UK–JP = United Kingdom–Japan Comprehensive Economic Partnership Agreement, CPTPP = Comprehensive and Progressive Agreement for Trans-Pacific Partnership, CSFTA CH–SG = China–Singapore Free Trade Agreement, CSFTA CL–SG = Chile–Singapore Free Trade Agreement, DEA = digital economy agreement, DEPA = digital economy partnership agreement, EP = economic partnership, EPA = economic partnership agreement, JSEPA = Japan–Singapore Economic Partnership Agreement, KSDPA = Korea–Singapore Digital Partnership Agreement, RCEP = Regional Comprehensive Economic Partnership, USMCA = United States–Mexico–Canada Agreement.

Note: Neither the list of the countries nor the list of agreements is comprehensive. The diagram serves only illustrative purposes of the relatively active countries in digital regulatory cooperation, focusing on Asia and the Pacific, as well as post-COVID-19 spike in the importance of digital regulatory cooperation and digital trade agreements. Effective 1 February 2021, ADB placed a temporary hold on sovereign project disbursements and new contracts in Myanmar.

Source: Based on dates of agreements as compiled by the volume editors.

Digital regulatory cooperation in Asia and the Pacific is crucial for several reasons. First, the high diversity in economic development across the region means that harmonized digital regulations can help bridge gaps between developed and developing countries. To put it differently, Asia and the Pacific might benefit the most when it comes to harmonized digital trade and regulatory cooperation. Second, the region's integration into global supply chains necessitates smooth cross-border transactions and payments with strong operational security, and this can only be achieved through coordinating and defragmenting regional regulatory policies, making the cross-border payment systems interoperable and standardized. Third, while cybersecurity and privacy concerns should ideally be dealt with on a global scale, which requires a unified approach, achieving regional consistency to ensure robust protection across borders might be a good starting point to move toward a larger global regulatory coherence.

The coexistence of different digital regulatory frameworks in the world backed by the PRC, European Union (EU), and United States (US) is indicative of the variety of preferences about what needs to serve as the backbone of those frameworks. Whereas the US model stresses the importance of free data flows to fully utilize the opportunities of digital trade, and the EU gives higher priority to the personal privacy, the PRC model focuses on cybersecurity. Nevertheless, many countries, mostly developed ones, continue to put in effort and lead various initiatives to engineer and develop regulatory frameworks that could effectively balance the interests of different parties, while being flexible enough to allow each to retain some sovereign control. This volume aims at contributing to a more structured discussion on this issue, providing a comprehensive mapping of the regulatory landscape and assessing its policy implications. The first chapter provides a full view of the variety of approaches, while subsequent chapters explore specific angles on digital trade, regulation, taxation, and standardization issues.

One of the highlights of this volume is the thorough examination in Chapter 2 of the DEPA, the first digitaltrade agreement. The advantages of DEPA being the first stand-alone and modular framework for digital trade regulation is founded on its innovative and adaptive nature. Modularity is a significant advantage since it gives the joining parties flexibility in adoption of specific sections of the agreement that best suit their unique digital trade environments and allow for smoother integration into the global digital economy. In addition, modularity not only encourages broader participation, but also ensures the agreement remains fresh, manageable, and responsive to the changes in the digital environment.

Another thought-provoking slice of the discussion is related to the evolution and future of digital trade standards. Standardization in digital trade, where data is the sole traveler across borders, serves a similar purpose as the usual standardization for traditional forms of trade of goods and services that are not in the digital economy. In the context of digital regulation, joining the same universe of standards forces members to speak the same language of terminology and definitions, and allows to increase the cross-border interoperability of local digital platforms.

Generally, standardization of any given field is already a challenging task both from technical and policy perspectives. However, it becomes even more complex once we localize the discussion around digital relations, given digital trade is based on exchange of data, communication, and other emerging technologies. Usually, standardization is only applicable to areas where there is a high level of maturity and stability in the underlying evolution of technology or business operations. Over time, the most robust definitions become crystalized and accepted universally. In contrast, emerging technologies initially come with volatile and ambiguous terminology. That is where the standardization becomes a challenge. While some layers of the substance that need to be standardized are evolving predictably, others are incredibly fluid and rapidly transforming. For example, standardization efforts might be highly effective in stable fields like telecommunication and 5G connectivity, but might easily become outdated if the tech is changing too actively. Once again, a good example is AI. It is already transforming the way things are designed, manufactured, advertised, and delivered globally, and having a huge impact on value chains across the world. The discussion becomes even more about detrimental effects if narrowed down to digital services. On the one hand, governments and international organizations are struggling to produce a well-shaped list of definitions and accurate description of the risks emerging from AI. On the other hand, leading countries pump in multibillion-dollar funding to take the lead in the AI horserace and gain an economic edge over the rest. While most seem to understand and recognize the potential risks, real efforts to make it safe remain overshadowed by economic motives. AI is evolving in giant steps and often unpredictably. So, while countries seek their way through these delicate trade-offs so they are not to be left behind, it is easy to be skeptical that standardization efforts on AI will achieve any near-term solution.

Another goal of this volume is to initiate deliberations around cross-border payment systems and shed light on the current situation in Asia and the Pacific. Cross-border payments and transactions, and more broadly financial systems, are the oil of international trade, especially when it comes to the trade of digital products. Current financial systems and cross-border payment systems are double-edged swords, as they open new markets while hacking away to overcome challenges such as financial stability, high costs, slow processing times, restricted access, and a lack of transparency.

One alternative paradigm of financial systems that is gaining traction is the move toward open finance and open banking, based on the broader concept of open data. The idea is to break the long-standing monopoly of financial institutions over consumer data and achieve better utilization by applying modern analysis and technology to provide consumer-tailored services and products. Although this is still practiced primarily among domestic financial institutions and banks, experiments are already underway in an attempt for these concepts to achieve international coverage.

Focusing on cross-border payments and understanding where the region stands, as well as touching on emerging paradigms such as open finance and banking naturally initiates a discussion around interoperability. Facilitated by standardized application programming interfaces, interoperability allows seamless communication between different financial systems, fostering a more integrated and efficient financial ecosystem. By exploring these themes, we try to provide big picture insights into the regulatory landscape and discuss the implications for policymakers and the private sector, aiming to enhance the efficiency and accessibility of international transactions and support the broader goals of digital trade.

Finally, we aim to continue discussions around cross-country taxation issues, international cooperation on harmonization efforts, and their effects on the digital economy. One of ADB's recently published volumes (ADB 2023) devotes a whole chapter to taxation and covers the topic in a broad context. In contrast, the discussion here focuses on taxation related to digital trade and the digital economy, addressing issues like the interplay between international tax and trade frameworks, the complexity of taxing digital activities, and the necessity for global cooperation.

The rapid expansion of digital activities in Asia, such as e-commerce, digital advertising, software development, and cloud computing, presents unique challenges. The current international tax system, developed before the digital era, is not equipped to tackle these challenges. New international tax rules are crucial for ADB's developing member economies and for businesses in the region and have potential to generate revenue and promote economic development. However, if the rules become too complex, they could be impediments to doing businesses. Further in this volume, a qualitative examination of the impact of international tax and investment frameworks on the digital economy is presented, highlighting the role of regional trade agreements in implementing digital tax rules. It is followed by policy recommendations to balance revenue generation, data protection, fair competition, and adherence to international standards.

In summary, the digital economy will undoubtedly play an increasingly dominant role in the future of economies, both globally and in Asia and the Pacific. This volume explores the importance of regulatory cooperation, and the opportunities embedded in successful digital trade policies and agreements. By understanding these dynamics, policymakers and the private sector can better navigate the complexities of the digital economy and unlock its potential for sustainable and inclusive growth.

Looking ahead, the rapid growth of digital technologies, alongside their deeper integration into trade systems, will continue to reshape the global economy. With that, transformation will bring new challenges that will require regulatory frameworks to evolve as well. Emerging technologies like generative AI, blockchain, and quantum computing promise to revolutionize the digital economy further, yet they also introduce complex regulatory and even ethical questions.

AI, for example, has long been a buzzword, attracting significant investment and financial resources. While many believed in a hype cycle that would eventually settle down, the reality turned out to be quite the opposite. Few expected the revolutionary impact that recent breakthroughs in generative AI would have. AI is already having wide-reaching effects, from transforming job markets and fully or partially replacing human workers in certain roles, to reshaping production and value chains by automating various operational tasks. It is also dramatically influencing marketing and sales strategies, driving personalized customer experiences, optimizing supply chains, and changing the competitive landscape across industries. The recent spike in generative AI has already been absorbed by a sizable share of industries globally, with the US leading the race by a noticeable margin (Figure I.5). At the same time, its rapid and widespread use brings up serious concerns around privacy, security, and governance.

**Figure I.5: Generative Artificial Intelligence Adoption by Organizations in the World, 2023**

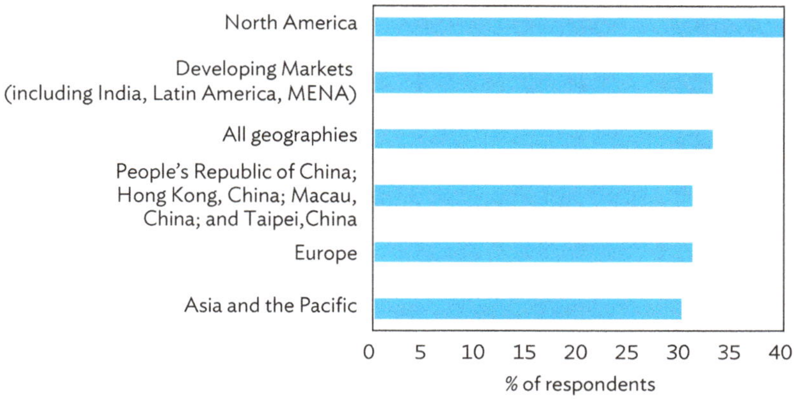


MENA = Middle East and North Africa.
Source: Chart: 2024 AI Index report, Stanford University, Human-Centered AI.

Similarly, blockchain technology offers significant opportunities for securing transactions and enhancing transparency in supply chains, financial services, and cross-border payments. Although it first gained attention as the foundation for cryptocurrencies, its applications extend way beyond the surface layer of crypto world and span across many industries. Blockchain can transform how data is shared and verified, reducing fraud and streamlining processes. It also promises to shift the focus from reliance on trust-based systems to trustless systems, where smart contracts can automatically enforce agreements once certain conditions are met. However, realizing its full potential requires substantial legal and regulatory reforms. The decentralized nature of blockchain raises complex questions about liability, security, and contract enforcement across borders. Regulatory frameworks must evolve to address issues such as data privacy, security, and interoperability while ensuring the technology can scale without limiting innovation.

Finally, alongside technological progress, geopolitical tensions will be a key factor influencing the future of digital trade and regulatory cooperation. How these tensions evolve—whether they escalate or ease—will shape future cooperation efforts, particularly in managing data flows, cybersecurity, and privacy.

Despite existing challenges and the continued fragmentation of geoeconomic relations, there are still efforts by like-minded countries to achieve transnational harmonization in selected areas of digital trade and regulation. A prominent example is the Joint Statement Initiative (JSI) on E-Commerce, which began in 2019, and which concluded negotiations in 2024 to create a framework for cooperation on digital trade issues (Box I.1).

### Box I.1: Joint Statement Initiative on E-Commerce

#### Background

The lack of progress in multilateral negotiations has led to several like-minded countries launching initiatives to advance discussions on key areas such as e-commerce, investment facilitation, micro, small, and medium-sized enterprises, and domestic regulation in services trade. These initiatives, including the Joint Statement Initiative (JSI) on E-Commerce, are open to all countries and aim to provide a renewed focus on plurilateral negotiations while multilateral discussions remain stalled. The JSI on E-Commerce has been co-convened by Australia, Japan, and Singapore, and seeks to address key gaps in global cooperation around digital trade.

#### Current Status of Negotiations

As of 25 June 2024, 91 World Trade Organization (WTO) members, representing 90% of global trade, have participated in these discussions.[a] Among them are eight Asian Development Bank (ADB) members, including Australia, Japan, the Republic of Korea, Singapore, the Philippines, Viet Nam, and Thailand. The negotiations were successfully concluded in July 2024, resulting in a comprehensive Agreement on Electronic Commerce. This represents a major achievement in advancing global digital trade particularly given the initial challenges and opposition from some members. The final agreement covers 13 key areas, including:

- Online consumer protection
- Electronic signatures and authentication
- Unsolicited commercial electronic messages (spam)
- Open government data
- Electronic contracts
- Transparency
- Paperless trading
- Cybersecurity
- Open internet access

*Continued on next page*

**Box I.1** *continued*

- Frameworks for electronic transactions
- Electronic invoicing
- Single windows for data submission
- Data privacy

While discussions initially faced contention on topics such as customs duties on electronic transmissions and cross-border data flows, the final agreement strikes a balance between flexibility and firm commitments. Notably, the moratorium on customs duties for electronic transmissions has been extended, and data privacy has been addressed through a flexible, yet robust, regulatory framework.

**Key Developments**

The finalized agreement avoided some contentious issues, such as data localization requirements and the protection of source code, which were heavily debated by the United States and other members. These elements were softened or excluded to allow for broader consensus among participants. One major challenge was integrating the agreement within the WTO framework. While some countries, opposed the use of Annex 4 (which allows plurilateral agreements under the WTO umbrella), a compromise was reached, allowing for opt-in participation while maintaining alignment with the broader multilateral system.

**Key Provisions**

- **Digital trade facilitation:** The agreement promotes the digitalization of trade processes, including electronic invoicing, paperless trading, and the creation of single windows for data submission. Transparency and the adoption of electronic payments are also encouraged.
- **Openness in electronic commerce:** Key provisions ensure access to the internet, promote open government data, and support the use of electronic contracts and signatures.
- **Trust and consumer protection:** The agreement strengthens consumer protection in online transactions, cybersecurity measures, and introduces flexible frameworks for personal data protection, similar to provisions in agreements like the Comprehensive and Progressive Agreement for Trans-Pacific Partnership..
- **Moratorium on customs duties:** The agreement extends the moratorium on customs duties for electronic transmissions, a long-standing issue in digital trade discussions. A review mechanism has been included, allowing for reassessment 5 years after the agreement's entry into force.

*Continued on next page*

**Box I.1** *continued*

- **Telecommunication and technology:** Provisions have been included to enhance access to telecommunication services and improve regulation, building on existing WTO frameworks to support the digital economy.

.

**Challenges and Future Outlook**

Despite this progress, some members, such as the People's Republic of China, the United States, and Indonesia, raised concerns about the permanent nature of the moratorium on customs duties and its implications for defining "electronic transmissions." The agreement also avoids binding provisions on data localization or cross-border data flows, which may be revisited in future discussions. Some countries are still undergoing domestic consultations to ratify the agreement, and its full implementation may take several years.

For developing countries and least developed countries, the agreement includes provisions for technical assistance and capacity-building to support implementation. However, the specifics of these support mechanisms are yet to be fully defined, and timelines for compliance remain flexible, with some countries granted up to 7 years.

ADB has actively encouraged its members to engage with the JSI, emphasizing its potential benefits for enhancing digital trade and for fostering economic integration in the Asia and Pacific region. ADB has provided capacity-building to policymakers to navigate the implications of the agreement and to equip them with the necessary tools for effective participation in digital trade negotiations. These efforts aim to ensure that members can fully leverage the opportunities presented by global digital trade.

[a] The members, in alphabetical order, are as follows: Albania; Argentina; Australia; Austria; Bahrain, Kingdom of; Belgium; Benin; Brazil; Brunei Darussalam; Bulgaria; Burkina Faso; Cabo Verde; Cameroon; Canada; Chile; the People's Republic of China; Colombia; Costa Rica; Côte d'Ivoire; Croatia; Cyprus; Czech Republic; Denmark; Ecuador; El Salvador; Estonia; Finland; France; Gambia; Georgia; Germany; Greece; Guatemala; Honduras; Hong Kong, China; Hungary; Iceland; Indonesia; Ireland; Israel; Italy; Japan; Kazakhstan; Kenya; the Republic of Korea; Kuwait, the State of; the Kyrgyz Republic; the Lao People's Democratic Republic; Latvia; Liechtenstein; Lithuania; Luxembourg; Malaysia; Malta; Mauritius; Mexico; Moldova, Republic of; Mongolia; Montenegro; Myanmar; the Netherlands; New Zealand; Nicaragua; Nigeria; North Macedonia; Norway; Oman; Panama; Paraguay; Peru; the Philippines; Poland; Portugal; Qatar; Romania; the Russian Federation; Saudi Arabia, Kingdom of; Singapore; Slovak Republic; Slovenia; Spain; Sweden; Switzerland; Taipei,China; Thailand; Türkiye; Ukraine; United Arab Emirates; the United Kingdom; the United States; Uruguay; and Viet Nam.

Source: Volume editors.

Digital trade is and will continue to expand in form and complexity, hence the issues addressed in this volume represent only a small part of the broader landscape. Future research must focus on keeping pace with technological advancements and the adoption of regulatory regimes, understanding the implications for firms and consumers, adapting to shifts in the geopolitical environment, both of which will have significant implications for trade and the digital economy. These evolving dynamics will require flexible and forward-looking approaches to ensure regulation and international cooperation keep up with the changing digital trade landscape. By doing so, countries will be better equipped to harness the opportunities of the digital economy while managing the associated risks.

The rest of the volume is organized as follows:

Chapter 1, "Trends in Domestic and International Digital Regulations in Asia and the Pacific" by Stephanie Honey, looks at the complex digital regulations in Asia and the Pacific. It shows how digital changes, sped up by COVID-19, need strong rules to support growth. The chapter points out differences in how countries manage electronic transactions, data protection, privacy, cybersecurity, and online consumer protection. It talks about the "regulatory overdrive" during and after the pandemic with new digital trade policies. This chapter maps out digital regulations across Asia and the Pacific and calls for updated rules to manage risks and boost the digital economy.

Chapter 2, "Digital Economy Partnership Agreement Provisions on Data Flow, Cybersecurity, and Privacy: Challenges and Policy Suggestions for Developing Countries" by Henry Gao, drastically changes the perspective and dives into the Digital Economy Partnership Agreement (DEPA). Gao contrasts DEPA to the respective provisions and chapters in CPTPP and RCEP, highlighting not only similarities, but also its flexible and inclusive approach. DEPA's modular design lets new members adopt parts that fit their needs, encouraging innovation. The chapter stresses the importance of working together on cybersecurity and privacy. Gao also talks about the challenges for developing countries with DEPA and how it can harmonize digital trade rules, underlining how DEPA can be a model for future digital trade deals. The language and the legal rigor of the discussion might entertain legal experts and other readers interested in delicate interpretation issues of certain chapters and provisions of the agreement.

Chapter 3, “Standards in the Age of Digital Trade: A Way Forward” by Jooyoung Kwak and Heejin Lee, focuses on the role of digital standards in trade. It looks at current digital trade deals and standards, especially for evolving areas like AI and 5G. The chapter discusses creating standards, the problems in doing so, and their potential impact on Asia and the Pacific. It highlights the need for private sector cooperation and international teamwork in standardization. The chapter also suggests ways to improve digital standards to support global trade.

Chapter 4, “Cross-Border Payments” by Martin Chorzempa, addresses the intricacies and potential improvements in cross-border payments, emphasizing their significance for global trade and financial inclusion. It examines current challenges, such as high costs, slow speeds, limited access, and lack of transparency, and highlights the need for robust public–private partnerships, regulatory harmonization, and innovative infrastructure. The chapter delves into the role of digital identity systems and the potential of central bank digital currencies (CBDCs) to streamline international transactions. It also reviews the landscape of cross-border payments in Asia, focusing on US dollar dominance, inefficiencies in correspondent banking, and the rise of digital agreements like DEPA and CPTPP.

Chapter 5, “Taxing the Digital Economy: Cross-Border Data and Trade Policies in Asia” by Julien Chaisse, looks at the tax challenges in the digital economy. The chapter discusses the need for new international tax rules to oversee digitalization. It examines how digital tax affects ADB’s developing member economies in Asia and the role of global tax rules. The chapter focuses on difficulties in measuring cross-border data flows and the creation of digital tax rules. It suggests policy actions for developing member economies, focusing on good corporate governance, transparency, risk management, and use of data. And finally, it highlights the need for fair digital tax systems to support the digital economy and ensure proper tax revenue.

# 1 Trends in Domestic and International Digital Regulation in Asia and the Pacific

Stephanie Honey

## Introduction

The COVID-19 pandemic has helped to turbocharge the shift to a more digitalized global economy. If done well, this promises to support inclusive growth, unlock new opportunities, improve productivity, and boost resilience (ADB 2022a and 2022b). Digital trade—that is, trade in digitally ordered and delivered goods and services—is far outpacing growth in other forms of trade, and digitalization is generating important savings in trade costs, particularly for developing economies (OECD 2023a).

Digital infrastructure, connectivity, and skills are critical elements in realizing the potential of digital trade, and an enabling regulatory and policy environment (including for trade policy) is essential. Recent empirical evidence shows that digital trade rules increase digital trade flows, especially flows of digitally deliverable services, and these benefits are magnified for low- and middle-income countries (Access Partnership 2023; Jiang et al. 2023; and Suh and Roh 2022).

There is both a pull and a push for regulatory action in the digital sphere. Well-designed regulatory settings, especially if interoperable with those in other jurisdictions, increase predictability and trust, create more equal conditions, and reduce costs and frictions for businesses and consumers. Regulation is also an important risk-mitigation strategy in a globalized world, helping to tackle external cybersecurity threats, manage cross-border anti-competitive behavior, and lessen protectionism.

On the other hand, regulatory heterogeneity, gaps, or restrictive measures are more likely to disadvantage developing economies and micro, small, and medium-sized enterprises (MSMEs), along with other groups, such as women entrepreneurs, who may be less well-equipped to meet the compliance costs and mitigate the economic risks that arise from siloed or unregulated approaches. Potential digital economy benefits are likely to be greater if a more holistic approach is pursued (ADB 2022b).

Domestic regulatory settings have an outsized influence on trade in the digital sphere. For example, behind-the-border measures governing privacy and data protection, cybersecurity, and online consumer protection all have impact on digital trade, and, depending on design, can effectively function as either nontariff barriers or enablers of flows of digital goods and services. Equally, regulations more explicitly concerned with cross-border trade, such as cross-border data flows and market access for digital goods and services, can also shape trade flows (International Monetary Fund et al. 2023).

A handful of economies in Asia and the Pacific are at the forefront of regulating the domestic and international digital economy. Others may lack basic regulatory building blocks, or favor unilateral approaches, and so may be largely absent from international trade negotiations (UNCTAD 2023). This chapter gives a snapshot of the current state of play in the region. The first part reviews the evolution of regulatory approaches to the digital economy. The second section discusses trends by subregion and country, while the third discusses underlying drivers of the different approaches. The fourth section reflects on how economies can optimize participation in and benefit from international cooperation on digital trade.

## 1.1. Domestic and International Regulation of the Digital Economy

### *Trends in Domestic Digital Governance*

Digital transformation is putting regulatory regimes under pressure. New business models, new types of goods and digitally delivered services, and complex new cross-border transactions may not be covered adequately, if at all, by existing regulation. Digitalization may also raise new risks—for example, around competition and inclusion—which current regimes are ill-equipped to handle. In any case, digital transformation may outpace regulators' ability to respond. This has resulted in a complex and evolving digital regulatory landscape in Asia and the Pacific (ADB 2022a).

A suite of initiatives from international institutions and academic bodies provides welcome granular information on aspects of digital regulation, which informs the discussion in this chapter.[7] However, despite these efforts, no single comprehensive source of information on domestic and trade digital regulation can be used to support policy formation and trade reform. In its May 2023 T20 Policy Brief, ADB recommended that comprehensive mapping be undertaken on national legislation, regulations, and international commitments, to establish a centralized "Digital Regulation and Information Repository" (ADB 2023).

### *Regulatory overdrive—but not by everyone*

The years since the pandemic period have seen considerable expansion-what could be described as regulatory overdrive—in digital economy governance (Evenett and Fritz 2022). Between 1 January 2020 and 31 May 2024, just over 1,600 policy or regulatory interventions affecting data governance were adopted or implemented, along with a similar tally of policy changes affecting content moderation, competition, consumer protection, authorization, registration and licensing, and over 700 interventions in other areas. Regulatory action has accelerated, particularly since 2022 (Figure 1.1).

**Figure 1.1: Policy Changes Proposed, Advanced, or Implemented in Digital Policy, 1 January 2020 to 30 April 2024**

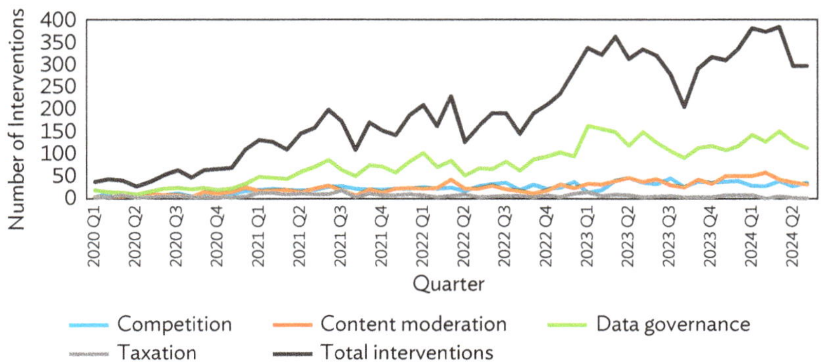


Source: Author, from Digital Policy Alert data, https://digitalpolicyalert.org/ (accessed 4 June 2024).

[7] These include the Global Cyberlaw Tracker of the United Nations Conference on Trade and Development (UNCTAD); the Regional Digital Trade Integration Index and "Legal TINA" of the United Nations Economic and Social Commission for Asia and the Pacific (UNESCAP); Global Trade Alert's Digital Policy Alert (DPA); the Digital Trade Integration project, an initiative coordinated by the European University Institute (EUI); the Digital Trade Inventory and Digital Services Trade Restrictiveness Index (DSTRI) of the Organisation for Economic Co-operation and Development (OECD); and the Trade Agreements Provisions on Electronic Commerce and Data (TAPED) of the University of Lucerne.

While Europe and the United States are the most active regulators, economies from Asia and the Pacific are also prominent. The People's Republic of China (PRC) ranked as the third most active jurisdiction globally. Others key economies in the region include Australia; Hong Kong, China; India; Japan; the Republic of Korea; New Zealand; and Singapore. The Association of Southeast Asian Nations (ASEAN) developing countries (Cambodia, Indonesia, the Lao People's Democratic Republic, Malaysia, the Philippines, Thailand, and Viet Nam) demonstrate moderate regulatory activity (Figure 1.2). In some major economies, digital regulations were put in place prior to 2020 and have not been updated.

**Figure 1.2: Most Active Jurisdictions in Asia and the Pacific for Digital Policy, 1 January 2020 to 30 April 2024**

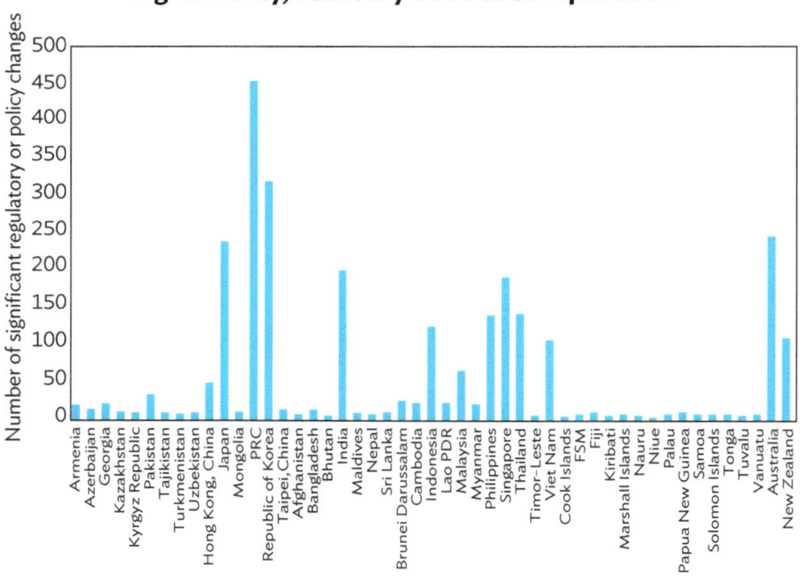


PRC = People's Republic of China, Lao PDR = Lao People's Democratic Republic, FSM = Federated States of Micronesia.
Source: Author, using Digital Policy Alert data. https://digitalpolicyalert.org/ (accessed 4 June 2024).

***The domestic regulatory landscape is complex***

A wide range of government agencies can be responsible for a dizzying array of regulatory issues. Inventories of digital regulation typically span more than a dozen major headings, with many more subsidiary topics. These include domestic data policies, cross-border data flows, content moderation, intermediary liability, registration and licensing, intellectual property rights, competition policy, online sales transactions (including payments) and business mobility, as well as a range of cross-cutting topics, such as telecoms infrastructure, quantitative restrictions on ICT goods and services, standards, foreign investment, public procurement, subsidies and industrial policy and taxation (EUI Digital Trade Index; UNCTAD Global Cyberlaw Tracker).

Compounding the analytical challenge, policy objectives for regulatory measures may not only include economic goals, such as development (including digital industrial policy), efficiency, competition, or intellectual property rights protection, but may also be concerned with public goods such as privacy, online harms, law enforcement, ensuring social stability, or protecting national security - which may affect trade even if this is not their primary aim.

### *Regulation is missing in some key areas for some Asian economies*

Figure 1.3 provides a snapshot of trends in the region across four important legislative areas: electronic transactions frameworks; data protection and privacy; consumer protection; and cybercrime legislation. Countries are grouped by subregion (but note that data was not available for all countries). Countries can receive a maximum score of 8 where legislation is in place in all four areas, or lower scores for draft or missing legislation. As can be seen from Figure 1.3, the region's advanced economies, most of Southeast Asia, and the PRC have enacted comprehensive legislation, while South Asia and Central Asia have only draft or missing legislation in some areas. None of the Pacific economies have consumer protection or privacy/data protection legislation in place, and some have no legislation in any of the four areas.

The European University Institute's Digital Trade Integration (DTI) database, which includes 26 economies in Asia and the Pacific, illustrates the long path for many economies in building out detailed regulatory settings for the digital economy.[8] While the developed and more advanced developing economies have extensive regulation in place across all 12 of the database's regulatory pillars, the overall volume and scope of regulation among the less-developed economies is significantly lower.

[8] The EUI DTI database includes Australia; Brunei Darussalam; Cambodia; the PRC; Hong Kong, China; India; Indonesia; Japan; Kazakhstan; the Kyrgyz Republic; the Lao PDR; Malaysia; Myanmar; Nepal; New Zealand; Pakistan; the Philippines; the Republic of Korea; Singapore; Taipei,China; Tajikistan; Turkmenistan; Thailand; Uzbekistan; Vanuatu; and Viet Nam (accessed 11 June 2024).

**Figure 1.3: Adoption of Key Digital Legislation by Regional Economies**

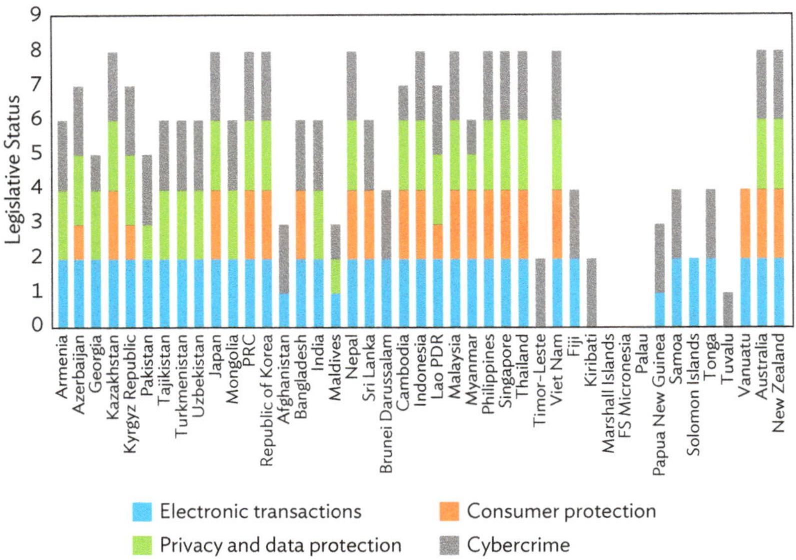


PRC = People's Republic of China, FS Micronesia = Federated States of Micronesia, Lao PDR = Lao People's Democratic Republic.

Note: For "Legislative Status," countries' legislation in each of the four areas is scored as follows: 2 = Legislation in place; 1 = Draft legislation being developed; 0 = No legislation (or no data available).

Source: UNCTAD Global Cyberlaw Tracker.https://unctad.org/topic/ecommerce-and-digital-economy/ecommerce-law-reform/summary-adoption-e-commerce-legislation-worldwide (accessed 4 June 2024)..

### *The regulatory environment is increasingly restrictive and heterogenous across countries*

Restrictiveness in the digital services environment has been increasing rapidly in the past decade. In 2023, among the 19 regional countries included in the OECD's Digital Services Trade Restrictiveness Index (DSTRI), scores ranged from 0.02 for Australia to 0.567 for Kazakhstan (with a score of zero representing an open regulatory environment for digital trade, and a score of 1 indicating a completely closed regime). According to the DSTRI, the most restrictive economies are Kazakhstan, the Lao PDR, and Cambodia, closely followed by the PRC, Pakistan, and Indonesia. In contrast, the least restrictive economies are Australia, Japan, the Republic of Korea, the Philippines, Malaysia, and New Zealand (Figure 1.4).

**Figure 1.4: Organisation for Economic Co-operation and Development Digital Services Trade Restrictiveness Index for Regional Economies, 2023**

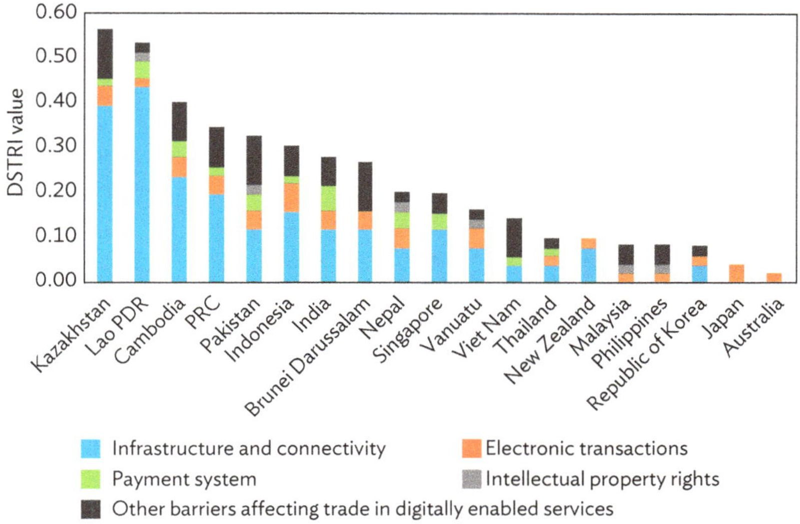


PRC = People's Republic of China, DSTRI = Digital Services Trade Restrictiveness Index, Lao PDR = Lao People's Democratic Republic.
Source: Author, using data from the OECD DSTRI (accessed 4 June 2024).

According to the DSTRI, the policy areas of greatest restriction are infrastructure and connectivity (including cross-border data flows and measures relating to interconnection into communications infrastructure), electronic transactions (such as electronic signatures not being recognized), and in some cases, payment systems (for example, restrictions on digital payments or internet banking). Other barriers include measures such as performance requirements, limitations on streaming, or restrictions on online advertising (OECD DSTRI, accessed 4 June 2024).

### *Data restrictions*

Regulations that restrict the flow of data are increasingly widespread (Cory and Dascoli 2021). These restrictions can apply both to the transfer of data across borders (data flow) and the processing and storage of data in the market (data localization). Such measures can be costly for businesses and economies, increasing inefficiency and creating significant trade barriers to small businesses (van der Marel, in ADB 2022c).

A range of different approaches are used by the region's economies. For example, of the 19 regional economies assessed in the UNCTAD *Digital Economy Report* 2021:

- Four use a regulatory "light touch" (free flow of data with minimal regulatory requirements—but may still impose certain restrictions in sensitive sectors such as defense or health);
- Eleven use a "prescriptive" approach (cross-border data flows are subject to compliance requirements, for example, in domestic data protection, particularly personal data, or privacy laws). Typically, prescriptive approaches include a conditional transfer requirement: around half use "hard" conditional transfers, and the other half an intermediate/soft approach.
- Two economies use a "restrictive" approach, two a "restrictive/guarded" approach and one a "guarded" approach. A "restrictive" approach means a complete or partial ban on data flows for reasons of public security, national security or data sovereignty. A "guarded" approach focuses on achieving domestic digital growth, for example, through strict data localization (UNCTAD 2021).

Similarly, in the International Telecommunications Union (ITU) ICT Regulatory Environment Tracker, while advanced regional economies' regulatory environment scores are generally high (indicating a more enabling environment), Central Asia, South Asia, and Southeast Asia have lower scores, and there is considerable variation within these groups on managing data flows, from "highly restrictive" to "light touch." At the other end of the spectrum, another group of economies may lack even basic data laws. Countries in this group are mainly from the Pacific, as well as Afghanistan, Cambodia, the Lao PDR, Nepal, and Sri Lanka (ITU ICT Regulatory Tracker, accessed 4 June 2024).

### *Restrictions in other areas*

Beyond data regulation, many economies have restrictive regulations in other areas which would reduce the potential benefits of e-commerce for the region. For example, in respect of online sales and transactions, many economies impose restrictions including local presence requirements to deliver digital services, have compulsory licensing regimes, place restrictions on e-payments, or limit access to online content. These types of measures add to costs and complexity in trade, particularly for small businesses (European University Institute Digital Trade Integration Project, accessed 4 June 2024).

There is also growing heterogeneity across countries, even where international standards may exist. The OECD's *Digital Trade Inventory* identifies 52 instruments that are directly relevant to digital trade, found in 24 forums including the World Trade Organization, the World Customs Organization, the International Organization for Standardization, and various United Nations bodies such as the UN Commission on International Trade Law (UNCITRAL). The uptake of these instruments varies significantly. Whereas there is relative coherence in trade facilitation, telecommunications and electronic transactions, in other areas, including privacy and cybersecurity, approaches are more fragmented (Nemoto and López González 2021).

Given global economic interconnectedness, these trends of regulatory fragmentation and restrictiveness potentially hinder the benefits of digital trade. Reductions in domestic barriers affecting digital trade are found to have a strong export-enhancing effect, increasing trade across countries at all levels of development (OECD 2023b). In contrast, "data nationalism" can be especially harmful for developing countries (UNCTAD 2021).

### *Trends in Regional Trade Agreements in Asia and the Pacific*

The architecture for global regulation in the digital economy is still a work in progress. Existing World Trade Organization (WTO) agreements form a baseline, but many WTO members consider that more comprehensive and modernized multilateral trade rules are needed. To that end, as of 25 June 2024, 91 WTO members, including 20 ADB regional economies were involved in negotiations of a "Joint Initiative on E-Commerce," with a view to conclude a plurilateral agreement on digital trade in 2024. As of January 2025, around 80 countries reached an agreement although the United States did not endorse the agreement yet, citing the need for further refinements, particularly concerning exceptions for essential security interests.

In December 2024, participants of the JSI on E-Commerce submitted a communication to the WTO General Council, proposing the formal incorporation of their agreement into the WTO framework. This underscores the participants' commitment to establishing comprehensive global rules governing digital trade. (WTO website, accessed 30 January 2025).[9]

Despite these advancements, some countries continue to express reservations about the JSI on E-Commerce, calling for further clarification of key definitions related to e-commerce trade in goods and services, as well as minor revisions.

Meanwhile, governance of digital trade has emerged primarily through regional trade agreements (RTAs) and, more latterly, digital economy agreements (DEAs). Out of 432 RTAs signed between January 2000 and November 2023, 214 contain provisions on digital trade and 122 have dedicated e-commerce chapters, with provisions increasing in scope and detail through the period (Burri, Vásquez Callo-Müller, and Kugler 2024). As Figure 1.5 shows, around half of the free trade agreements, RTAs, and digital economy agreements negotiated by ADB regional economies include at least one digital trade provision, with a handful of ADB regional economies particularly active in negotiating such provisions (ADB 2022b).

**Figure 1.5: Trade Agreements, Digital Provisions, and Chapters in ADB Regional Economies**

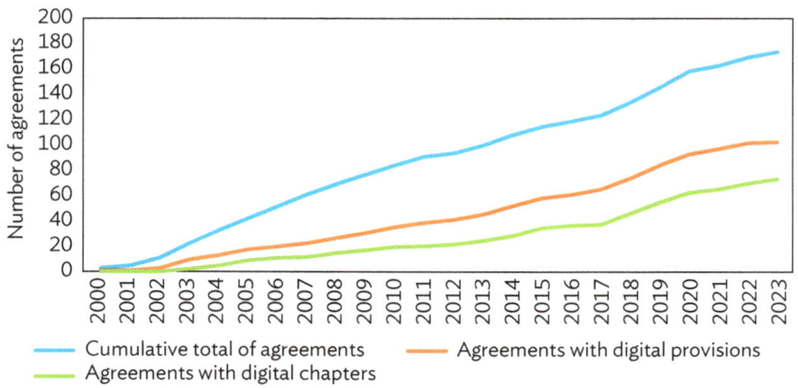


Note: The cumulative total of agreements includes free trade agreements, regional trade agreements, and various upgrades, protocols and other elements, and digital economy agreements.
Source: Author, using data from Trade Agreements Provisions on Electronic Commerce and Data November 2023 edition (accessed 4 June 2024).

9 Economies include Australia, Brunei Darussalam, the PRC, Georgia, Hong Kong, China; Indonesia; Japan; Kazakhstan; the Republic of Korea; the Kyrgyz Republic; the Lao PDR; Malaysia; Mongolia; Myanmar; New Zealand; the Philippines; Singapore; Taipei,China; Thailand; Viet Nam. Regarding India's position, see: India and South Africa. 2021. The Legal Status of "Joint Statement Initiatives" and their Negotiated Outcomes. WT/GC/W/819, General Council. 1–2 March 2021, dated 19 February 2021.

Participation in these agreements varies significantly across different subregions (Figure 1.6). The most active participants are the more developed economies, particularly Singapore, which has driven not only digital provisions and chapters, but also the development of dedicated “digital-only” DEAs discussed further below. Other active participants include Australia, New Zealand, the Republic of Korea, and Japan.

**Figure 1.6: Participation in Agreements with Digital Elements by ADB Regional Economies**

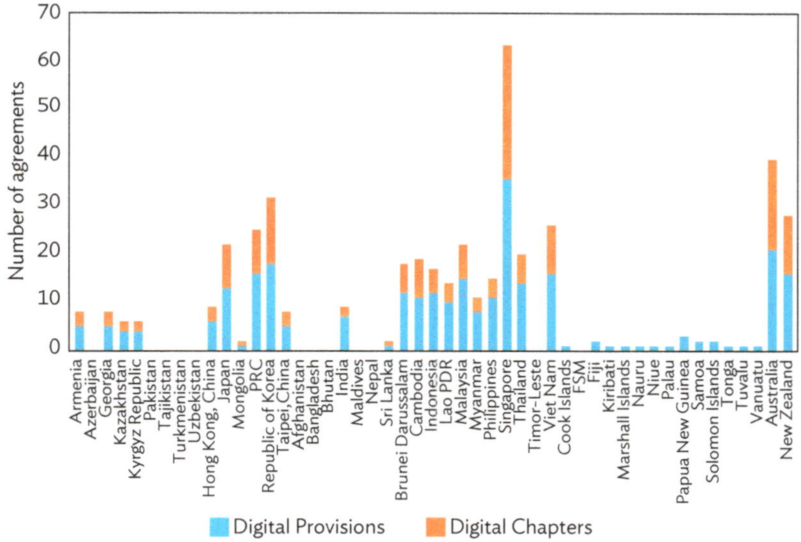


PRC = People’s Republic of China, Lao PDR = Lao People’s Democratic Republic, FSM = Federated States of Micronesia.
Source: Author, using data from Trade Agreements Provisions on Electronic Commerce and Data November 2023 edition (accessed 4 June 2024). Note that the cumulative total of agreements includes free trade agreements, regional trade agreements, and various upgrades, protocols and other elements, and digital economy agreements.

Other Parties in these agreements and negotiations include not only regional partners, particularly from Southeast Asia, but also middle powers, such as Australia and Japan, and large developed countries from outside the region, including the United States and Canada. For example, these countries engage through bilateral agreements, the Comprehensive and Progressive Agreement for Trans-Pacific Partnership (CPTPP), and the Indo Pacific Economic Framework (IPEF) negotiations. More recently, the European Union (EU) and United Kingdom have increased their trade agreement footprint in the region through bilateral agreements with, variously, Australia, New Zealand, Singapore, and the Republic of Korea.

Among the developing economies in Asia and the Pacific, the most engaged are in Southeast Asia, primarily through the Association of Southeast Asian Nations (ASEAN) as a bloc. The PRC is also notable (and East Asian economies are active). In contrast, in the Pacific, Central Asia, and a large majority of South Asian countries, participation is generally low.

### *RTA templates*

A key template in the region is the CPTPP signed in 2018 (and its 2016 predecessor Trans-Pacific Partnership Agreement, identical at least in digital trade rules terms), which involved seven regional economies. Whereas earlier agreements largely focused on specific sector rules, the CPTPP for the first time brought together and codified a small core of key data governance rules and digital trade facilitation measures, including free data flow and a prohibition on forced data localization (with exceptions); principles on access to the internet; personal information/data protection; online consumer protection; spam (unsolicited commercial electronic messages); e-authentication (including e-signatures); paperless trading; and cooperation on cybersecurity (Figure 1.7).

**Figure 1.7: "Core" Comprehensive and Progressive Agreement for Trans-Pacific Partnership Digital Trade Provisions in Agreements Involving ADB Regional Countries**

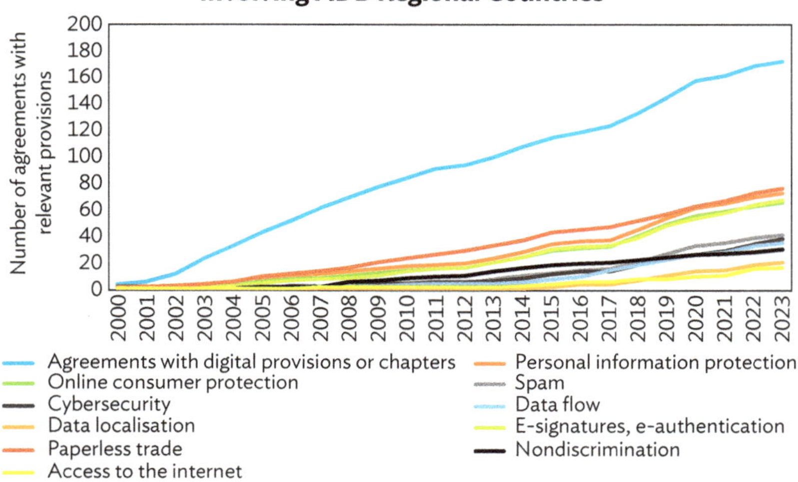


Source: Author, using data from Trade Agreements Provisions on Electronic Commerce and Data November 2023 edition, accessed 4 June 2024. Note that the cumulative total of "agreements with digital provisions or chapters" includes free trade agreements, regional trade agreements, and various upgrades, protocols and other elements, and digital economy agreements.

Market access is also critical to the ability of trading partners to realize digital trade opportunities. In RTAs including CPTPP and its successors, market access commitments are primarily made through services chapters, although some provisions that contribute to access are also included in the e-commerce chapters.

These e-commerce provisions include rules for not imposing customs duties on electronic transmissions, commitments on nondiscriminatory treatment of digital products, and provisions on principles for access to and use of the internet. However, in contrast to the core CPTPP provisions listed above, uptake of the latter two elements has been low in both RTAs and DEAs, with only 30 (out of around 175) agreements including nondiscrimination provisions and only 16 including provisions on access to the internet (TAPED, accessed 4 June 2024).

On the key issue of data governance, there has been a significant increase in adoption of data flow and data localization rules (Figure 1.8). These broad trends, however, mask significant variations in the nature of the commitments made, as Figure 1.8 also shows, with a year-by-year accounting of the degree to which these provisions are legally binding ("legal bindingness"). This is consistent with the wide variability in domestic regulation discussed in the preceding section.

**Figure 1.8: Data Governance Trends in Digital Trade Provisions Among ADB Members**

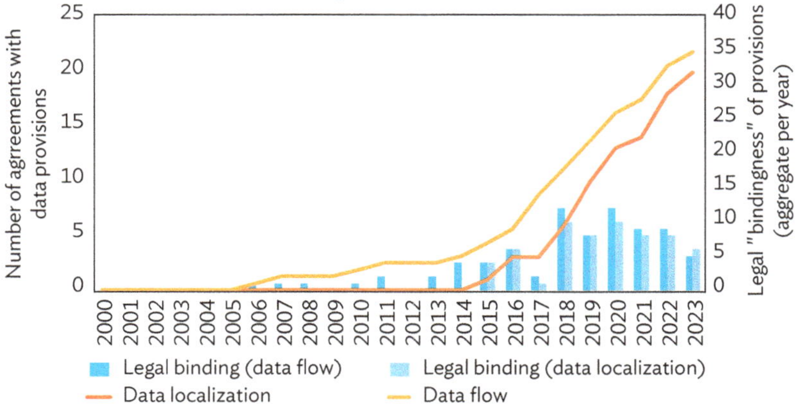


Source: Author, using data from Trade Agreements Provisions on Electronic Commerce and Data November 2023 edition (accessed 4 June 2024). Note that the cumulative total of agreements includes free trade agreements, regional trade agreements, and various upgrades, protocols and other elements, and digital economy agreements. Note that the measure of "Legal bindingness" (the degree to which provisions are legally binding) is scored 0 where provisions are absent, 1 for nonbinding/soft law commitments, and 2 for binding/hard law commitments.

In some cases, for example, in CPTPP and many DEAs, there is a strong presumption of free flows of data with circumscribed exceptions for legitimate public policy reasons (and a further qualification that restrictions must not constitute a disguised or arbitrary restriction on trade). Similarly, there is typically a general prohibition of forced data localization, again with limited exceptions for public policy reasons. Several other economies are seeking to join CPTPP, including the PRC and Taipei,China, which may broaden the influence of this model.

In contrast, in RCEP (2020), involving 15 regional economies, data flow and localization provisions include considerable "policy space," providing a self-judging flexibility to restrict or curtail data flow and the location of data processing and storage (ADB 2022b). Several other regional economies have indicated their interest in joining, including Bangladesh; Hong Kong, China; and Sri Lanka. The third "template," developed by the EU, until recently did not include data governance provisions, relying instead on the "human rights" protection offered by the General Data Protection Regulation (ADB 2022a, 2022c). However, more recent RTAs concluded by the EU in the region, including with New Zealand, show more engagement on data governance.

***Digital Economy Agreements***

Since 2019, the action on digital trade rules has shifted significantly from RTAs to dedicated digital-only DEAs (Burri, Vásquez Callo-Müller, and Kugler 2024). Although often discussed as separate agreements, in some cases, these DEAs are in fact an update to an existing RTA—as, for example, in the Singapore DEAs with Australia, the United Kingdom, and the Republic of Korea.

Stand-alone DEAs include the 2020 Digital Economy Partnership Agreement (DEPA) among Singapore, New Zealand, the Republic of Korea, and Chile; the 2019 US–Japan Digital Trade Agreement; the 2019 ASEAN E-Commerce Agreement (and its current negotiations for a Digital Economy Framework Agreement); digital partnerships the EU has negotiated with Singapore, Japan, the Republic of Korea, and Canada since 2022; the MERCOSUR E-Commerce Agreement; and the United Kingdom–Ukraine Digital Trade Agreement. These stand-alone DEAs do not typically include specific market access elements other than on customs duties and nondiscrimination.

The DEA model has driven significant expansion of the scope of digital trade rules. This new template is also reflected in the e-commerce chapters of very recent RTAs, such as the United Kingdom–Australia and United Kingdom–New Zealand FTAs. In essence, this new model looks to enable "trade in the digital economy," encompassing end-to-end enablement of digital trade transactions, and bringing in a range of other issues relating to consumer and business trust, inclusion for a range of underserved groups such as small businesses, women, and Indigenous entrepreneurs, and developing economies in the region; and technological innovation.

Figure 1.9 illustrates this expanding list of covered issues.

**Figure 1.9: Expansion of the Scope of Regional Trade Agreements and Digital Economy Agreements: An Illustrative Chart**

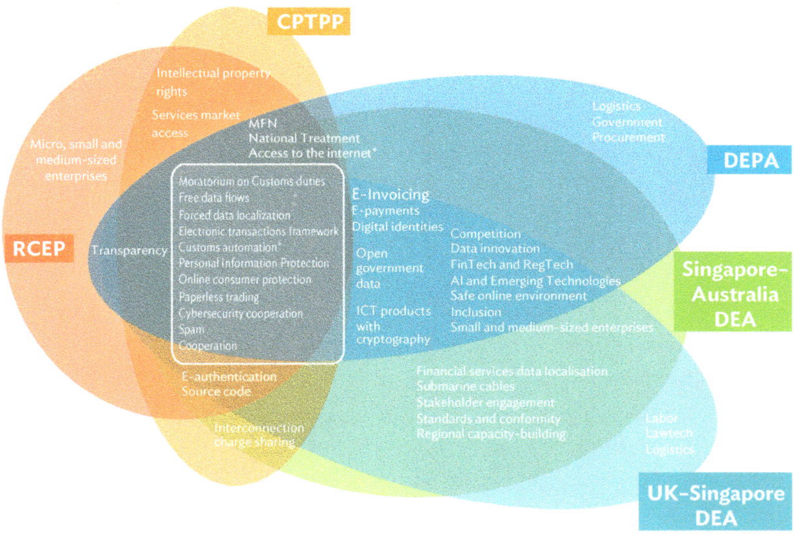


CPTPP = Comprehensive and Progressive Trans-Pacific Partnership, DEA = Digital Economy Agreement, DEPA = Digital Economy Partnership Agreement, ICT = information and communication technology, MFN = Most Favored Nation, RCEP = Regional Comprehensive Economic Partnership.
* not in RCEP.
Source: Author, using data from Trade Agreements Provisions on Electronic Commerce and Data November 2023 edition (accessed 4 June 2024).

Regional countries have increasingly adopted elements of this broader DEA template, particularly for measures that reduce trade and transaction costs for both digital trade (such as digitally delivered services) or digitally enabled trade (such as digitalized trade administration documents for goods trade (Figure 1.10).

**Figure 1.10: Digital Trade Provisions Aimed at Reducing Trade and Transaction Costs**

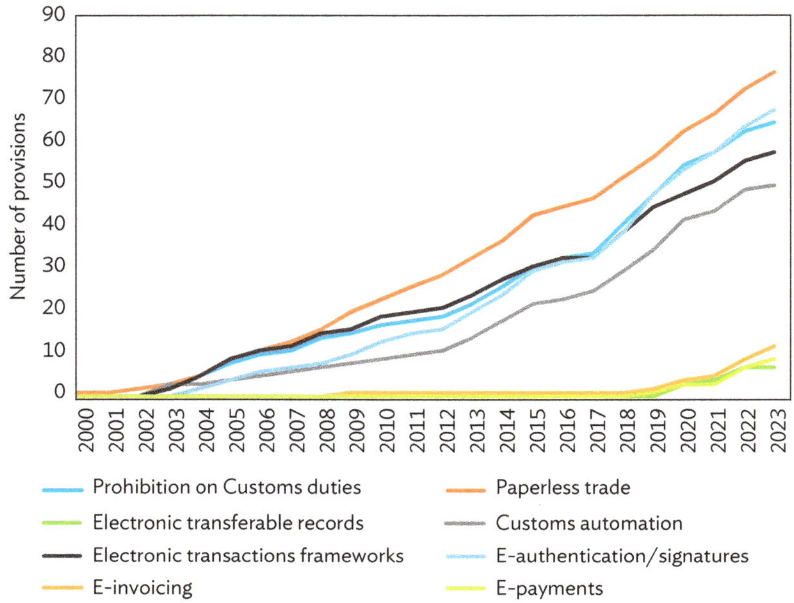


Source: Author, using data from Trade Agreements Provisions on Electronic Commerce and Data (accessed 4 June 2024).

Such measures include provisions covering the non-imposition of customs duties on electronic transmissions, paperless trade, electronic transferable records, customs automation, principles on access to the internet, domestic electronic transactions frameworks (and relatedly, references to United Nations model laws, including the Model Law on E-Commerce and the UN Electronic Communications Convention), e-invoicing, e-payments, and electronic signatures. More coherent and well-designed regulatory guardrails in these areas can help to reduce costs and increase trade opportunities for MSMEs.

Similarly, there is increasing uptake of provisions drawn from the DEA template relating to "trust," such as data protection (including personal information protection), online consumer protection, spam, and cybersecurity (Figure 1.11).

**Figure 1.11: Provisions on Digital Trust in Asia and the Pacific**

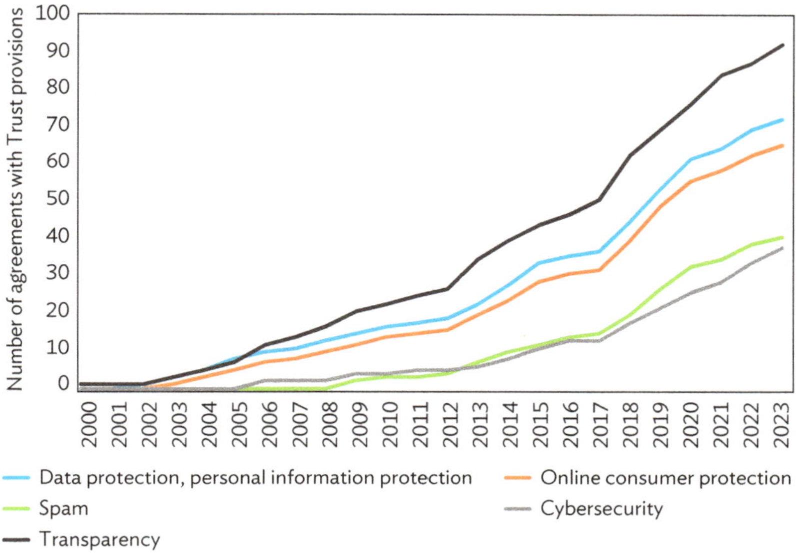


Source: Author, using data from Trade Agreements Provisions on Electronic Commerce and Data November 2023 edition (accessed 4 June 2024).

Beyond these elements are several novel provisions, including measures on logistics, government procurement and lawtech; provisions that reflect the broader societal context for digital trade (inclusion, SMEs, stakeholder engagement, a safe online environment, and capacity-building), and even digital infrastructure such as submarine cables (ADB 2022b).

A key concept in these new agreements is the importance of enabling greater regulatory coherence and interoperability to optimize opportunities in the digital economy. DEAs favor internationally agreed upon standards and conformity assessment, as well as the use of institutional mechanisms such as mutual recognition (for example, in payments or digital identities). This is a critical concept in addressing fragmentation: rules should be designed to enable interoperability across jurisdictions whose approaches to digital regulation are diverse (ADB 2022b).

In many cases, these commitments are made only on a best-endeavors basis, or identified as areas for future cooperation, meaning that the "legalization" of undertakings in these areas remains a work in progress. In fact, this approach of seeking to develop hard law through deliberate cross-border regulatory cooperation (via DEAs) offers a potentially more agile and fit-for-purpose regulatory model for the digital economy, and particularly in new and emerging policy areas, than more traditional approaches (ADB 2022b).

In the case of the DEPA, the agreement is an "open plurilateral" which includes a formal accession process, under which the Republic of Korea has acceded, and the PRC and others have applied to join. Over time, this could help to narrow the regulatory heterogeneity across the region as more economies join. The DEPA is also designed in thematic "modules" which other countries can use as models, helping to create more regulatory coherence across markets (ADB 2022b).

### *Summary of Regional Digital Regulation Trends*

As discussed earlier, economies in Asia and the Pacific take different approaches to digital regulation. Some have detailed frameworks and participate actively in international collaboration and discussions while others have gaps in regulation, relatively higher compliance costs, or restrictive policies that limit the potential gains from digital trade.

Broadly, digital regulation in the region falls into three main groups:

- **Comprehensive and open frameworks:** Some advanced economies have well-developed digital regulations. They allow cross-border data flows under clear conditions and have strong privacy and cybersecurity rules. These economies are also part of multiple trade agreements and regional digital initiatives.
- **Developing frameworks with some gaps:** Many economies have basic regulations, but lack comprehensive coverage in key areas like consumer protection or data privacy. Some have partial restrictions on data flows, requiring businesses to meet certain conditions when it comes to transferring data abroad. These economies often engage in trade agreements selectively.
- **Minimal or highly restrictive regulations:** A few economies have either little regulation or strict controls on digital trade, such as mandatory data localization or government-imposed limits on online content. These restrictions create barriers for businesses and make international digital trade more difficult.

The variety of regulations reflects different domestic priorities—security, economic competitiveness, oversight of digital services, to name a few. International and regional efforts to improve regulatory compatibility continue, but differences remain.

Next, we examine the underlying drivers behind these regulatory approaches, looking at the economic, political, and institutional factors influencing digital economy policies across the region.

## 1.2. Underlying Drivers of Country Approaches to Digital Economy Regulation

Regulation of the digital economy is complex and challenging, but there is a strong case for seeking greater regional regulatory coherence to create a more predictable, certain, stable, seamless, and low-cost trade environment for businesses, and a more trusted and secure environment for consumers. It is useful to examine the underlying motivations behind national approaches to digital regulation to explore how current differences can be bridged.

In some cases, economies' approaches are clearly linked to their geographical location: for example, the economies of Central Asia share a similar approach. In other cases, geography is less relevant than are factors such as economic drivers (for example, overall level of development, the size of the domestic market, trade profile, and the level of technological development), an economy's geopolitical orientation, sociocultural factors and their domestic regulatory capacity—or several such factors combined. Often, it is not a matter of a single narrative, but rather a nuanced set of priorities and concerns.

Economic drivers play a key role in shaping the position of active digital economy regulators, especially those involved in international digital trade negotiations, with interest in fostering the largest possible seamless digital market, aiming to create opportunities for their exporters while leveraging imported digital services to enhance productivity and growth.

These economies, often characterized by robust exports of both goods and services, stand to benefit from digital trade facilitation measures, such as paperless trade, e-invoicing, or platform-based goods exports, as well as from enabling regimes for digitally delivered services. Economies with vibrant and innovative local sectors engaged in emerging technologies such as fintech, AI, or digital identities tend to benefit from well-functioning and competitive markets, including from free flows of data. Therefore, such economies tend to oppose data localization, though some may impose conditionality on data transfers in line with public policy goals such as privacy and regulatory oversight or access to certain types of data such as financial services or health. In the international sphere, economies with these characteristics typically advocate for and engage in ambitious RTAs and innovative DEAs that take a "holistic" view in terms of topic coverage and geographical scope, and favor interoperability. They may not necessarily have the economic or political heft to be "rule-makers" in their own right, but instead support innovative DEA models.

Other relatively advanced developing economies, especially in Southeast Asia, have a similar set of drivers and priorities, but with stronger domestic development orientation. These countries may have challenges regarding regulatory capacity or achieving economic inclusion, which limit the scope of regulation, their appetite to expose domestic sectors to competition, and/or their ability to engage in a wide range of RTAs and/or DEAs. In some cases, however, trade negotiations can be a deliberate strategy to help with capacity-building and domestic policy reform (for example, in Viet Nam).

On the other hand, while others may similarly have economic development goals, these may be oriented more to creating domestic champions rather than coherent external markets—in effect, a "digital industrial policy." In India, Indonesia, and the PRC, for example, the digital economy is seen as a potent enabler of economic development, but the sheer size of the domestic digital economy in these countries means that they prioritize the domestic market over creating opportunities to operate in global markets.

While it is a large global digital services exporter, India's regulatory model focuses on maximizing the economic and social benefits of data and data-driven sectors (Mishra 2023). Data regulations appear to ensure that local data are used primarily to develop domestic digital startups (UNCTAD 2021).

Similarly, the PRC has a vibrant, innovative and very large domestic digital economy. It has many "tech giants" which have succeeded not only domestically, but also in global markets. Their strong performance has been enhanced by government intervention to restrict foreign competition in the digital economy and undertake strategic investment to generate domestic competition and foster domestic champions (UNCTAD 2021). The PRC is also a leading exemplar of digitally enabled goods exporting, for example, through e-commerce platforms, meaning that its restrictive approach on data flows suits its domestic agenda while not impeding its digitally enabled export model, which is less concerned with data flows than it would be if based on digital services exports.

These "digital industry policies" have been successful to some extent for India and the PRC, thanks to the size of their domestic markets and their willingness to intervene with tailored policy and regulatory measures, including subsidies. However, such an approach is unlikely to translate easily to countries with a much smaller domestic market, fewer resources, and less capacity for intervention.

Furthermore, just as is the case in respect of conventional industry policy, protectionist measures may lead to inefficiencies and a lack of innovation, by shielding domestic firms from global competition and technology and intangible spillover effects—ultimately to the detriment of domestic consumers and small domestic firms that consume digital services or are engaged in global value chains. There are also likely to be impacts on the economy overall, particularly given the strong enabling effect of digitally delivered services on productivity and growth (ADB 2022c). Economies following an autarkic approach may miss out on creating export opportunities for their own tech businesses in other markets because they are not engaged in the global digital economy.

Leaving the economic dimension aside, some economies in the region may also prioritize national security and public stability considerations. This can mean seeking to safeguard "policy space" to regulate data-driven sectors, including a lot of government oversight on both data governance and online content. For example, the PRC favors a generally restrictive approach to data, including online content, for reasons of national security, cyber-sovereignty, and social stability.

Where institutional capability is high in many of the economies discussed, for others in the region, regulatory capacity is a significant limiting factor. This applies most strongly to economies in the Pacific, which face a range of hurdles in growing the digital economy, including infrastructure, digital literacy, financing, and capability. The Pacific E-Commerce Initiative, a multistakeholder partnership to support Pacific Islands Forum countries, has developed a regional e-commerce strategy which includes advocacy for regulatory capacity-building and development (UNCTAD 2022). Other less-developed economies in Asia and the Pacific face similar challenges, including the Lao PDR, Timor-Leste, Maldives, Sri Lanka, and some in Central Asia.

## 1.3. Optimizing Participation in International Cooperation

As the discussion in this chapter has highlighted, to maximize the benefits of the digital economy, regulatory approaches need to be agile and responsive; seek to balance a complex mix of commercial interests, innovation, and legitimate public policy concerns; and to the extent possible, seek to achieve interoperability with other economies. Ensuring that regulation is "fit for purpose" along these lines is vital given the broader context of rising global fragmentation (Evenett and Fritz 2022).

Achieving more coherent regulatory approaches is a daunting challenge in the context of the region's regulatory heterogeneity, regulatory gaps, and in some cases, overly restrictive approaches. It is also a challenge given the large potential universe of regulatory measures. The next section attempts to sketch out priorities for action.

### *Identifying "Core" Regulatory Building Blocks*

This chapter so far has illustrated a possible intersection between key elements of the evolving digital trade rules template and the "core" regulatory building blocks that developing countries will need to regulate and promote digital trade, not only to benefit domestic consumers and businesses, but also to participate effectively in future digital trade negotiations.

These building blocks can be divided into thematic categories, including: (i) market access; (ii) data regulation; (iii) measures to enhance trust in digital trade; (iv) measures to reduce trade and transaction costs; and (v) cooperation and stakeholder engagement. Table 1.1 identifies these elements and gives a rationale for their inclusion.

There are, of course, many other areas of high importance: in some, such as competition policy, whereas cooperation would help to create more effective responses, equal treatment for businesses, and more consumer choice, it is also true that few economies have established regulation specific to the digital economy, and provisions in trade agreements are scanter. Developing countries also face potentially significant implementation and enforcement costs. At the right time, this should be a priority for action.

**Table 1.1: Proposed "Core Regulatory Building Blocks" for Digital Trade**

| Key elements in digital trade rules | Domestic regulation or policy | Rationale |
|---|---|---|
| **(i) Market access, competition, and inclusion** | | |
| Market access | Regulations relating to imports of digital goods and services, particularly regarding when customs duties are not imposed. | Maintaining the current prohibition on Customs duties is critical for growth and productivity, and for affordable MSMEs/ consumer access to digital goods and services. |
| **(ii) Data regulation** | | |
| Data regulation (data flows, data localization) | Regulation of cross-border transfer of data for the conduct of business, requirements on the location for the processing and storage of data. | Well-designed policies minimize regulatory friction so enhances digital trade flows, while still preserving legitimate policy space; enhance the ability (and lowers the costs) of MSMEs to access digital services; supports innovation and economic growth. A patchwork of approaches across the region can have trade impacts and create operational uncertainty for businesses. |
| **(iii) Trust** | | |
| Personal information protection, data protection, privacy | Regulation on data protection and/or privacy (governing the collection, use and/or sharing of personal or other types of data). | Increases consumer and business confidence in digital trade, may reduce business compliance costs (if interoperable), safeguards important rights and the "social license to operate."<br>Only around half of ADB regional countries have data protection laws in place, with less coverage in South Asia and the Pacific. |
| Online consumer protection | Application to consumers engaged in digital trade of regulations for the protection of consumers, the prevention of deceptive and fraudulent practices, and recourse for consumer disputes. | Increases consumer and business confidence in digital trade, safeguards consumer rights.<br>Only around one-third of regional economies have such legislation in place. |
| Spam | Regulation of unsolicited commercial electronic communications. | Builds consumer confidence, may help to mitigate cybersecurity risks. |

*Continued on next page*

**Table 1.1** *continued*

| Key elements in digital trade rules | Domestic regulation or policy | Rationale |
|---|---|---|
| Cybersecurity | Regulations and policies relating to cybersecurity, including establishing entities responsible for cyber responses and mitigation, policies for collaboration with other entities. | Critical to trust for consumers, businesses, and governments (part of the "social license to operate"); supports increased adoption of digital tools by MSMEs and participation in digital trade. About four-fifths of regional economies have cybersecurity legislation in place or under preparation. Failure to act exposes economies, businesses, and consumers to significant risk—and many cyber threats are cross-border, requiring coordinated international responses. |
| Transparency on e-commerce regulation | Can be achieved through policy rather than regulation. | Increases business opportunities and confidence, and consumer access to digital services. Helps to mitigate nontariff barriers and disguised protectionism. |
| **(iv) Trade and transaction costs** | | |
| Electronic transactions frameworks and laws | Regulatory frameworks for electronic transactions, including the acceptance of electronic copies of documents. | A prerequisite for conducting commercial transactions online, typically establishing legal equivalence between paper-based and electronic documents. Reduces transaction costs for digital trade, including through the adoption of international model laws such as UNCITRAL Model Laws on Electronic Commerce or Electronic Transferable Records, and the UN Convention on the Use of Electronic Communications in International Contracts. About three-quarters of ADB developing economies have or are developing such legislation, although the Pacific is lagging. |
| Paperless trade, customs automation | Regulations recognize the legal validity of (and ideally promote the use and acceptance of) electronic copies of required trade documents; policies to promote adoption and integrated solutions (e.g., for trade and finance documentation). Policies to support the automation of customs procedures and the establishment of digital Single Windows (may also require regulatory change). | Reduces trade costs and enhances timeliness in trade, reduces fraud and delays—especially for goods trade, so is important even for less "digital" economies in the region. |

*Continued on next page*

**Table 1.1** *continued*

| Key elements in digital trade rules | Domestic regulation or policy | Rationale |
|---|---|---|
| E-authentication, e-signatures | Regulation of the legal validity of e-signatures, authentication, and digital certificates. | Reduces transaction costs and increases security of transactions, building business and consumer confidence. |
| E-payments | Regulation of payments do not discriminate against digital supply. | Reduces transaction costs for businesses, supports greater participation in digital trade—an essential element in all digital trade transactions, and especially valuable for MSMEs and developing economies without accessible traditional financial services. International interoperability and cooperation can help make payments more efficient and more secure. |
| Standards | Policy (and where necessary, regulation) to adopt international standards as far as possible and participate in their development. | Reduces compliance costs, supports greater interoperability and participation in digital trade. Important for developing economies to have a voice in standards-setting to ensure that they are fit for purpose. |
| **(v) Cooperation** | | |
| Cooperation on digital trade | Policies to support greater domestic innovation (for example, by establishing regulatory sandboxes) and cross-border cooperation on digital trade and emerging technologies; policies for ongoing engagement with stakeholders. | Fosters greater regulatory coherence and innovation, reducing compliance costs for MSMEs and consumers; enhances innovation; builds the "social license to operate" and enables more fit-for-purpose policy and regulatory design (including in rapidly emerging areas such as generative AI). An important pathway to regulatory capacity-building for developing economies. |
| MSMEs | Policies to support MSME access to the internet, capacity-building, and skills development. | Enhances ability of MSMEs to participate in digital trade. |

AI = artificial intelligence, MSMEs = micro, small, and medium-sized enterprises.
Source: Author, adapting Access Partnership 2023. Figures on regional cyberlaw from the UNCTAD Global Cyberlaw Tracker (accessed 11 June 2024); other notes on trade provisions from Trade Agreements Provisions on Electronic Commerce and Data.

In other areas, such as telecommunications infrastructure and competition, government procurement, intellectual property rights, content regulation, and foreign direct investment, these form part of broader domestic policy development. Though crucial, these are bigger conversations than just digital trade. In yet others, particularly some of the more innovative areas from DEAs such as artificial intelligence, open government data and digital identities, and some of the more practical "digital tools" that could help businesses, such as e-invoicing, while these need to be addressed, getting the basic building blocks in place first should be the priority.

### *Using International Cooperation to Build Capacity*

Several possible channels can support regulatory capacity-building for digital trade, such as tailored Aid-for-Trade program (ADB 2022). However, developing and least-developed countries can potentially also leverage other forms of international cooperation, including through trade agreements, to boost these efforts.

Settings such as the ASEAN Economic Community, the Asia-Pacific Economic Cooperation (APEC) forum, and the E-Commerce Capacity Building Framework for developing and least-developed countries established in early 2023 under the WTO Joint Initiative on E-Commerce, and the World Bank's pilot Digital Advisory and Trade Assistance Fund, are important forums to deepen understanding of the nuances of good regulatory practices in the digital economy, at least for participating countries. Other international bodies including UNCITRAL, UNCTAD, and the United Nations Economic and Social Commission for Asia and the Pacific, provide a forum to refine best practices.

Just as importantly, modern RTAs and new DEA-style initiatives can be valuable incubators for new approaches. In the case of RCEP, a mechanism is included for "targeted cooperation which will help Parties to implement or enhance their electronic commerce legal framework, such as research and training activities, capacity building, and the provision of technical assistance."[10] In the ASEAN E-Commerce Agreement, cooperation was proposed on a range of elements—which has laid some valuable groundwork for the current negotiations on a Digital Economy Framework Agreement (Tham 2021). The Singapore-Australia DEA similarly explicitly provides for regional capacity-building.

[10] RCEP, Article 12.4.

The new DEAs (and potential upgrades to existing RTAs such as CPTPP) also provide an important coordination mechanism. They typically identify many issues for further cooperation and engagement among participants, potentially offering an opportunity for shared learning and regulatory co-design. The emphasis on interoperability in these agreements also means that countries need to invest less time and resource in regulatory harmonization, and focus instead on enabling, interoperable outcomes established by DEA mechanisms.

In this context, the DEPA stands out from other DEAs: as an open plurilateral, it has the potential to form the foundation of outcomes among a much broader group of economies, rather than the "closed set" of a bilateral DEA. As discussed, many of the trade negotiations in the region only include a limited number of countries, and often not those most in need of regulatory development. The DEPA could broaden this population substantially.

It is critical that developing countries take part in the design of new regulatory approaches in a way that reflects their own priorities, constraints, and potential (Mishra 2022). This does not necessarily point to a one-size-fits-all approach, since different economies will have a different set of concerns and characteristics. Regardless, unilateral and restrictive approaches are unlikely to support inclusive growth in many economies and would add to the costs and frictions felt by MSMEs, underserved groups, and economies overall, including when seeking to enforce poorly designed, noninteroperable regulatory approaches. On the other hand, an open regulatory environment magnifies the benefits of digital connectivity for international trade (IMF et al. 2023).

In short, there can be a valuable interplay between domestic regulatory efforts and engagement in cross-border regulatory conversation that enriches both exercises. Developing countries should prioritize participating in international forums, including trade negotiations, wherever possible.

# APPENDIX: INVENTORY OF DIGITAL REGULATION BY SUBREGION, ASIA AND THE PACIFIC

| Country | UN MLEC | Electronic transaction legislation | Consumer protection legislation | Data protection and privacy legislation | Cyber-crime | ITU ICT Regulatory Tracker: Score (out of 100) | Data flow regulatory model | Local data storage | Regulated conditions on data transfers | Regulatory scale | Purpose of regulatory measures on data, where known (aggregated) |
|---|---|---|---|---|---|---|---|---|---|---|---|
| **Central Asia** | | | | | | | | | | | |
| Armenia | | Y | *No data* | Y | Y | 87.5 | Prescriptive | | | | |
| Azerbaijan | | Y | *Draft* | Y | Y | 64.5 | Prescriptive | | Y | Conditional transfer: Intermediate | National security, data protection, law enforcement |
| Georgia | | Y | *No data* | Y | Draft | 90.5 | Prescriptive | | Y | Conditional transfer: Hard | Data protection, privacy |
| Kazakhstan | | Y | Y | Y | Y | 53 | Prescriptive | Y | Y | Partial localization conditional transfer | Data security, data protection |
| Kyrgyz Republic | | Y | *Draft* | Y | Y | 70 | Prescriptive | | Y | Conditional transfer: hard | Data protection |
| Pakistan | Y | Y | *No data* | *Draft* | Y | 88.5 | Restrictive/ guarded | Y | Y | Strict localization | Regulatory access, public security, national security, data protection, economic development |

*Continued on next page*

**Appendix** *continued*

| Country | UN MLEC | Electronic transaction legislation | Consumer protection legislation | Data protection and privacy legislation | Cyber-crime | ITU ICT Regulatory Tracker: Score (out of 100) | Data flow regulatory model | Local data storage | Regulated conditions on data transfers | Regulatory scale | Purpose of regulatory measures on data, where known (aggregated) |
|---|---|---|---|---|---|---|---|---|---|---|---|
| Tajikistan | | Y | *No data* | Y | Y | 14 | | | | | |
| Turkmenistan | | Y | *No data* | Y | Y | 6.7 | | | | | |
| Uzbekistan | | Y | *No data* | Y | Y | 16.8 | | | | | |
| **East Asia** | | | | | | | | | | | |
| People's Republic of China | Y | Y | Y | Y | Y | 63 | Restrictive | Y | Most transfers not permitted | Mostly strict localization and conditional transfer: hard | Cybersecurity, national security, public security, protection of data, protection of sensitive data |
| Japan | | Y | Y | Y | Y | 73.5 | Favouring light touch/ prescriptive | | Some data | Conditional transfer: Hard | Data protection and privacy |
| Republic of Korea | Y | Y | Y | Y | Y | 70.2 | Prescriptive but not too much | | Varies | Localization and conditional transfer: Intermediate | Public security, national security, data protection and privacy |
| Mongolia | | Y | *No data* | Y | Y | 81.5 | | | | | |

*Continued on next page*

**Appendix** *continued*

| Country | UN MLEC | Electronic transaction legislation | Consumer protection legislation | Data protection and privacy legislation | Cyber-crime | ITU ICT Regulatory Tracker: Score (out of 100) | Data flow regulatory model | Local data storage | Regulated conditions on data transfers | Regulatory scale | Purpose of regulatory measures on data, where known (aggregated) |
|---|---|---|---|---|---|---|---|---|---|---|---|
| **South Asia** | | | | | | | | | | | |
| Afghanistan | Y | Draft | | | Y | 68.3 | | | | | |
| Bangladesh | Y | Y | Y | | Y | 64.5 | Probably light touch | Y | | | |
| Bhutan | Y | Y | Y | Y | Y | 62.7 | | | | | |
| Maldives | Y | *Draft* | | *Draft* | *Draft* | 51.3 | | | | | |
| Nepal | | Y | Y | Y | Y | 60 | | | | | |
| Sri Lanka | Y | Y | Y | | Y | 61.3 | | | | | |
| **Southeast Asia** | | | | | | | | | | | |
| Brunei Darussalam | Y | Y | | | Y | 71.5 | | | | | |
| Cambodia | Y | Y | Y | Y | *Draft* | 68 | | | | | |
| Indonesia | | Y | Y | Y | Y | 62 | Restrictive/ guarded | Y | | Strict localization and conditional transfer: Hard | Public security, national security, regulatory access, regulatory oversight |
| Lao PDR | Y | Y | *Draft* | Y | Y | 36.7 | | | | | |
| Malaysia | Y | Y | Y | Y | Y | 85 | Prescriptive | | | | |

*Continued on next page*

**Appendix** *continued*

| Country | UN MLEC | Electronic transaction legislation | Consumer protection legislation | Data protection and privacy legislation | Cyber-crime | ITU ICT Regulatory Tracker: Score (out of 100) | Data flow regulatory model | Local data storage | Regulated conditions on data transfers | Regulatory scale | Purpose of regulatory measures on data, where known (aggregated) |
|---|---|---|---|---|---|---|---|---|---|---|---|
| Myanmar | | Y | Y | *Draft* | *Draft* | 63.5 | | | | | |
| Philippines | Y | Y | Y | Y | Y | 69.2 | Light touch | | Y | Free flow of data (accountability-based) | Data protection and privacy |
| Singapore | Y | Y | Y | Y | Y | 93.5 | Light-touch | | | Free flow of data (accountability-based) | Data protection and privacy |
| Thailand | Y | Y | Y | Y | Y | 85.5 | Prescriptive | | Y | Conditional transfer: Intermediate | Data protection and privacy |
| Timor-Leste | | No data | No data | | Y | 55.5 | | | | | |
| Viet Nam | Y | Y | Y | Y | Y | 70.8 | Tending to Restrictive | Y | Unclear | Partial localization | National security, cybersecurity, social order, public safety |
| **The Pacific** | | | | | | | | | | | |
| Cook Islands | | Y | Y | Y | | | | | | | |
| FSM | | *No data* | Y | *No data* | | 51 | | | | | |
| Fiji | Y | Y | Y | | Y | 62 | | | | | |

*Continued on next page*

**Appendix** *continued*

| Country | UN MLEC | Electronic transaction legislation | Consumer protection legislation | Data protection and privacy legislation | Cyber-crime | ITU ICT Regulatory Tracker: Score (out of 100) | Data flow regulatory model | Local data storage | Regulated conditions on data transfers | Regulatory scale | Purpose of regulatory measures on data, where known (aggregated) |
|---|---|---|---|---|---|---|---|---|---|---|---|
| Kiribati | Y | *Draft* | Y | | Y | 49.5 | | | | | |
| Marshall Islands | | No data | No data | | | 15.5 | | | | | |
| Nauru | | | No data | | Y | 48.2 | | | | | |
| Niue | | Y | *No data* | | | | | | | | |
| Palau | | No data | No data | No data | | | | | | | |
| Papua New Guinea | Y | *Draft* | *No data* | | Y | 60 | | | | | |
| Samoa | Y | Y | Y | | Y | 73.5 | | | | | |
| Solomon Islands | | Y | Y | | | 81 | | | | | |
| Tonga | | Y | Y | | Y | 46.8 | | | | | |
| Tuvalu | | | | | *Draft* | 9.5 | | | | | |
| Vanuatu | Y | Y | Y | | | 77 | | | | | |
| Oceania | | | | | | | | | | | |
| Australia | Y | Y | Y | Y | Y | 94.5 | Light touch | | No health data transfers | Free flow of data (accountability) Strict localization (health data) | Data protection and privacy, protecting sensitive personal data |

*Continued on next page*

**Appendix** *continued*

| Country | UN MLEC | Electronic transaction legislation | Consumer protection legislation | Data protection and privacy legislation | Cyber-crime | ITU ICT Regulatory Tracker: Score (out of 100) | Data flow regulatory model | Local data storage | Regulated conditions on data transfers | Regulatory scale | Purpose of regulatory measures on data, where known (aggregated) |
|---|---|---|---|---|---|---|---|---|---|---|---|
| New Zealand | Y | Y | Y | Y | Y | 89.5 | Prescriptive but mild | | No tax, company data transfers | Strict localization (tax and company data) and conditional transfer: Intermediate | Regulatory access to data, data protection and privacy |

LAO PDR = Lao People's Democratic Republic, FSM = Federated States of Micronesia.
Sources:
Column 2: United Nations Commission on International Trade Law, UNCITRAL Model Law on Electronic Commerce (MLEC), status page (accessed in February 2023).
Columns 3 - 6: UNCTAD Global Cyberlaw Tracker (accessed in February 2023); additional information regarding the Pacific from: Pacific E-Commerce Initiative Pacific Region E-Commerce Assessment, December 2020.
Sources:
Column 7: ITU ICT Regulatory Tracker (accessed in March 2023). The ICT Regulatory Tracker is an evidence-based tool which pinpoints the changes taking place in the ICT regulatory environment. It is a composed metric based on 50 indicators covering regulatory authority, regulatory mandates, regulatory regime, and competition framework for the ICT sector. It covers over 190 countries and economies.
Columns 8–12: UNCTAD Digital Economy Report 2021, Annex II.
Columns 13–14: Asian Development Bank. 2022. *Aid for Trade in Asia and the Pacific: Leveraging Trade and Digital Agreements for Sustainable Development*; Burri, M., M. Vásquez Callo-Müller, and K. Kugler. 2024.
The Evolution of Digital Trade Law: Insights from TAPED. *World Trade Review*.

## References

Access Partnership. 2023. Economic Impact of Adopting Digital Trade Rules: Evidence from APEC Member Economies. APEC Committee on Trade and Investment. March.

Agarwal, B. and N. Mishra. 2022. Addressing the Global Data Divide through Digital Trade Law. *Trade, Law & Development*. 14 (2).

Asian Development Bank (ADB). 2022a. *Asian Economic Integration Report 2022: Advancing Digital Services Trade in Asia and the Pacific.*

_______. 2022b. *Aid for Trade in Asia and the Pacific: Leveraging Trade and Digital Agreements for Sustainable Development.*

_______. 2022c. *Unlocking the Potential of Digital Services Trade in Asia and the Pacific.*

_______. 2023. Building an Information-Sharing Mechanism to Boost Regulatory Frameworks on Cross-Border Data Flows. *T20 Policy Briefs*. May.

The Asia Foundation. 2024. *Digital Trade Agreements in Asia and the Pacific*. March.

Burri, M., M. Vásquez Callo-Müller, and K. Kugler. 2024. The Evolution of Digital Trade Law: Insights from TAPED. *World Trade Review* (2024), pp. 1–18.

Burri, M., M. Vásquez Callo-Müller, and R. Polanco. 2022. TAPED—Trade Agreements Provisions on Electronic Commerce and Data, Codebook.

Cory, N. and L. Dascoli. 2021. How Barriers to Cross-Border Data Flows Are Spreading Globally, What They Cost, and How to Address Them. Information Technology and Innovation Foundation. July 2021.

Economic and Social Commission for Asia and the Pacific (ESCAP). 2022. *Asia-Pacific Digital Transformation Report 2022: Shaping our Digital Future.*

_______. 2022. *Asia-Pacific Digital Trade Regulatory Review 2022.*

Evenett, S. J. and J. Fritz. 2022. *Emergent Digital Fragmentation—The Perils of Unilateralism: A Joint Report of the Digital Policy Alert and Global Trade Alert*. CEPR Press.

Ferracane, M. 2022. The Digital Trade Integration Database: Description of Pillars and Indicators. *RSC Working Paper* 2022/70, European University Institute, Robert Schuman Centre for Advanced Studies.

International Monetary Fund (IMF)-Organisation for Economic Co-operation and Development (OECD)-United Nations (UN)-World Bank Group-World Trade Organization (WTO). 2023. *Digital Trade for Development.*

Jiang, T. et al. 2023. Do Digital Trade Rules Matter? Empirical Evidence from TAPED. *Sustainability*. 2023 15. 9074.

Mishra, N. 2022. Can Trade Agreements Narrow the Global Data Divide? A Novel Agenda for Digital Trade. Hinrich Foundation.

______. 2023. Data Governance and Digital Trade in India—Losing Sight of the Forest for the Trees? In *Data Sovereignty*, edited by A. Chander and H. Sun. Oxford University Press.

Mitchell, A. and N. Mishra. 2023. A New Digital Economy Collaboration in the Indo-Pacific: Negotiating Digital Trade in the Australia–India CECA. *Journal of World Trade*. p. 57 (1).

Nemoto, T. and J. López González. 2021. Digital Trade Inventory: Rules, Standards and Principles. *OECD Trade Policy Papers* No. 251. Organisation for Economic Co-operation and Development.

Organisation for Economic Co-operation and Development (OECD). 2023a. Of Bytes and Trade: Quantifying the Impact of Digitalisation on Trade. *OECD Trade Policy Papers* No. 273.

______. 2023b. *Key Issues in Digital Trade*. OECD Global Forum on Trade 2023, Making Digital Trade Work for All. October.

Pacific E-Commerce Initiative. 2020. *Pacific Region Regional E-Commerce Assessment 2020.*

Suh, J. and J. Roh. 2022. The Effects of Digital Trade Policies on Digital Trade. *The World Economy*. 2023. 46. 2383–2407.

Sutthivana, N., W. Anukoonwattaka, and Y. Duval. 2023. *Navigating the Interplay: Digital Trade Provisions and Sustainable Development Aspects*. Economic and Social Commission for Asia and the Pacific.

Tham, Siew Yean. 2021. “Digital Commitments in ASEAN’s Free Trade Agreements.” ISEAS Yusof Ishak Institute, *Perspective* 2021. (163). p. 4.

United Nations Conference for Trade and Development (UNCTAD). 2016. *Data Protection Regulations and International Data Flows: Implications for Trade and Development.*

______. 2021. *Digital Economy Report 2021: Cross-Border Data Flows and Development: For Whom the Data Flow.*

______. 2022. *Digital Economy Report Pacific Edition 2022: Towards Value Creation and Inclusiveness.*

______. 2023. *E-Commerce and Digital Economy Programme Year in Review 2022—Looking Beyond Current Crises: Boosting Digital Readiness in Developing Countries.*

Vásquez Callo-Müller, M. and K. Kugler. 2023. *Digital Trade, Development and Inequality*. Symposium on Digital Trade and International Law. Cambridge University Press.

World Bank Group. 2023. *Digital Progress and Trends Report.*

### *Databases*

Burri, M., M. Vásquez Callo-Müller, and K. Kugler, Trade Agreements Provisions on Electronic Commerce and Data (TAPED). https://digitaltradelaw.ch/taped/.

Digital Policy Alert (DPA). https://digitalpolicyalert.org/.

European University Institute (EUI), "Digital Trade Integration Project" database. https://dti.eui.eu/database/.

International Telecommunication Union ICT Regulatory Tracker. https://app.gen5.digital/tracker/metrics.

United Nations Conference on Trade and Development (UNCTAD). Global Cyberlaw Tracker. https://unctad.org/topic/ecommerce-and-digital-economy/ecommerce-law-reform/summary-adoption-e-commerce-legislation-worldwide.

United Nations Economic and Social Commission for Asia and the Pacific (ESCAP) (2022), *Regional Digital Trade Integration Index (Version 1): A Guide.*

United Nations Economic and Social Commission for Asia and the Pacific (ESCAP). *Regional Digital Trade Integration Index* database. https://dtri.uneca.org/escap/trade-integration.

# 2 Digital Economy Partnership Agreement Provisions on Data Flow, Cybersecurity, and Privacy: Challenges and Policy Suggestions for Developing Countries

Henry Gao

## Introduction

With the growing popularity of digital trade provisions in free trade agreements, different policy models have emerged. Depending on their approaches to three provisions—data flows, cybersecurity, and privacy protection—three models are in use. The first is a US model which prioritizes the free flow of data across borders. Then an EU model emphasizes the protection of privacy or personal information, and a third, the model followed by the People's Republic of China (PRC), stresses the importance of cybersecurity.[11] Many free trade agreements cover these issues, but many do not go deeply into some of these issues, while some totally omit certain issues.

In contrast, the Digital Economy Partnership Agreement (DEPA) between Singapore, New Zealand, and Chile provides the most comprehensive treatment of all these issues and goes further. It would be a mistake to regard the DEPA as just another trade agreement. Rather, the DEPA is a pioneering framework that addresses rapidly evolving challenges and opportunities of the digital age. As the first of its kind, the DEPA is designed to tackle issues that traditional trade agreements overlook. It covers emerging areas like data flows, digital identities, and AI governance. A detailed examination is essential to appreciate how DEPA sets new standards and precedents for future digital trade agreements. DEPA provisions touch upon multiple facets of the digital economy, from e-commerce to digital payments, data privacy, and more. These elements are interconnected, and their implications are far-reaching, impacting businesses, governments, and individuals across borders.

[11] For a detailed analysis of the three models, see Gao (2023).

This chapter is not just about covering the basics of the DEPA. Instead, it is about unpacking the layers of complexity and innovation that make this agreement a game-changer in the global digital economy. The DEPA introduces novel approaches to digital governance, such as the use of regulatory sandboxes and cooperative frameworks. These innovations deserve a deep dive because they represent a shift in how digital economies might be regulated globally, offering a glimpse into the future of international digital cooperation. Moreover, many of DEPA's provisions contain nuances that are not immediately obvious. By delving into its specific paragraphs and clauses, one can uncover subtleties that reveal the true intent of the agreement. This level of scrutiny is necessary to understand the real impacts of DEPA and the challenges that the agreement might pose.

## 2.1. Data Flows

DEPA's provision on data flows is contained in "Module 4: Data Issues." This module includes three substantive provisions, covering personal information protection, data flow, and data localization. Below is the provision on data flow:

*Article 4.3: Cross-Border Transfer of Information by Electronic Means*

*The Parties affirm their level of commitments relating to cross-border transfer of information by electronic means, in particular, but not exclusively:*

*"1. The Parties recognise that each Party may have its own regulatory requirements concerning the transfer of information by electronic means.*
*2. Each Party shall allow the cross-border transfer of information by electronic means, including personal information, when this activity is for the conduct of the business of a covered person.*
*3. Nothing in this Article shall prevent a Party from adopting or maintaining measures inconsistent with paragraph 2 to achieve a legitimate public policy objective, provided that the measure:*
   *(a) is not applied in a manner which would constitute a means of arbitrary or unjustifiable discrimination or a disguised restriction on trade; and*
   *(b) does not impose restrictions on transfers of information greater than are required to achieve the objective."*

### *Affirmation of Existing Commitments*

The opening paragraph of the provision is interesting. By stating "[t]he Parties affirm their level of commitments," the provision implies that the obligation on data flow only reaffirms the Parties' existing commitments and alleviates the concern that the Parties have to assume new obligations. Use of the plural "commitments," along with the phrase "in particular" implies there are many possible variations of the commitments on data flow. This reading is further supported by the addition of "but not exclusively," which means that the language on data flow in the DEPA is first among equals, but not the only possible formulation of the obligation on data flow.

The opening paragraph is followed by a specific example of the substantive obligation on data flow, which is copied from the Article on data flow in the Comprehensive and Progressive Agreement for Trans-Pacific Partnership (CPTPP) word for word.[12] This is not surprising, given that the three Parties to the DEPA—Singapore, New Zealand, and Chile —were the three original Parties to the Trans-Pacific Strategic Economic Partnership Agreement (TPSEP),[13] the predecessor to the Trans-Pacific Partnership (TPP) and then the CPTPP.[14] The CPTPP is now one of the most influential free trade agreements and its chapter on electronic commerce has become a leading model chapter. Parties to the DEPA had the incentive to expand the reach of the CPTPP model by adopting its language.

On 15 July 2023, the DEPA Parties signed the Protocol to the DEPA,[15] which removed the opening paragraph of Article 4.3, but kept the rest of the provision intact.

### *No Uniform Regulatory Approach*

The DEPA's opening paragraph is followed by a set of substantive provisions, with the first paragraph sets the tone by acknowledging that "[t]he Parties recognize that each Party may have its own regulatory requirements concerning the transfer of information by electronic means." This short sentence confirms two things:

12 CPTPP Article 14.11.

13 See Gao (2010) for a history of the TPSEP.

14 See Gao (2012) for a description of the evolution from the TPSEP to the TPP.

15 The protocol can be found at https://www.mfat.govt.nz/assets/Trade-agreements/DEPA/DEPA-Protocol-signed-version.pdf.

First, it affirms each Party's right to regulate data transfer. This is quite significant in terms of legal obligations as it means that the right to regulate is a fundamental right, rather than just an exception to the obligation to allow free flow of data. In other words, a Party has the power to impose regulatory requirements on data transfer, and such a right to regulate is not an exception to the general obligation to allow data flow, as will be mentioned later in this chapter.

Second, the short sentence not only affirms the Parties' right to regulate, but explicitly allows for a diversity of approaches on data flow, as it confirms that "each Party may have its own regulatory requirements." This means that, instead of having to conform to a specific regulatory approach, each Party may adopt the approach which fits its situation best. This is especially good news for developing countries, as they might have unique circumstances that demand nontraditional approaches to data transfer regulations.

### *Minimum Standard*

Despite the allowance for diversity of approaches to data transfer, the DEPA also follows the example of the CPTPP in setting a minimum standard for cross-border transfer of data—i.e., "Each Party shall allow the cross-border transfer of information by electronic means, including personal information, when this activity is for the conduct of the business of a covered person."

This forms the core obligation in the Article by requiring Members to allow "the cross-border transfer of information by electronic means." The provision also explicitly states that it applies to all data including personal information (but do note the exception on personal information protection, which this chapter goes on to explain).

The provision on free flow of data is often misunderstood as an absolute requirement to allow all types of cross-border data transfer for all purposes. This is not the case. Instead, it is subject to several important restrictions:

First, the data transfer activity shall be "for the conduct of the business of a covered person." While the DEPA does not provide the definition of "covered person," one can refer to the definition in the CPTPP, which is where the provision came from. According to CPTPP Article 14.1, "covered person" means a covered investment, investor, or service supplier of a Party. This means that if a country does not wish to allow the cross-border data transfer in a given sector, it could do so legitimately by not including the sector in its schedule of commitments. Moreover, to the extent that a data transfer is not for business purposes, such as those provided on a free basis, it might also be restricted as it is arguably not a "covered investment." It is worth noting that, in the protocol signed by the DEPA parties in May 2023, the language of "covered person" has been replaced with "person of a Party," which is defined in Article 1.3 as a national or an enterprise of a Party. This filled the gap on the lack of definition of "covered person" and removed ambiguity about the exact scope of the "covered person."

Second, the definition for "covered person" under CPTPP Article 14.1 explicitly excludes financial services, which means that restrictions could be imposed on the flow of financial data. This is duly copied into the DEPA, which also carved out financial services in Article 1.1.2(b).

Third, according to CPTPP Article 14.2, the e-commerce chapter does not apply to government procurement or "information held or processed by or on behalf of a Party, or measures related to such information, including measures related to its collection." This leaves a wide exception for the information relating to the government. Again, this exclusion is also repeated in DEPA Article 1.1.2.

### *Public Policy Exception*

The DEPA article also includes a public policy exception, which explicitly affirms that the article shall not "prevent a Party from adopting or maintaining measures inconsistent with paragraph 2 to achieve a legitimate public policy objective." Again, this language is taken from CPTPP Article 14.11, which itself is modeled on the corresponding provisions on general exception under the General Agreement on Tariffs and Trade (GATT) and the General Agreement on Trade in Services (GATS), and leaves government with wide discretion to regulate cross-border information flow for a wide variety of purposes.

### *Is the Obligation on Data Transfer Binding or Subject to Dispute Settlement?*

The qualifications on the data flow obligation in the CPTPP are also copied into the Regional Comprehensive Economic Partnership (RCEP), the mega free trade agreement between 15 countries in Asia and the Pacific: the 10 ASEAN member states (Brunei Darussalam, Cambodia, Indonesia, the Lao PDR, Malaysia, Myanmar, the Philippines, Singapore, Thailand, and Viet Nam) plus Australia, the People's Republic of China, Japan, New Zealand, and the Republic of Korea that entered into force in January 2022.

Due to its diverse membership, the e-commerce chapter of the RCEP is not of as high standard as the CPTPP. It still includes the fundamental provisions, such as on trade facilitation and data flows. In addition to the qualifications on the data flow obligation like the CPTPP, the RCEP further includes a separate exception for security measures under Article 12.15. Moreover, the exceptions provision under the RCEP also goes one step further than the CPTPP by explicitly stating that, for the general exception, "the necessity behind the implementation of such legitimate public policy shall be decided by the implementing Party," and for the security exception, the measures "shall not be disputed by other Parties." Coupled with the exclusive carve-out of the RCEP e-commerce chapter from the dispute settlement mechanism under Article 12.17, the provision on free flow of data is not legally enforceable and supposed to apply only on a best endeavor basis.

It is interesting that even as the DEPA copies the substantive obligations on data flow from the CPTPP in terms of the binding force and application of the dispute settlement mechanism, it initially adopted the approach of the RCEP. This was achieved through two provisions hidden in the Agreement: First, DEPA Annex I records the Parties' understanding that four Articles "do not create any rights or obligations between or among the Parties under this Agreement," which include the provisions on data flow and data localization. Second, in the DEPA module on dispute settlement, Annex 14-A explicitly carves out these two provisions from the application of the dispute settlement mechanism in the module, including both the mediation mechanism and arbitration mechanism.

The lack of binding force and availability of the dispute settlement mechanism might be regarded as a design defect, but it can also be regarded as a unique feature of the DEPA for the following reasons:

First, as small countries, the three signatories of DEPA are fully aware that they cannot just force specific models on other countries like the big powers. Instead, they understand that the power of persuasion from an innovative model might work better than the powers of binding legal obligation and formal dispute settlement mechanism. This is what happened to the predecessor to the CPTPP, the TPSEP, which the same three countries had started. It can be said that they are replicating the success formula again.

Second, at a broader level, the DEPA's soft approach is not unique. It can be seen as the continuation of two traditions in the region—i.e., the ASEAN way (Woon 2012) and the open regionalism championed by the APEC. Both traditions reject the top–down, one-size-fits-all approach in favor of a bottom–up, consensus-first approach that allows members to move at varying pace. Given the complexity in the region, such an approach might be more realistic.

On the other hand, it could also be argued that the exclusion from dispute settlement simply results from all the original DEPA Parties having been Parties to the CPTPP, which does apply the dispute settlement chapter to these provisions. Thus, it does not make sense for them to apply the dispute settlement mechanism to these provisions, which is unnecessary, but may add further complications. However, this needs to change when countries that are not CPTPP members join the DEPA, as otherwise this would result in a lack of enforceability against the new parties. This is confirmed by the Protocol to the Digital Economy Partnership Agreement: Approval of Final Outcome and Authority to Sign, released by the Cabinet Economic Development Committee of the New Zealand government on 15 August 2023. The approval noted that amendments were needed to "provide legal certainty and transparency of commitments for accession candidates that are not members of the CPTPP, and to make them legally enforceable in the same manner as other DEPA commitments" (New Zealand Cabinet Economic Development Committee 2023).

With the signing of the Protocol on 15 July 2023, the data flow provision, along with provisions on data localization, nondiscrimination, and cryptography, are all subject to binding dispute settlement. However, as the DEPA is a stand-alone agreement rather than part of a bigger free trade agreement such as the CPTPP which includes other market access chapters, the utility of the dispute settlement mechanism might be more limited than some might think. This is because, under a normal FTA, the party winning a dispute can resort to trade sanctions to force the losing party to comply with the dispute settlement panel decision. Yet, under DEPA, there is no such sanctions to force the losing party to be subject to the same types of trade sanctions as under a normal FTA.

### *Challenges for Developing Countries*

As mentioned, the DEPA provision on data flow does not mandate free cross-border data flow for all kinds of data, but only data transfer activity "for the conduct of the business of a covered person." Legally speaking, this means that a country is not obliged to allow data flow for activities outside of the conduct of business covered under its commitments on services or investment. In practice, however, it would be difficult to implement this without broader data flow restrictions that apply across the board. Moreover, due to the pressures from negotiating partners in the negotiation of trade agreements, many countries might not be able to say no to the data flow provision. Thus, many countries might choose to agree to broad rules on free flow of data, but this may raise several challenges.

The first concerns economic or commercial challenges. The provision on free flow of data could enable the flow of different types of valuable data such as consumer data, transactional data, operational data, and big data, which are key to AI and machine learning. With free data flow, companies can more easily enter different markets and expand between them without needing to overhaul their data management strategies for each country. This makes it economically viable for giants to enter smaller or emerging markets that previously had been inaccessible because of regulatory hurdles. Access to diverse data sets from different countries fuels innovation. For instance, companies can develop new products or services that cater specifically to regional preferences or needs, using insights gleaned from data collected across different countries. This also allows for faster iteration and deployment of new technologies across multiple markets.

Ultimately, smooth data flows can also help tech giants achieve economies of scale, reducing costs and improving efficiencies. This is particularly important for companies that rely on massive data processing capabilities, such as cloud service providers. Thus, with facilitative data flow provisions, foreign tech giants will rush in. As they have more experience in e-commerce and more resources (especially financial), they might take over the market and leave little space for local firms. This is the case not only for global tech giants such as Amazon, Alibaba, and Uber, but also for regional tech giants such as Lazada, Shopee, and Grab, which have become the dominant players in almost all Southeast Asia.

One counterargument to the negative impacts of foreign tech giants is that they will also provide more jobs, but this might not be the case. Instead, while they might create more low-skill jobs such as delivery drivers, they do not necessarily create more high-skill jobs such as engineers. Instead, senior management for the local branch are often helicoptered from abroad. Worse still, they might poach the entrepreneurs and engineers from local startups and transfer them to other countries, further exacerbating the brain drain.

The second concern is regulatory challenges. Given the importance of data in every aspect of the modern economy, one significant consideration for regulatory supervision in every country is access to data. If data are not stored locally, this would make it hard for the regulators to have the necessary data to assess the regulatory risks and implement the necessary regulatory requirements. In some economies, regulatory authorities have introduced data localization measures to enhance monitoring and regulatory access (Parsheera 2022). For instance, central banks may require "unfettered supervisory access" to data to strengthen oversight, while insurance regulators may mandate data localization for policyholders information to facilitate regulatory access. Additionally, cybersecurity agencies may require organizations to maintain secure logs of their ICT systems for a specified period within national jurisdictions.

Such concerns are not limited to developing countries. Instead, even developed countries such as the US used to share them. This is reflected in the TPP chapter on e-commerce, which explicitly carved out financial services by stating explicitly that the term "covered person" does not include "financial institution" or a "cross-border financial service supplier."[16] Such language was supported by the US Treasury Department, Federal Reserve, and the Federal Securities and Exchange Commission, despite strong corporate opposition to data localization requirements.[17] This stance was informed by unpleasant experience during the 2008–2009 global financial crisis, when US regulators struggled to access necessary data. Thus, the Treasury wanted to preserve the ability of US regulators to enforce similar restrictions in the future. This cautionary approach is copied into the DEPA, where Article 1.1 notes that the Agreement does not apply to financial services except for Article 2.7 on Electronic Payments.

The third set of challenges concerns security. Such challenges may arise either because data is stored remotely, which can lead to data breach risks, or because giant foreign corporations control the digital infrastructure

[16] TPP, Article 14.1.

[17] CRS INSIGHT, TPP Financial Services Data Flows. 3 June 2016 (IN10498). https://sgp.fas.org/crs/row/IN10498.pdf.

and to meet regulations may have to disclose certain data to their home governments. This is illustrated by the notorious PRISM program revealed by Edward Snowden. In view of such challenges, many countries have put various safeguards in place. Some safeguards aim to limit foreign surveillance, for example, by mandating all email service providers operating in a given country to host their servers locally, a requirement that was underpinned by the Snowden affair (Parsheera 2022). Other regulations go beyond local storage to promote indigenous technology. For example, in 2014, banking regulators in the People's Republic of China issued several documents to make the information technology in the sector "secure and controllable." These included several requirements. Foreign providers of tech products and services were required to establish technology research and development (R&D) and service centers within the PRC to hold indigenous intellectual property rights controlled by its citizens, legal entities, or institutions. They had to file their source codes for registration with the Information Technology Department of the China Banking Regulatory Commission. Furthermore, they were required to control their supply chain risks, which could mean extending location requirements to suppliers of the direct providers of such products and services (King and Wood Mallesons 2015).

### *Policy Suggestions for Developing Countries*

Following signing of the DEPA protocol in July 2023, the provision on data flow is subject to the dispute settlement mechanism and a binding obligation. Thus, developing countries seeking accession to the DEPA should start reviewing their data flow regimes to prepare for eventual implementation, which should include the following components:

First, recognizing that cross-border data flow is a necessity for e-commerce firms to operate. If a country does not allow the free flow of data, this would create additional burdens for e-commerce platforms, sellers, and buyers—and may drive them away to other countries. Thus, developing countries shall review their existing legislation and remove unnecessary obstacles to data flow.

Second, at the same time, any country understandably could have legitimate concerns over potential problems created by data flows across borders and impose restrictions. However, in enacting restrictions, the government shall make sure the measures are limited, so that e-commerce players do not face unnecessarily burdensome commitments.

More specifically, a developing country shall develop its data flow regime in two steps:

The first step is to put in place proper legal framework for data flows, which may include introducing new laws and reviewing existing laws to better fit the need for data flow regulation.

In the second step, the government shall start reviewing the types of data or activities subject to data flow restrictions, the different types of restrictions that may be adopted, and carefully delineate restrictions on data flow by separating those on personal info protection, cybersecurity, public policy, and so on. It shall also make plans to progressively reduce the list of activities/ data subject to the restrictions.

## 2.2. Cybersecurity

DEPA provisions on cybersecurity feature in Module 5, on Wider Trust Environment. Module 5 includes the following two provisions:

*Article 5.1: Cybersecurity Cooperation*

1. *The Parties have a shared vision to promote secure digital trade to achieve global prosperity and recognise that cybersecurity underpins the digital economy.*

2. *The Parties further recognise the importance of:*
   - *(a) building the capabilities of their national entities responsible for computer security incident response;*
   - *(b) using existing collaboration mechanisms to cooperate to identify and mitigate malicious intrusions or dissemination of malicious code that affect the electronic networks of the Parties; and*
   - *(c) workforce development in the area of cybersecurity, including through possible initiatives relating to mutual recognition of qualifications, diversity and equality.*

*Article 5.2: Online Safety and Security*

1. *The Parties recognise that a safe and secure online environment supports the digital economy.*
2. *The Parties recognise the importance of taking a multi-stakeholder approach to addressing online safety and security issues.*

3. *The Parties shall endeavour to cooperate to advance collaborative solutions to global issues affecting online safety and security.*

### A Shared Vision on Cybersecurity

Article 5.1 starts by affirming the Parties' shared vision to promote cybersecurity, which is premised on the crucial role of cybersecurity in underpinning the digital economy, which, in turn, would help to achieve global prosperity. Without cybersecurity, neither the providers nor the users of digital trade would be willing to engage in the digital economy, which would lead to the decline of the sector. This understanding is further affirmed in the first paragraph of Article 5.2, which states that "[t]he Parties recognise that a safe and secure online environment supports the digital economy."

### Broad Scope

Cybersecurity could include the security of the private networks of digital trade firms and the security of public networks, such as internet service providers and telecommunication companies. The CPTPP provision on cybersecurity covers both private and public networks by noting the importance of "(a) building the capabilities of their national entities responsible for computer security incident response; and (b) using existing collaboration mechanisms to cooperate to identify and mitigate malicious intrusions or dissemination of malicious code that affect the electronic networks of the Parties."[18] In contrast, the RCEP provision on cybersecurity covers only cybersecurity issues concerning private networks.[19] This could be because the RCEP includes extensive exceptions on public policy and security, which are broad enough to cover cybersecurity issues concerning public networks.[20]

In this regard, the DEPA adopts the CPTPP model by covering both the public and private networks, which is a better approach given that the DEPA does not have extensive exceptions on public policy and security like the RCEP. This is confirmed by the adoption of "a multi-stakeholder approach to addressing online safety and security issues," which presumably would cover both public and private stakeholders.

---

[18] Article 14.16.

[19] Article 12.13.

[20] See, for example, the exceptions under Articles 12.14 and 12.15.

### *Capacity Building and Collaboration*

Unlike the physical realm, digital economy has no borders. Thus, cybersecurity issues often are not confined within national borders. Recognizing the global nature of issues affecting online safety and security, the DEPA calls for Parties to "cooperate to advance collaborative solutions." Such collaboration would occur across two levels:

(1) National, where it is a multistakeholder collaboration involving both public and private actors.
(2) International, when it would involve collaboration between national authorities from different Parties "to identify and mitigate malicious intrusions or dissemination of malicious code that affect the electronic networks of the Parties."

Capacity building is a major part of such collaboration. It includes building the capabilities of public actors (i.e., each Parties' "national entities responsible for computer security incident response") and private actors ("workforce development in the area of cybersecurity").

It is also worth noting that the DEPA, following the traditions of both the CPTPP and RCEP, does not require the establishment of new mechanisms for collaboration on cybersecurity. Instead, the DEPA emphasizes that this will be achieved "using existing collaboration mechanisms." This could help alleviate the concerns of new entrants on the need to establish new mechanisms.

### *Workforce Development*

Given their small internal markets, it might not be practical for each of the three DEPA Parties to develop its own cybersecurity workforce. The DEPA solves this problem by calling for workforce development in the sector "through possible initiatives relating to mutual recognition of qualifications, diversity and equality." This could be achieved through mutual-recognition agreements, which fit the overall theme of the DEPA in promoting interoperability. By pooling markets, the DEPA not only helps to expand the potential size of the market for cybersecurity experts, but also could give them a head start if the qualifications and standards for cybersecurity in DEPA countries becomes the de facto regional or even global standard with the future expansion of the DEPA, through initiatives such as the WTO's Joint Statement Initiative on E-commerce and the Indo-Pacific Economic Framework.

### *Challenges for Developing Countries*

DEPA provisions on cybersecurity are not by themselves a major challenge for developing countries as the agreement is mainly couched in nonbinding, best endeavor language. However, this does not mean that cybersecurity issues may be ignored, as firms trading digital services would regard the absence of a necessary regulatory framework as a red flag for entering the market.

While regulations on cybersecurity are essential to safeguard digital infrastructure and protect sensitive data, developing countries should be careful to not resort to overly broad or rigid cybersecurity regulations, as these can lead to several problems:

#### ***Stifling innovation***

Broad and stringent regulations may discourage innovation and hinder growth of the digital economy. Startups and small businesses, which often drive innovation, might struggle to comply with complex requirements, leading to reduced technological advancement and economic growth.

One recent example comers from Thailand's 2019 Cybersecurity Act, legislation that some internet freedom activists have criticized as a form of "cyber martial law" (Tanakasempipat 2019). The Act covers a wide range of issues from slow internet connections to major attacks on critical infrastructure, and empowers the National Security Council to override existing procedures with its own law in a cybersecurity crisis. The law also allows the National Cybersecurity Committee to summon and question individuals, enter private property without court orders in case of serious cyber threats, and sets up Cybersecurity Regulating Committee to access data and networks, seize devices, and impose penalties for noncompliance, without needing court warrants in "emergency cases."

Similarly, Viet Nam's 2019 Cybersecurity Law obliges online service providers to remove or block content deemed against the state's interests, which can lead to arbitrary censorship and limit freedom of expression, while also creating compliance challenges for businesses to navigate ambiguous content restrictions (Nguyen 2019).

***Reduced access to foreign investment and technology***

Strict and ambiguous cybersecurity regulations can discourage foreign investors from entering the market. Uncertainty about compliance and potential legal risks might lead investors to seek out more favorable investment environments, slowing down economic development. One example in this regard is Viet Nam's Decree 53 in 2022, which requires not only local storage, but also local offices for service providers that are considered to have not sufficiently complied with government guidelines. Such excessive regulations not only deter technology companies from entering developing country markets, but also make it impossible for local firms to tap international markets by using the services of foreign digital technology service providers. This, in turn, may limit access to cutting-edge technologies and digital services, further widening the technology gap between developed and developing countries.

Besides being a challenge for businesses, cybersecurity concerns can also create significant challenges for governments and regulators. First, cybersecurity enforcement is often quite technical and demands significant resources to implement, which can be especially challenging for developing countries with limited institutional capacity and enforcement mechanisms. For example, Cambodia employs extensive surveillance and monitoring practices, including monitoring online communications. These not only infringe on citizens' privacy rights and discourage open communication, but also require the government to put in place necessary hardware, software, and enforcement capacity, diverting resources from more pressing needs such as education, health care, and infrastructure development.

These implementation challenges can lead to two possible scenarios. The first is where regulations exist on paper, but are not effectively implemented or monitored, or only selectively enforced on an arbitrary basis. This could result in an uncertain regulatory environment for businesses, making it harder to make investment decisions or even to operate on a day-to-day basis. The second choice is to resort to what one might call "blunt force regulations" or "arbitrarily, suddenly imposing restrictions." Van der Kamp (2023) describes these as "crude, one-size-fits-all" rules using "highly coercive means." An example is internet shutdowns. While not a traditional cybersecurity regulation, such shutdowns demonstrate how excessive control over digital infrastructure can disrupt access to critical services and impede economic activities.

Developing countries should strike a balance with cybersecurity regulations that are targeted, flexible, and risk-based. This approach would encourage responsible cybersecurity practices while minimizing negative impacts on innovation, economic growth, and digital inclusion. Collaboration with international partners and learning from best practices can also help avoid some of the pitfalls associated with broad regulations.

### *Cybersecurity Challenges Arising from Data Localization Requirements*

Among regulations that could pose cybersecurity problems, data localization requirements are a prime example. They not only increase operating costs for e-commerce firms by obligating them to use or locate computing facilities in the host country, but also increase security risks for firms because additional computing facilities provide more possibilities for security breaches. On the other hand, it can be argued that data localization requirements help to generate business opportunities for domestic firms and create local jobs. However, because the big international e-commerce firms impose stringent data security requirements, local firms may not always have the resources to capture these opportunities. This might create conflicts with workforce development provision of the DEPA, as greater competition between security firms as a result of pooling the market could, in turn, squeeze out local firms.

DEPA's provision on data localization is Article 4.4, which is copied from Article 14.13 of the CPTPP. It states the key obligation as: "No Party shall require a covered person to use or locate computing facilities in that Party's territory as a condition for conducting business in that territory." Like the earlier provision on data flow, "a covered person" is also changed to "a person of a Party" pursuant to the protocol signed in July 2023.

As with the provision on the free flow of data, the CPTPP data localization provision is also subject to several important restrictions:

First, the obligation only applies to cases where "a person of a Party" is "conducting business in that Party's territory." This means that a country wishing to require data localization in a given sector could do so legitimately by not including the sector in its schedule of commitments.

Second, the carve-outs for financial services and government-related data also apply to the ban on data localization, while Article 14.13 also includes a public policy exception in the same vein as Article 14.11. This reflects concerns of the US Federal Reserve, which worried that offshore data storage could make financial regulation difficult. Similarly, while the ban on data localization is copied into the RCEP, the security exception also applies and it is self-determined by the Party invoking the exception.

Given the severe lack of capacity in all areas of digital trade, especially concerning cybersecurity, the provision on capacity building would be good news for developing countries. At the same time, their lower development level means they are likely to have difficulty in participating in Mutual Recognition Agreements (MRAs). This might make it hard for them to participate in DEPA workforce development initiatives.

## 2.3. Personal Information Protection

DEPA's provision on personal information protection is contained in Module 4: Data Issues, alongside the provisions on data flow and data localization. The wording of the provision is as follows:

1. *The Parties recognise the economic and social benefits of protecting the personal information of participants in the digital economy and the importance of such protection in enhancing confidence in the digital economy and development of trade.*
2. *To this end, each Party shall adopt or maintain a legal framework that provides for the protection of the personal information of the users of electronic commerce and digital trade. In the development of its legal framework for the protection of personal information, each Party shall take into account principles and guidelines of relevant international bodies.*
3. *The Parties recognise that the principles underpinning a robust legal framework for the protection of personal information should include:*
   *(a) collection limitation;*
   *(b) data quality;*
   *(c) purpose specification;*
   *(d) use limitation;*
   *(e) security safeguards;*
   *(f) transparency;*
   *(g) individual participation; and*
   *(h) accountability.*
4. *Each Party shall adopt nondiscriminatory practices in protecting users of electronic commerce from personal information protection violations occurring within its jurisdiction.*

5. *Each Party shall publish information on the personal information protections it provides to users of electronic commerce, including how:*
   *(a) individuals can pursue remedies; and*
   *(b) businesses can comply with any legal requirements.*
6. *Recognising that the Parties may take different legal approaches to protecting personal information, each Party shall pursue the development of mechanisms to promote compatibility and interoperability between their different regimes for protecting personal information. These mechanisms may include:*
   *(a) the recognition of regulatory outcomes, whether accorded autonomously or by mutual arrangement;*
   *(b) broader international frameworks;*
   *(c) where practicable, appropriate recognition of comparable protection afforded by their respective legal frameworks' national trustmark or certification frameworks; or*
   *(d) other avenues of transfer of personal information between the Parties.*
7. *The Parties shall exchange information on how the mechanisms in paragraph 6 are applied in their respective jurisdictions and explore ways to extend these or other suitable arrangements to promote compatibility and interoperability between them.*
8. *The Parties shall encourage adoption of data protection trustmarks by businesses that would help verify conformance to personal data protection standards and best practices.*
9. *The Parties shall exchange information on and share experiences on the use of data protection trustmarks.*
10. *The Parties shall endeavour to mutually recognise the other Parties' data protection trustmarks as a valid mechanism to facilitate cross-border information transfers while protecting personal information.*

### CPTPP Roots and Scope

Like the provisions on data flow and cybersecurity, the DEPA provision on personal information protection largely copies the language from Article 14.8 of the CPTPP. Out of the 10 sentences in Article 4.2 of DEPA, 6 are taken word for word from the CPTPP, while the rest further elaborate existing obligations under the CPTPP.

There are two approaches when it comes to the protection of personal data. The first is through comprehensive legislation governing personal data protection, with the EU's General Data Protection Regulation (GDPR)[21] being the leading example. The second approach is sector-specific, where the protection is guaranteed only for sectors with specific personal data protection laws.[22] The second approach is the preferred stance of the US, which adopted it for the CPTPP. This is why Parties to the DEPA are required only to "adopt or maintain a legal framework that provides for the protection of the personal information of *the users of electronic commerce and digital trade*" (emphasis added), rather than adopting a comprehensive personal data protection law.

To avoid any doubt, the DEPA also includes a footnote, again copied from the CPTPP, which states explicitly that "a Party may comply with the obligation in this paragraph by adopting or maintaining measures such as a comprehensive privacy, personal information, or personal data protection laws, sector-specific laws covering data protection or privacy, or laws that provide for the enforcement of voluntary undertakings by enterprises relating to data protection or privacy." This gives the Parties wide discretion in developing legal framework and does not limit them to specific models of personal data protection.

### *International Guidelines*

By allowing diverse approaches to personal data protection, the DEPA makes it easier for the Parties to comply with the obligation. At the same time, divergent regulations could raise the compliance costs for digital trade firms to navigate different and sometimes even conflicting regulatory regimes. To alleviate this problem, the DEPA calls for Parties to "take into account principles and guidelines of relevant international bodies." This again is in line with the spirit of the DEPA to promote interoperability.

By referring to "international bodies" rather than "national bodies," DEPA implies that the benchmark should be some internationally agreed upon guidelines rather than guidelines of specific countries. In practice, the most likely candidate for such guidelines would be the APEC Cross Border Privacy Rules (CBPR), rather than the GDPR championed in Europe. The CBPR takes a more flexible approach to privacy regulation as a

21 *EU General Data Protection Regulation (GDPR)*: Regulation (EU) 2016/679 of the European Parliament and of the Council of 27 April 2016 on the protection of natural persons with regard to the processing of personal data and on the free movement of such data, and repealing Directive 95/46/EC (General Data Protection Regulation), OJ 2016 L 119/1.

22 See Gao (2023) for a discussion of the difference between the two approaches.

voluntary, enforceable code of conduct designed to facilitate cross-border data transfers among participating APEC economies while ensuring a high standard of data protection. Companies that choose to take part in the CBPR must demonstrate compliance with the APEC Privacy Framework principles, such as notice, choice, integrity, security, and accountability. Certification is managed by accredited accountability agents within the APEC region, who monitor and enforce compliance.

### *A "Robust Legal Framework"*

To make sure that the legal framework for the protection of personal information is robust enough, the DEPA expands on the CPTPP obligation by spelling out what a "robust legal framework" should include. The elements it lists cover (a) collection limitation; (b) data quality; (c) purpose specification; (d) use limitation; (e) security safeguards; (f) transparency; (g) individual participation; and (h) accountability. The first five set the substantive requirements on the collection and use of data, while the last three focus on procedural safeguards. This makes it harder for the data controllers and processors to abuse data as it shines a spotlight on what they do. Together, the elements represent the broad consensus of most of the existing personal data protection laws, and can provide good guidance to developing countries looking to develop their own legal framework.

### *Nondiscrimination*

At the end of the day, personal information protection is about the rights of the users. Traditionally, users do not have a role in trade regulations, which mainly protect the interests of producers and their products. This is also reflected in the DEPA, which includes a clause on the nondiscriminatory treatment of digital products.[23] The provision on personal information protection extends the obligation to "users of electronic commerce." This covers both local and foreign users who suffer from personal information protection violations occurring within the jurisdiction. In practice, this would lengthen the reach to both local and foreign suppliers of e-commerce, such that foreign e-commerce providers are not discriminated against in the name of personal information protection.

[23] Article 3.3.

### *Remedy and compliance*

It is a well-known legal maxim that there is no right without a remedy. Thus, the DEPA explicitly specifies that the personal information protection laws shall specify how individuals can pursue remedies. Moreover, recognizing that prevention works better than cure, DEPA also calls for Parties to publish information on how businesses can comply with legal requirements, so that businesses can set up the necessary compliance mechanism and not inadvertently run afoul of the law.

### *Interoperability*

As mentioned, if diverse approaches to personal information protection to be allowed, then this could lead to divergent regulatory regimes or even conflicts. DEPA partly addresses this problem by requiring Parties to "take into account principles and guidelines of relevant international bodies." That by itself is not enough: there might be different international guidelines and variations even when countries adopt the same guidelines. Thus, the DEPA also calls for each Party to "pursue the development of mechanisms to promote compatibility and interoperability between their different regimes for protecting personal information." This is consistent with the DEPA objective to promote interoperability, which was mentioned 10 times in the DEPA (and mentioned a further 4 times using the word "interoperable"). Compatibility and interoperability are usually achieved in two ways: through mutual recognition, or having compatibility and interoperability harmonized with international standards. Both ways are mentioned in the DEPA, which was also copied from the CPTPP.

In addition, the DEPA also specifically refers to one method of recognition. That is, "appropriate recognition of comparable protection afforded by their respective legal frameworks' national trustmark or certification frameworks," as well as "other avenues of transfer of personal information between the Parties." This is followed by another sentence which calls for the Parties to exchange information on how the mechanisms are applied in their respective jurisdictions and explore ways to extend these or other suitable arrangements to promote compatibility and interoperability.

### *Data Protection Trustmarks*

Data Protection Trustmark (DPTM) is a voluntary enterprise-wide certification scheme by the Government of Singapore, which was announced at the wake of a major cybersecurity incident when the personal information of more than 1.5 million patients of SingHealth was stolen on 21 July 2018 (Su 2018). By providing certifications for organizations to demonstrate accountable data protection practices, the DPTM assures users that their personal data are being securely handled. To promote the adoption of data protection trustmarks, the DEPA includes three sentences, which respectively calls for the adoption of data protection trustmarks by businesses, exchange information on and share experiences on the use of data protection trustmarks, and mutually recognize the other Parties' data protection trustmarks as a valid mechanism to facilitate cross-border information transfers while protecting personal information.

### *Implementation Challenges for Developing Countries*

As has been explained, the DEPA's approach to personal information protection balances diverse regulatory strategies and promotes interoperability. It also encourages the adoption of data protection trustmarks to improve cross-border data flows while maintaining user privacy. Although these provisions aim to enhance personal information protection in the digital economy, nations would need to overcome several obstacles to achieve effective implementation.

#### ***Resource constraints***

Developing countries often have limited financial and human resources to establish and maintain robust legal frameworks for personal information protection. The development and enforcement of privacy regulations can be costly, particularly for establishing mechanisms for transparency, individual participation, and accountability.

#### ***Lack of infrastructure***

Effective personal information protection requires appropriate technical infrastructure, including secure data storage, encryption, and cybersecurity measures. Developing countries may struggle to establish and maintain the necessary technological infrastructure to safeguard personal data.

### *Compliance costs*

If privacy regulations are too strict, they will greatly increase the cost of doing business for everyone, and especially for micro, small, and medium-sized enterprises that would have to incur the same one-off costs of hiring and training staff members as bigger companies.

### *Cultural considerations*

Countries in Southeast Asia traditionally have mostly rural communal societies, which do not have the same concepts of privacy as Western urban-based individualist societies. Thus, the need to build public awareness and educating individuals about their privacy rights in the digital sphere is crucial. However, the most vulnerable populations are typically much less informed about their privacy rights and less equipped to protect their personal data. This makes it hard for developing countries to inform citizens about these rights and empower them to exercise control over their personal data. Another challenge is that many countries in the region are multicultural. This makes it difficult to tailor privacy regulations tailored to the cultural and linguistic context of each country. Developing countries, therefore, may find it challenging to strike a balance between adopting internationally recognized principles and making sure that these principles align with local norms and customs.

## *Lack of Regulatory Expertise*

The biggest problem for regulation in many developing countries is the lack of expertise in this area, given that privacy started out as a Western concept and might be ill-suited for the specificities of the local environment. This also explains why many developing countries do not even have general laws on personal information protection, let alone for personal information protection in the digital economy. One obvious solution to the regulatory gap is copying from pieces of foreign legislation, but then the risk is that they just copy regulations without much thinking, which might raise other problems. For example, a regulation on data protection modelled after the EU's GDPR *could include provisions that allow the government to restrict the transfer of personal data by data controllers to certain countries or territories for processing there.*[24] However, one key difference is that such a regulation

[24] See The Digital Personal Data Protection Bill. 2023. https://prsindia.org/files/bills_acts/bills_parliament/2023/Digital%20Personal%20Data%20Protection%20Bill,%202023.pdf.

may not clearly define the established principles or criteria to evaluate the legitimacy of data transfers, which could lead to considerable legal ambiguity, *as is seen in some recent legal frameworks* (Manne and Baeczentewicz 2023). This is not the case under the GDPR, which clearly spelled out ways that such cross-border transfer might be allowed—i.e., either pursuant to an adequate decision that applies to the whole country (Article 45), or where the controller or processor has provided appropriate safeguards (Article 46). The lack of such mechanism might not be a big problem for a Party like the EU, which due to its fragmented market does not have big e-commerce players. However, for a country with big e-commerce ambition, blindly copying such extremely restrictive personal data regulation will stifle the development of its domestic e-commerce market.

#### ***International cooperation***

The DEPA also provides for international cooperation among its members, but such opportunities might be difficult for developing countries to harness because of their limited regulatory capacity. Without sufficient capacity to effectively design, implement, and enforce regulations that align with international standards and obligations, many developing countries may find it hard to reach consensus on common standards, rules, and requirements with other countries.

### *Policy Suggestions for Developing Countries*

A big challenge for many developing countries is that they not only lack online consumer and personal information protection laws, but also do not even have consumer and personal information protection laws in general. Thus, they would need capacity building for personal information protection, not only for the government to understand the need for a proper regulatory framework, but also for business and consumers to understand the range of their respective rights and obligations. Their low level of regulatory capacity would mean that developing countries would also face challenges in participating in mutual recognition agreements.

In the formulation of online personal information protection laws, developing countries shall focus on the following issues:

First, avoiding languages which are too general and try to specify the obligations or exceptions as detailed as possible. Second, given the sensitivity of personal data, the law shall separate the protection of personal data from other data, as the EU GDPR and Personal Data Protection Law in the PRC has done. This would ensure that personal data protection is put in place properly.

The third point is that the law shall focus on issues particularly relevant to e-commerce, such as the abuse or leakage of personal data of e-commerce users, the local storage of certain data, and the cross-border transfer of personal data. As mentioned, it would be useful to work out different use scenarios of different types of data, and design legal mechanisms to deal with each individual scenarios of data protection. These different data use scenarios shall be clearly delineated without internal contradictions or inconsistency.

## 2.4. Architectural Issues

One of the major innovations of the DEPA is its modular approach, which does two things. First, it keeps the Agreement flexible,[25] in that new members do not have to accept all modules, but may pick and choose from existing modules. Second, it turns the Agreement into a "living agreement" with new modules that the Parties might add in future to address emerging issues.

Putting this together with the explicit rejection of the binding force and application of the dispute settlement system to key provisions such as on data flow—as discussed earlier in this chapter—the DEPA's modular approach ensures maximum innovation for ambitious Parties, while retaining maximum flexibility for Parties that want to take a more cautious regulatory approach. This could be good news, especially for developing countries looking to accede to the DEPA. At the same time, when it comes to specific accessions, the situation might be more complicated. For example, the Singapore government, in a submission to the APEC, noted that two key considerations for new accessions are whether the new member is "willing and ready to fulfill all the obligations in the DEPA," and "[w]hat collaborative projects would you like to explore with the DEPA parties." Therefore, the reality is that developing countries seeking to join the DEPA might still have to overcome significant hurdles, despite some key obligations in the DEPA not being binding in nature.

[25] APEC, Digital Economy Partnership Agreement, submitted by Singapore, 2021/CTI/WKSP9/007 Session 4.2, http://mddb.apec.org/Documents/2021/CTI/WKSP9/21_cti_wksp9_007.pdf.

Another issue is the relationship between the DEPA and other agreements or provisions related to the digital economy that are included in trade agreements. This is a real concern as all three founding Parties of the DEPA are also active in free trade agreements, with each party to more than a dozen FTAs, many of which include chapters or provisions on digital trade. Anticipating the issue, the DEPA explicitly addresses the problem in Article 1.2 by spelling out the relationship between the DEPA and other Agreements:

1. *Recognising the Parties' intention for this Agreement to coexist with their existing international agreements, each Party affirms:*
   (a) *in relation to existing international agreements to which all Parties are party, including the WTO Agreement, its existing rights and obligations with respect to the other Parties; and*
   (b) *in relation to existing international agreements to which that Party and at least one other Party are party, its existing rights and obligations with respect to that other Party or Parties, as the case may be.*
2. *If a Party considers that a provision of this Agreement is inconsistent with a provision of another agreement to which it and at least one other Party are party, on request, the relevant Parties to the other agreement shall consult with a view to reaching a mutually satisfactory solution. This paragraph is without prejudice to a Party's rights and obligations under Module 14 (Dispute Settlement).*

In other words, the DEPA is supposed to coexist with other free trade agreements. In case of inconsistencies between the DEPA and another agreement involving two Parties to the DEPA (such as CPTPP or RCEP), the Parties would consult with each other to reach a mutually satisfactory solution. However, any Party may bring a dispute settlement case under the DEPA. One problem with this provision is that it only covers existing agreements, not future agreements. This might not be a major problem in practice, since if a DEPA Party negotiates a new agreement with digital trade provisions, it is likely to try to ensure obligations of the new agreement are consistent with its DEPA obligations.

This might not hold true in two scenarios: The first scenario is when a new DEPA Party, such as the PRC, negotiates another agreement, as it does not have the same incentive as the original Parties to the DEPA to give priority to the DEPA model. The second scenario is when DEPA Parties negotiate trade agreements with a major power, such as the US, in the new Indo-Pacific Economic Framework Agreement, which can dictate terms different from the existing DEPA provisions. In those cases, there might be a need to amend the DEPA by resorting to the procedure under Article 16.3. However, by then, the amendment might not be necessary as the DEPA might have already achieved its historical mission of inspiring new digital economy agreements. This is just what happened to the TPSEP (also started by the three original Parties to the DEPA) on conclusion of the CPTPP.

## 2.5. Conclusions

Despite these many challenges, many ways still exist for developing countries to mitigate the potential adverse impacts of these provisions, either through national policy actions, or through technical assistance from the international community. Suggestions include:

### *Learn from the good regulatory practices of other countries*

Many of the digital economy problems facing developing countries are not new. Instead, they most likely have already been encountered by other countries and solved. An example discussed earlier is the carve-out for financial services under the CPTPP the emanated from the concerns of US financial regulators. However, it is worth noting that the US regulators have since found new way of dealing with the problem, which is provided for in the following provisions under *Article 17.18: Location of Computing Facilities of the United States–Mexico–Canada Agreement (USMCA):*

2. *No Party shall require a covered person to use or locate computing facilities in the Party's territory as a condition for conducting business in that territory, so long as the Party's financial regulatory authorities, for regulatory and supervisory purposes, have immediate, direct, complete, and ongoing access to information processed or stored on computing facilities that the covered person uses or locates outside the Party's territory.*
3. *Each Party shall, to the extent practicable, provide a covered person with a reasonable opportunity to remediate a lack of access to information as described in paragraph 2 before the Party requires the covered person to use or locate computing facilities in the Party's territory or the territory of another jurisdiction.*

In other words, the key to effective financial regulation is not the location of the data, but whether the regulators have "immediate, direct, complete, and ongoing access" to such data. Thus, to the extent that any country believes that data localization is the only solution to address regulatory concerns, they might have to review their regulatory approach. At the same time, it is understandable that some developing countries might not have the technical capacity to gain immediate access to data located in foreign facilities, but then the solution should lie in building the necessary digital infrastructure or removing barriers to cross-border data flows to facilitate such access.

In this regard, even for developed countries, their positions are often not static, but are constantly evolving. One of the latest examples is when the US withdrew its support for provisions such as free flow of data and prohibition on data localization in October 2023 (Broadbent 2023). While the US has not given the exact reasons for such policy shift, it seems the move was motivated mainly by the need to enforce its labor and competition laws. However, as mentioned earlier, the enforcement of such laws could be justified by various exceptions clauses commonly found in the digital trade chapters of free trade agreements. These typically allow measures taken for valid public policy reasons. In any event, developing countries should pay close attention to the evolving international landscape and then adjust their positions accordingly.

### *Developing countries should harness private sector capacity*

On cybersecurity issues, the private sector has developed many ways to deal with the potential security risks without resorting to draconian one-size-fits-all blunt regulations. Despite the evolving cybersecurity landscape as new threats emerge and technology advances, private companies are continuously adapting their cybersecurity strategies. One obvious way is to rely on established cloud service providers like Amazon Web Services (AWS), Microsoft Azure, and Google Cloud, which have developed robust security measures to protect data stored on their platforms. Another way comes through using Multi-Factor Authentication (MFA). This adds an additional layer of security by requiring users to provide multiple forms of verification before gaining access to a system. Many companies have implemented MFA to prevent unauthorized access to accounts and sensitive data. Blockchain technology may also be used to strengthen cybersecurity by providing a decentralized and tamper-resistant ledger. It has been applied to secure transactions, supply chain management, and identity verification.

The third suggestion is to work with nongovernment organizations (NGOs). One major challenge to policymaking in many countries is the collective action problem. As Mancur Olson explained in his seminal work, *The Logic of Collective Action* (Olson 1965), while individuals have incentives to collectively pursue common goals, larger groups face a "free rider" problem where some individuals benefit from the group's efforts without contributing. This dynamic leads to the underprovision of public goods, as individuals opt to free ride rather than bear the costs of contributing. But this collective action problem can be overcome by NGOs who dedicate themselves to worthy causes such as privacy protection.

Most of the work in the area is done by international NGOs, which are often well-funded and have significant experience, such as the work of Privacy International in the Philippines (Zhu 2022). At the same time, local NGOs can also play important roles, such as the efforts by Bloggers Association of Kenya (BAKE) to push the boundaries of privacy protection through litigation with the support of rights group Article 19 (Freedom House 2022). Whether or not the work was initiated by international or local NGOs, it is important to recognize that, at the end of the day, the local population must build enough awareness to have ideas such as privacy protection taken root within the country.

Addressing these challenges requires a comprehensive and context-specific approach, which can be met by technical assistance activities organized by international donors, which can take the following forms:

- **Workshops and seminars**: Organize workshops and seminars to educate government officials, policymakers, and stakeholders about the importance of data flow, cybersecurity, and privacy protection. These events can provide an overview of the challenges and best practices, and the main regulatory models on each issue.
- **Professional development programs**: Establish programs that offer specialized training to industry professionals in areas such as cybersecurity, data protection, and data flow. These programs can enhance local expertise and knowledge.
- **Cybersecurity awareness campaigns**: Start public awareness campaigns to educate citizens about cybersecurity risks, safe online practices, and the importance of protecting their personal data. As mentioned earlier, such campaigns can be conducted by industry groups and NGOs working together.

Besides such technical assistance activities, developing country governments could also benefit from inputs from stakeholders to formulate and implement various laws. Such inputs can be gathered through consultations with citizen groups, NGOs, industry associations and representatives, and international organizations during the drafting phase, where industry groups are brought in to find ways to minimize regulatory impacts while ensuring regulatory objectives are met and integrating privacy impact assessments into policymaking to ensure that new technologies and initiatives respect the privacy rights of individuals.

By implementing these ideas, developing countries can strengthen their capabilities in data flow, cybersecurity, and privacy protection, and contribute to a safer and more secure digital environment for their citizens and businesses. In turn, developing countries can also take part in international agreements such as the DEPA, and they can use the Agreement to build up their domestic regulatory framework on these issues.

## References


Broadbent. 2023. USTR Upends U.S. Negotiating Position on Cross-Border Data Flows. https://www.csis.org/analysis/ustr-upends-us-negotiating-position-cross-border-data-flows.

Freedom House. 2022. Kenya: Freedom on the Net 2022 Country Report. https://freedomhouse.org/country/kenya/freedom-net/2022.

Gao, H. 2010. The Trans-Pacific Strategic Economic Partnership Agreement: A Critical Analysis *Legal Issues of Economic Integration.* 37 (3). pp. 221–240. https://ink.library.smu.edu.sg/sol_research/958.

_______. 2012. From the P4 to the TPP: Transplantation or Transformation? In *The Trans-Pacific Partnership: A Quest for a Twenty-First Century Trade Agreement,* edited by C. L. Lim, D. K. Elms, and P. Low. Cambridge University Press.

_______. 2023. Data Sovereignty and Trade Agreements: Three Digital Kingdoms. In *Data Sovereignty: From the Digital Silk Road to the Return of the State*, edited by A. Chander and H. Sun. Oxford Academic. Oxford University Press. https://doi.org/10.1093/oso/9780197582794.003.0010.

King and Wood Mallesons. 2015. China Strengthening Bank IT Regulation (Zhongguo Jiaqiang Yinghang IT Jianguan). *China Law Insight.* 17 March 2015. (Chinese language). https://www.chinalawinsight.com/2015/03/articles/finance/□□□□□□i t□□□□/ (accessed 17 August 2023).

Manne, G. and M. Baeczentewicz. 2023. "Keeping Data Flowing Is in India's Interest." *The Times of India*. 28 March. https://timesofindia.indiatimes.com/blogs/voices/keeping-data-flowing-is-in-indias-interest/.

New Zealand Cabinet Economic Development Committee. 2023. Protocol to the Digital Economy Partnership Agreement: Approval of Final Outcome and Authority to Sign. 15 August 2023. https://www.mfat.govt.nz/assets/OIA/OIA-2023/PR-2023-0280-DEPA-Collated-Docs.pdf.

Nguyen, D T U. 2019. "Vietnam's New Cyber Law Will "Chill" Innovation, Investment: BSA." *Bloomberg Law*. 3 January. https://news.bloomberglaw.com/privacy-and-data-security/vietnams-new-cyber-law-will-chill-innovation-investment-bsa.

Olson, M. 1965. *The Logic of Collective Action: Public Goods and the Theory of Groups*. Cambridge and Harvard University Press.

Paine, J. 2022. Data Localization Rules Will Set Back Vietnam's Digital Economy. Opinion, *Nikkei Asia*. 30 September. https://asia.nikkei.com/Opinion/Data-localization-rules-will-set-back-Vietnam-s-digital-economy.

Parsheera, S. 2022. What's Shaping India's Policy on Cross-Border Data Flows? In *Data Governance, Asian Alternatives: How India and Korea Are Creating New Models and Policies,* edited by E A. Feigenbaum and M R. Nelson. Carnegie Endowment for International Peace. https://ssrn.com/abstract=4344111.

Su, J. 2018. "What Is Singapore's New Data Protection Trustmark Certification (DPTM) All About?" *Zegal Singapore*. 30 July. https://zegal.com/en-sg/blog/post/what-is-singapores-new-data-protection-trustmark-certification-dptm-all-about/.

Tanakasempipat, P. 2019. Thailand Passes Internet Security Law Decried as "Cyber Martial Law." *Reuters*. 28 February. https://www.reuters.com/article/us-thailand-cyber-idUSKCN1QH1OB.

Van der Kamp, D. 2023. Introduction: Clean Air at What Cost? In *Clean Air at What Cost?: The Rise of Blunt Force Regulation in China.* Cambridge Studies in Law and Society. pp. 1–27. Cambridge University Press. doi:10.1017/9781009152655.001.

Woon, W. 2012. *Dispute Settlement the ASEAN Way.* https://cil.nus.edu.sg/wp-content/uploads/2010/01/WalterWoon-Dispute-Settlement-the-ASEAN-Way-2012.pdf.

Zhu, N. 2022. "How Privacy Organizations Build a Better Society." Blog, *Internxt*. 12 April. https://blog.internxt.com/how-privacy-orgs-improve-society/.

# 3 Standards in the Age of Digital Trade: A Way Forward

Jooyoung Kwak and Heejin Lee

## Introduction

Digital services and platform businesses increasingly operate globally, and the routine exchange of data across borders gives rise to "digital trade." As standards play a critical role in improving interoperability and reducing barriers in the trade of goods and services across borders, "digital standards" are expected to play a similar role in digital trade.

The term "digital standards" is used in diverse contexts besides digital trade, including discourse on the standardization of digital, critical, and emerging technologies. For example, the US National Standards Strategy for Critical and Emerging Technology in May 2023 announced a list of 14 technologies and applications that standardization could be applied to. Among them, 10 standards[26] can be called "digital technologies," including "Communication and Networking Technologies," "AI and Machine Learning," "Digital Identity Infrastructure and Distributed Ledger Technologies," and "Cybersecurity and Privacy." The rest are all closely related to, and supported by, digital technologies. Hence, there is a strong case for embedding digital standards in all of these technologies and applications.

The tendency for integrating standards is also found in digital trade. Technology has been used in trade well before digital trade came into wide use. The United Nations/Electronic Data Exchange for Administration, Commerce and Transport (EDIFACT) is an example of the facilitation of trade by information and communication technology (ICT) that is already

---

[26] Among the listed technologies, those except clean energy generation and storage, biobanking and carbon capture, removal, utilization and storage are regarded as digital or digital-related.

common. Digital trade includes another increasingly important aspect of trade: the cross-border flow of digital goods. Products and services become digitalized and transferred across borders in the form of data. In current usage of the term "digital trade," the cross-border flow of data has attracted the most attention. EDIFACT is a type of standard. In digital trade, standardization for the facilitation of trade is increasingly needed and expanding in scope. Digitalization and transfer of products and services in the form of data also require further standardization to be operational in different regions and countries on a global scale.

Another often used term is "digital trade standards." The ASEAN-Australia Digital Trade Standards (DTS) Initiative is an example.[27] Although "digital trade standards" can be interchangeable with the term "digital standards," this chapter uses "digital trade standards" to refer to "digital documentation accompanying goods traded across borders and used to access markets, signify ownership of a good, and claim payments, among other functions" (Suominen 2023, p. 3) rather than general rules and principles surrounding digital technologies.

The "Digital Standards Initiative" of the International Chamber of Commerce (ICC) aims to establish "a globally harmonized digital trade environment." However, an exact and agreed upon definition of digital standards has yet to be made. Absent a common definition, this chapter uses "digital standards" to refer to technical standards related to digital technologies in a trade agreement. In this light, digital standards can provide the technical foundation for how the digital trade principle can be implemented.

There is still some overlap in that digital standards issues match issues involving digital trade standards as digital services and platform applications serve consumers all over the world, with data generated from services crossing borders. Even as we may use "digital trade standards" in a narrow sense, in practice, the two terms are often used interchangeably.

This chapter is organized as follows. First, the current digital standards are introduced with a focus on their main features. Specifically, four "digital" trade agreements—the Digital Economy Partnership Agreement (DEPA), the Australia–Singapore Digital Economy Agreement (ASDEA), the Digital Economy Agreement between the United Kingdom and Singapore (UKSDEA), and the Korea–Singapore Digital Partnership Agreement (KSDPA)—are discussed. Next, current efforts to set AI and

[27] https://asean-au-dts.org/.

5G communication standards for the sector are illustrated in relation to the implications for Asia. As the digital trade agreements have several standard-related provisions, these provisions that appear particularly on the DEPA and DEA are introduced with the challenges and the solutions for policymakers. Because compliance in the private sector is highly important in fostering digital trade, a brief note about the challenges and recommendation for private participation in both implementation/compliance and development/improvement of the standards is suggested. Finally, recommendations to improve digital standards in digital trade are suggested.

## 3.1. Development of Digital Standards: Trends and Main Features

Countries are still negotiating some issues in conventional/traditional agendas relating to digital trade. A well-known point of contention is the duty-free moratorium on electronic transmissions. Developing countries and advanced economies argue that the moratorium brings disproportionate or unbalanced gains for different countries[28]

Another issue of note is the cross-border transferability of data and data localization. Whereas some countries still do not allow outbound data transfer or insist that servers are localized, recent digital trade agreements tend to include data transfer provisions and discourage data localization.

Digital trade was first discussed in an independent trade agreement with the signing of the US–Japan Digital Trade Agreement (USJDTA) in 2019. Prior to that, digital trade was regarded as being complementary to trade of commodities and services. The establishment of trade agreements specific to digital trade is a current global trend. Among them are the DEPA, the ASDEA, the UKSDEA, and the KSDPA. With their focus on fundamental aspects of digital trade, these deals go beyond the limits of a free trade agreement (FTA), and advocate for free digital trade. The characteristics of each are illuminating to the discussion in this chapter. [29]

---

[28] At the 12th World Trade Organization (WTO) Conference, an extension of the "moratorium on customs duties on electronic transmission" was adopted. This moratorium, which exempts electronic transmissions from tariffs, was adopted as part of the WTO's Declaration on Global Electronic Commerce during the second Ministerial Conference in 1998 and has been extended at subsequent ministerial conferences. Regarding the moratorium policy, developing countries believe that if they are permanently unable to impose tariffs on electronic transmissions, they will suffer significant loss of revenue. They argue that tariff policies need to be revised for the development of their underdeveloped digital industries.

[29] This subsection is based on Kwak (2021).

### *Digital Economy Partnership Agreement (DEPA)*

The DEPA, signed between New Zealand, Singapore, and Chile in 2020, represents a new form of trade agreement created to promote trade utilizing digital technology and to establish norms for the digital economy. The DEPA establishes norms and cooperation among member countries for the proliferation of electronic trade and the creation of a stable data business environment. Accordingly, the DEPA reflects issues about digital trade such as data transferability and data location. Its provisions are categorized into digital trade facilitation, data trades (free data transferability and data protection), reliability and security for digital trade, and cooperation over new digital technologies and governance.

The three signatory countries are members of the Comprehensive and Progressive Agreement for Trans-Pacific Partnership (CPTPP), which came into effect in 2018, and so their norms for digital trade standards are already exacting. Therefore, the content of the DEPA is not especially unique. Instead, what stands out about the DEPA is its adoption of a modular approach, which merits explanation.

In traditional FTA negotiations, various chapters, specific clauses, tariff schedules, and so on, are negotiated to form a single agreement. In contrast, the DEPA modularizes norms related to business and trade facilitation, digital products, data issues, consumer trust, digital identity, new technologies, innovation, digital economy, cooperation with small and medium-sized enterprises, digital inclusion, transparency, and dispute resolution. Third countries can join the DEPA by adopting all or some of these modules, utilize specific modules in other trade agreements, or revise domestic regulations by incorporating specific modules.

The DEPA's modular approach, which encourages the development of innovative digital technologies while minimizing the adverse impact of digital trade on the domestic economy, is expected to play a role in shaping international digital trade norms. With the modular approach, a country can join up to only the provisions it needs. In this sense, DEPA is a flexible methodology.

### *Australia-Singapore Digital Economy Agreement (ASDEA)*

Australia and Singapore have entered into another form of international agreement specializing in digital trade.[30] Both countries previously introduced an e-commerce chapter in their 2003 bilateral FTA and positioned themselves as pioneers in digital trade by participating in the CPTPP. They formed the Australia and Singapore Digital Economy Agreement (ASDEA) to replace the e-commerce chapter of the bilateral FTA as a means to respond more nimbly to the rapidly evolving digital trade environment.

This DEA includes numerous provisions related to digital infrastructure and digital technology which are not common in earlier digital trade agreements. For example, the ASDEA has an independent article on electronic authentication and electronic signature, whereas the DEPA does not include these provisions. An article on the internet interconnection charge sharing is also a new feature of the ASDEA. It also adds new provisions regarding digital infrastructure, including clauses related to a secure online environment and submarine cables.

Both countries have also agreed to participate in international efforts to establish ethical standards for artificial intelligence (AI) and to encourage its commercial use. In addition, they have committed to working together to develop technological standards that promote digital trade and enhance cooperation for financial technology (FinTech) and regulatory technology (RegTech).[31] Given that the DEPA only includes FinTech cooperation, the inclusion of RegTech in the ASDEA is a new element in digital trade agreements.

While both the DEPA and the ASDEA advocate free location of computing facilities, the ASDEA also specifies the computing facilities to be used in financial services. Stakeholder participation is also a new feature.

Overall, Australia and Singapore are adapting to a new trade environment and pursuing regulations that are friendly to digital technologies. From this perspective, ASDEA is considered a strong fit for the digital age.

---

30 This subsection reflects Kwak (2021).

31 RegTech, short for Regulatory Technology, refers to the use of technology, particularly software and data analytics, to help financial institutions and other regulated industries comply with government regulations efficiently and at a lower cost. The goal of RegTech is to streamline and automate regulatory compliance processes, reducing the risk of noncompliance and associated penalties while also improving operational efficiency.

### *Digital Economy Agreement between the United Kingdom and the Republic of Singapore (UKSDEA)*

The UKSDEA amends certain aspects of the bilateral FTA between the United Kingdom and Singapore, notably replacing the FTA's entire Section F of Chapter 8, which dealt with e-commerce-related matters, with more substantive content related to digital trade and the digital economy. Furthermore, the UKSDEA revised provisions related to customs and trade facilitation to adopt a single window system, allowing traders to submit customs documents required for goods export, import, and transit in one place.

On the digital economy, the UKSDEA covers a wide range of binding regulations on cooperative elements in emerging and innovative areas, as specified in the foundational "cornerstone of the digital economy" section. It also addresses binding regulations related to three memorandums of understanding, which cover digital identity, digital trade facilitation, and cybersecurity and were exchanged in November 2021, as well as extensive cooperation elements outlined in a joint letter on FinTech and customs cooperation that was exchanged on in February 2022.

The UKSDEA is the first digital economy agreement between an Asian country and European country. It connects the two nations as global high-tech and service hubs for expanding growth of the digital economy. In the increasingly interconnected digital world, this agreement is something of a model for countries in different regions.

The main feature of the agreement is its 11 modules with binding regulations across three core dimensions: (i) end-to-end digital trade development, which includes electronic payment and paperless trade; (ii) reliable data transfer and support, covering the cross-border transfer of financial services data and the prohibition of data localization, including financial services, as well as regulations for submarine cables; and (iii) trust for digital system and the facilitation of participation in the digital economy, which includes regulations on cryptography, source code protection, and online consumer protection.

The UKSDEA is another step forward in provisions for legal services in connection with technologies following the ASDEA, in which Australia and Singapore agreed to establish a detailed framework specifically for the use of technology in the provision of legal services. The UKSDEA includes commitments related to technology in legal services because these are one of the services applicable to its drive to facilitate cross-border services.

### *Digital Partnership Agreement Between the Republic of Korea and Singapore (KSDPA)*

The KSDPA builds on the FTA between the Republic of Korea and Singapore that came into effect in 2006. The FTA's e-commerce chapter contained four brief provisions covering definitions of e-commerce, the scope of application, the electronic supply of services, and digital products. The KSDPA adds layers of assurance of the FTA provisions and widens the scope of digital trade norms in e-commerce facilitation, digital business promotion, and online consumer protection. At the same time, it strengthens cooperation in emerging digital technologies.

E-commerce facilitation covers provisions on duty-free electronic transmissions, electronic authentication, electronic signatures, electronic invoicing, electronic payment, paperless trade, and express shipment. Digital business promotion includes provisions for nondiscrimination on digital products, cross-border data transfers, and prohibitions on localized computing facilities and the publication of source codes. It also covers cooperation on AI, FinTech, and standards for the digital economy.

The elaboration and extension of cooperation enshrined in the bilateral FTA is the main feature of the KSDPA. For instance, the agreement adds cooperation clauses on AI (Article 14.28), FinTech (Article 14.29), and digital economy standards (Article 14.31), as well as encryption techniques used in ICT products (Article 14.17) and source code (Article 14.19).

## 3.2. Select Digital Standards: Trends and Implications for Asia

As AI comes into wider use, countries are increasingly discussing how to support its development and diffusion. Issues of ethics and standards are up for debate, as is building an institutionally secured mechanism for AI governance. The DEPA and the ASDEA emphasize AI ethics and governance and put forward provisions for cooperation between countries adopting AI ethics, along with governance guidelines. Since AI will come to influence all data that crosses borders, it is becoming more and more relevant to digital trade. In this vein, it is crucial to explore trends in AI standards.

Telecommunication technologies are also important since they constitute a key infrastructure factor for digital trade. They impact opportunities for digitalization and innovation, which, in turn, affect conditions for businesses to compete in Asia and the Pacific. Therefore, it is also necessary to review recent trends in 5G standards and the region's participation in creating them.

### *AI Standards*

Activities are underway to establish international standards for AI, ranging from defining what AI is to classifying related technologies, with standardization bodies leading these efforts. Their actions are expected to contribute to the sharing and enabling of AI technologies across the globe. The primary group leading international standardization efforts for AI is known as the ISO/IEC JTC1 SC42 (Artificial Intelligence). Abbreviated as SC42, this public standards development organization was established by the first Joint Technical Committee (JTC1) at its Vladivostok Plenary in November 2017. The scope of SC42 covers AI-related standardization activities and feeds back into the JTC1, which guides contributions not only to its own standards subcommittees, but also through to the International Organization for Standardization (ISO) and the International Electrotechnical Commission (IEC).

When standardized guidelines, quality management, error reduction, and other requirements for operating systems employing AI technologies are established, they strengthen interoperability between systems. Moreover, harmonizing international standards helps improve the reliability of AI technology products and services. AI standardization aims to develop the "fundamentals" for various applications. By maintaining the broadened scope and the abstracted values, standards can be applied to technical development and the fast expansion for AI technology.

Within SC42, several key working issues and activities are notable. First, proposals for new and technically important AI standards have been submitted. In particular, machine learning-related initiatives have been substantiated. At the same time, it is clear that competition among participating countries for leadership roles in important technical areas has become intense, especially since a country chairing initiatives such as a standards-setting group can gain political clout as a result.

Second, SC42 maintains collaborative relationships with other technical committees within ISO and IEC, including the JTC1 subcommittees.

Technical committees like ISO/TC204 (Intelligent Transport Systems) and IEC/TC215 (Health Informatics) are important since these are areas where AI applications hold particular promise. Their work fosters collaboration and development. Private standards and forums are also pertinent. Efforts are being made to expand the intersections between AI technologies and various industry and technical domains. Within the WG4 (Use Cases) technical committee, work is ongoing to create technical reports about industry-specific use cases.

As the global AI market continues to grow, a wider range of tangible and intangible technology service markets will integrate with industries that benefit from AI technologies, such as autonomous vehicles and factory automation. The AI market is diverging into different areas within manufacturing and services. Opportunities for AI in manufacturing include autonomous vehicles, intelligent robotics, and smart factories. In services, applications are significant for medical AI, intelligent education, FinTech, and smart services. The trend for splitting these sectors has led to a competitive race for leadership within the AI industries of the world.

Reflecting the trend, the American National Standards Institute (ANSI) recently established programs under ISO/IEC JTC1/SC42, including health informatics (ISO/IEC AWI TS 17847). And in 2024, the Standardization Administration of China (SAC) led the establishment of a new technical committee for smart shipping.

### *5G and Advanced Communications*

The current landscape for 5G and advanced communication standardization is that 5G is being improved in parallel with the development of next generation 6G services. The rollout of 5G mobile communication, with its initial standardization (Rel-15) completed by 3GPP in 2018, has led to widespread commercialization in many countries, and a rapid increase in subscribers. Subsequently, 3GPP finalized the secondary 5G standard (Rel-16) in June 2021. This was submitted to the Radiocommunication Sector of the International Telecommunication Union (ITU-R), with official approval received within months for it to become the IMT (International Mobile Telecommunications)-2020 standard.

5G has been developed to fulfill requirements such as ultra-high speed, ultra-low latency, and extensive connectivity. It encompasses technologies supporting not only enhanced data services, but also new services. At present, 3GPP is working on Rel-18, which includes 5G-Advanced standardization, with the aim of pushing 5G standardization further by covering a range of technologies for ongoing performance and service improvements that pave the way for 6G. 5G-Advanced standardization was completed by March 2024.

Alongside 5G-Advanced standards, the ITU-R has established a road map for standardization of 6G, an effort labeled the IMT-2030 standard and also known as the Global 6G Vision. The road map encompasses vision definition, requirements identification, technical proposals, performance evaluations, and standard approvals. The formation of a 6G Vision's working group in March 2021 culminated in completion of the Framework Recommendation of IMT-2030 in June 2023. Discussions have also started on new frequencies for 6G.

To secure leadership in the upcoming 6G era, interested nations, academia, and industry stakeholders have submitted proposals on requirements, frequencies, and technologies for inclusion in the 6G Vision Recommendation to the Vision Working Group. Discussions on these proposals mostly take place within national standards organizations.

Mobile telecommunication standardization follows a 10-year cycle to transition into the next generation. Following the initial standardization for each generation, the focus is on responding to market demands through mid-generation standards. These typically coincide with significant industry reinvestment.

### *Implications for Asia*

Australia, the People's Republic of China (PRC), India, Japan, the Republic of Korea, and Singapore are taking part in the discussions over IEC JTC1 SC42 (Artificial Intelligence) and have P (voting right) membership. Countries in Asia and the Pacific are major stakeholders in AI standardization and can influence the procedure for setting AI standards relating to digital trade agreements. Their strong presence implies that the region can take a lead, including through embedding digital standards in the provisions of digital trade agreements. These can be referred to in agreements expected to come in other regions. In this process, efforts to engage developing countries are required in Asia as well as in other regions. Developing countries are often underrepresented in standardization. As digital standards and digital trade norms are being made, it is time for them to participate more actively and contribute. As developing countries can become "digital deciders" in digital standards and digital trade, they need to be encouraged and supported for more participation to make their voice heard (Bergsen et al. 2022).

Also, international standardization activities and infrastructure enhancement are needed for AI to make progress. High-quality data and relevant standards are crucial for the AI industry's growth. Development of a domestic AI ecosystem requires close monitoring of the industry, including where demand for AI emerges and staying up to date with domestic and international progress to identify the standardization needs of related technologies. The proactive introduction of international AI standards and the development of national or organizational standards are also needed if the industry is to thrive.

Digital trade agreements are preparing AI ethics and standards. However, societal concerns such as safety issues related to automation and replacement, and structural problems over the quality and reliability of data processing are constantly brought up. Solutions need to be explored.

Since developing countries in Asia do not participate in discussions on AI rules and standards, nor on 5G and next generation communication technology standards, they remain followers who cannot capture full value from the technological development. Therefore, their capability to receive benefits from standardization of emerging technologies needs to be improved.

An example of an initiative to share standardization benefits comes from Australia. Standards Australia is running a program called International Standards Integration for Critical and Emerging Technologies in Southeast Asia.[32] The program, which spans 2022 to 2025, is building knowledge and practical skills to support development of standards for critical and emerging technologies through a range of bilateral and regional activities.

## 3.3. Digital Standards Provisions in Digital Trade Agreements and Impacts on Digital Trade

Provisions in digital trade agreements related to technical standards also include technical regulations and conformity assessment. Technical standards are essential for evaluating the performance of

[32] https://www.standards.org.au/engagement-events/international/critical-emerging-technologies.

technologies necessary for digital trade standards enabling cross-border transactions such as paperless trade, e-invoicing, or digital payments. Digital trade standards have been discussed for a long time, and for some market needs such as e-payment, standards started to be developed when the technology emerged—that is, even before digital trade negotiations began. However, contents related to standards, regulations, and conformity assessment are recent inclusions.

Provisions on standards, technical regulations, and conformity assessment first appeared with the DEPA. Article 10.3 (Information Sharing) specifies in clause 3(e) that information-sharing may include details of *"technical regulations, standards, or conformity assessment procedures related to digital trade."* In later digital trade agreements (ASDEA, UKSDEA, and KSDPA), the provisions for those are manifested in the independent articles.

Negotiations over ASDEA, UKSDEA, and KSDPA were concluded through 2020 and 2021. Since Singapore was involved in all three, they share some similar highlights. The agreements acknowledge the important role of standards in the digital economy and encourage parties to develop standards that facilitate the digital economy. Participating countries must cooperate on accepting standards, technical regulations, and conformity assessments, and share information about efforts taken that are related to them.

Table 3.1 summarizes standard-related provisions in the three digital trade agreements. Digital trade standards are the most recent component in digital trade agreements, given that standards, technical regulations, and conformity assessments are gaining more importance in digital trade. With technologies already part of our daily lives, digital trade has taken place outside of global digital trade norms. As dialogue deepens between governments, each dimension of digital trade will be related to standards, technical regulations, and conformity assessments. For example, the agreements specify certain technical standards that should be met for interoperability or security in the dimensions of electronic authentication, electronic payments, paperless trading, data innovation, and digital identities. As the digital industries make technical progress, more dimensions will require standards to facilitate digital trade.

**Table 3.1: Standard-Related Provisions in Digital Trade Agreements**

| Agreement | Article | Summary of provisions |
|---|---|---|
| DEPA | No independent article. | • Information sharing is mentioned in relation to standards, technical regulations, and conformity assessment. |
| ASDEA | Article 30. Standards and conformity assessment for digital trade. | • Recognition of standards for the well-functioning digital economy.<br>• Active participation in regional and international bodies to development and adoption of standards to support digital trade.<br>• Standards cooperation among involved parties in the areas of AI ethics and AI governance.<br>• Recognition of the conformity assessment results.<br>• Information sharing. |
| UKSDEA | Article 8.61-D. Standards and conformity assessment. | • Recognition of standards for the well-functioning digital economy.<br>• Participation in international forum development of digital trade-related standards.<br>• Recognition of the conformity assessment results.<br>• Participation of government and nongovernment bodies for standards, technical regulations, and conformity assessment procedure.<br>• Information sharing. |
| KSDPA | Article 14.31: Standards, technical regulations and conformity assessment procedures for digital economy. | • Recognition of standards for the well-functioning digital economy.<br>• Participation in regional, multilateral, or international fora development of digital trade-related standards.<br>• Recognition of the conformity assessment results.<br>• Participation of government and nongovernment bodies for standards, technical regulations and conformity assessment procedure.<br>• Information sharing. |

AI = artificial intelligence, ASDEA = Australia–Singapore Digital Economy Agreement, DEPA = Digital Economy Partnership Agreement, KSDPA = Korea–Singapore Digital Partnership Agreement.
Source: Provisions in each agreement.

## 3.4. Standardization Mechanisms and the Relevance to Digital Standards

Standard development organizations (SDOs) are usually configured as three tiers: international, regional, and national standards. International standards are adopted by international standardization bodies for use by the public. The major international SDOs that prepare and release international standards are the ITU, the ISO, and the IEC. Each has its own areas of specialty. ITU works on the telecommunication standards, IEC on the electronics and electrical standards, and ISO for the rest. However, as technologies increasingly converge and become more complex, SDOs often work together in joint technical or scientific committees.

Regional SDOs also exist. These make regional standards available for public use, such as in countries in the EU. In Europe, regional SDOs include the European Telecommunications Standards Institute (ETSI), the European Committee for Standardization (CEN), and the European Committee for Electrotechnical Standardization (CENELE).

Individual countries also have standardization bodies. National SDOs are not necessarily government units. For example, American National Standards Institute (ANSI) or British Standards Institution (BSI) are renowned for their leading roles in guiding the direction of standardization. Nongovernment bodies are also involved. They collaborate with businesses, research institutes, consumers, academia, and other stakeholders to reflect domestic conditions and enable mutual usage. Nongovernment SDOs include Telecommunications Industry Association (TIA) in the United States, China Communication Standards Association in the PRC, and the automobile association Verband der Automobilindustrie in Germany.

Standards-making mechanisms vary. International, regional, or national standards can be categorized by the standard-making mechanism into de jure and de facto standards, or forum/consortium standards. De jure standards are released by the official SDO. The SDO may allow a technical/scientific committee to be established after considering a proposal from an industry association. Committee members develop details for the standard and the SDO formally acknowledges them. Conversely, a market-leading technology surviving competition becomes a de facto standard that is benchmarked and mimicked by technologies that succeed it. Forum/consortium standards are made by a set of firms organized in one technical field. Table 3.2 summarizes what these mechanisms look like in practice.

**Table 3.2: Standard Types per Standard-Setting Mechanism**

| | De jure standards | Forum or consortium standards | De facto standards |
|---|---|---|---|
| Standard-setting mechanism | Proposal to the official SDOs, setting up a technical committee, and committee member agreement. | Ad hoc organizations or consortium formed to exchange opinions or influence standardization for a specific technical field. | Recognition is achieved based on being the best technology in a market. |
| Acting SDOs | International, regional, and national official SDOs. | W3C,[a] IETF,[b] OMA,[c] CSA-IoT,[d] Bluetooth,[e] World DMB Forum,[f] and so on. | IEEE,[g] 3GPP,[h] ASME,[i] ASTM,[j] SAE,[k] and so on. |
| Characteristics | Standardization through the transparent and open procedure. | Responsive and flexible standardization reflecting market demand, with competition in standardization by multiple organizations in the same field. | The product that emerges victorious in the market competition becomes the standard. |

[a] The World Wide Web Consortium (https://www.w3.org).
[b] Internet Engineering Task Force (https://www.ietf.org).
[c] OMA SpecWorks, previously Open Mobile Alliance (https://omaspecworks.org).
[d] Connectivity Standards Alliance-Internet of Things, formerly the Zigbee Alliance (https://csa-iot.org). The organization used to focus on publish the Zigbee standards, to be used for high-level communication protocols and now develops Matter, an intellectual property-based open standard.
[e] The Bluetooth Specific Interest Group (https://www.bluetooth.com/specifications/). It oversees standards and specifications for the Bluetooth technology.
[f] World Digital Multimedia Broadcasting Forum (https://www.worlddab.org). It facilitates adoption and implementation related to digital broadcasting radio technologies.
[g] Institute of Electrical and Electronics Engineers (https://www.ieee.org). Some of the IEEE works is standard development in electrical engineering, electronics engineering, and other related technologies.
[h] The Third Generation Partnership Project (https://www.3gpp.org/about-us/introducing-3gpp). It works on development of telecommunication standards.
[i] The American Society of Mechanical Engineers (https://www.asme.org). It promotes the machinery and the multidisciplinary research, including standard development.
[j] The American Society of Testing Materials (https://www.astm.org). It develops standards for raw materials, products, services, and systems in the areas of steel, metals, chemicals, and construction materials.
[k] Society of Automotive Engineers (https://www.sae.org/about). It develops standards for automobiles and aerospace engineering.

Table 3.1 illustrates that digital trade standards in the provisions of digital trade agreements usually appear with technical regulations and a conformity assessment, and typically are discussed within an institutional context. Table 3.2 illustrates that digital [technology] standards address specific technologies to be developed in a forum/consortium or determined by the market. Despite the essential role of nongovernment organizations in developing standards, intergovernment organizations still matter for disseminating digital [trade] standards. Digital trade standards should be agreed upon and coordinated among countries, and as such are more likely to go through government channels of communication like the ISO.

## 3.5. Digital Trade Standards in Selected Trade Agreements

Trade agreements enshrine provisions for digital trade standards in addition to other (nondigital) standards, technical regulations, and conformity assessment. They stress the importance of standards, but differences in the types of obligation for the adoption of standards are subtle yet meaningful, depending upon the intended function. Details follow of digital trade standards relating to each function, along with descriptions of their unique challenges and policy recommendations for addressing them.[33]

### *Electronic Payments*

In general, digital trade agreements do not cover service trade issues like financial services.[34] However, electronic payments in the finance sector are central to discussions on digital trade, and as such are expected to become more important. These provisions aim to promote efficient and secure electronic payment systems and improve the interoperability and interconnection of payment infrastructure. To achieve this, they require international standards to be considered and deployed. The DEPA provisions impose an obligation to consider internationally agreed upon payment standards, while ASDEA provisions mandate Australia and Singapore to adopt the ISO 20022 international standard.[35] ISO 20022 is distinctive because it specifies a particular international standard for electronic payments.

Nevertheless, the DEPA and DEA member countries may use different electronic payment systems in their own territory, including digital wallets, mobile payment apps, and traditional banking systems. Harmonizing these systems can be complex. To ensure interoperability that allows cross-border payments to be made without friction, member countries should develop and promote common standards for electronic payment protocols and technologies. Spreading ISO 20022 beyond Australia and Singapore may be one such feasible option.

[33] This section is based on Kim (2021).

[34] Information is based on DEPA Article 2.7(a) and ASDEA Article 11.

[35] ISO 20022 is an international standard to determine a universal financial industry message scheme, used for electronic data exchange among financial institutions and financial service participants.

### *Electronic Invoicing*

Electronic invoicing is promoted to enhance the efficiency, accuracy, and reliability of e-commerce.[36] Moreover, to ensure cross-border interoperability of electronic invoices, the agreements oblige the use of international standards, guidelines, or recommendations when available. Typically, international expansion of the electronic invoicing system requires best practices to be developed and shared. Furthermore, ASDEA is noteworthy for specifying Pan European Public Procurement Online (PEPPOL) as a standard for electronic invoicing and demanding the introduction of a system based on these standards. PEPPOL was developed to support the procedure for cross-border electronic procurement in the EU.

However, several potential challenges have emerged. Having different taxation and value-added tax (VAT) regulations across member countries is inconvenient for business. Integrating electronic invoicing seamlessly with financial systems, such as accounting and payment platforms, is another task that is difficult in practice. Countries should establish standardized processes and guidelines for tax reporting and VAT compliance in electronic invoicing. Countries should develop common integration standards and protocols to facilitate the exchange of electronic invoices with financial systems. Although electronic invoicing is a part of digital trade, it should be harmonized with current and nondigital financial systems.

### *Paperless Trade*

While the introduction of a single window system is promoted in the context of trade facilitation norms, recent digital trade negotiations have introduced provisions to establish interconnected and trusted networks.[37] Trade administration documents like Sanitary and Phytosanitary (SPS) certifications and import/export data have increasingly been transformed into machine-readable electronic formats and electronic data. The trend encourages data exchange systems based on internationally recognized standards to ensure connectivity and uninterrupted operation.

In this context, DEPA acknowledges the importance of open standards. However, it is worth noting that these regulations primarily recognize the significance of standards without mandating specific details for their implementation. Recent normative changes focus on the need to share

36 Information is based on DEPA Article 2.5 and ASDEA Article 10.

37 Information is based on DEPA Article 2.2 and ASDEA Article 12.

information, experiences, and best practices related to data exchange systems, and on fostering cooperation.

Paperless trade significantly reduces administration costs. Despite the benefits, it may take time to implement fully. Different countries may have varying standards and regulations, including on document formats, data exchange protocols, and digital signatures. Also, it may be costly to shift from traditional trade administration.

Standards like the United Nations Commission on International Trade Law's Model Law on Electronic Transferable Records (MLETR) provide a framework to facilitate paperless trade across countries. Given the administration costs, MLETR is expected to alleviate the documentation burden and encourage both offline and digital trade. Adoption is slow, but more countries are trying to align their domestic institutions with MLETR.

Paperless trade also requires a capacity of online system use. Therefore, it may be burdensome for small businesses that lack the resources and expertise to respond to the transition. Paperless trade further extends to the problem of digital divide since not all countries or businesses have the same digital infrastructure and capabilities. Bridging the digital divide among DEPA and DEA member countries is essential. Unless these issues are resolved, resistance to the transition from traditional paper-based trade to digital processes is likely, particularly among established businesses and government agencies. When developing countries are involved, capacity building programs need to be designed and implemented for digital trade. A good example is the ASEAN-Australia Digital Trade Standards (DTS) Initiative.[38]

### *Electronic Signatures and Electronic Authentication*

Electronic signature and electronic authentication have received strong support in FTA e-commerce negotiations and more recently in World Trade Organization (WTO) e-commerce negotiations.[39] The key regulations guarantee that parties involved in e-commerce can choose electronic authentication methods and recognize the legal validity of electronic signatures.[40]

---

38 https://asean-au-dts.org/.

39 Information is based on ASDEA Article 9.

40 Korea–US FTA Article 15.4, CPTPP Article 14.6, USMCA Article 19.6, USPDTA Article 10, and ASDEA Article 9. The DEPA does not have provision.

The ASDEA encourages the use of interoperable electronic authentication and permits requirements for electronic authentication methods to meet specific performance standards or obtain certification from a legal authority. This underscores the respect for national standard adoption authority in adopting, for example, international standards like the United Nations Commission on International Trade Law's Model Law on Electronic Signatures, although both Australia and Singapore support the use of electronic authentication to facilitate electronic commerce as a major part of digital trade. Fundamentally, where an agreement has a provision on electronic authentication, this suggests that the countries involved are committed to institutionalization of electronic signature and authentication.

However, different national legal frameworks make the adoption of electronic signature and authentication difficult to enforce across member countries of a trading group. Technical challenges may also have an impact. First, electronic signature solutions may not always be compatible across borders, making it difficult for businesses to engage in seamless cross-border transactions. Policymakers are, therefore, advised to promote use of widely accepted electronic signature standards like Public Key Infrastructure (PKI) and to adopt common technical protocols that ensure interoperability.

Second, technical stability is particularly important. Ensuring the authenticity and security of electronic signatures is crucial. Cyberattacks and identity theft can undermine trust in digital transactions. Policymakers should implement robust authentication mechanisms, including multi-factor authentication (MFA) and biometrics, to enhance security. Member countries can also collaborate on cybersecurity measures.

## *Digital Identity*

Countries and international institutions cooperate to strengthen the technical interoperability of digital identity and to develop technical standards through digital trade negotiations. For digital identity provisions, they impose fundamental obligations for technical interoperability and the development of common standards. Specific compliance requirements include the signing of agreements on mutual recognition, international standards development, and cooperation in sharing best practices related to policies, regulations, technologies, and security standards.[41]

[41] Information is based on DEPA Article 7.1 and ASDEA Article 29.

Although digital identity is expected to facilitate electronic transactions and digital trade, it is important to maintain a balance between security and user privacy. Ensuring that user data are protected while still allowing for efficient digital identity verification can be complex. Unauthorized access or data breaches can have severe consequences. Eventually digital identity should be backed up by a robust security framework that includes encryption, multifactor authentication, and continuous monitoring to mitigate security concerns. Regular security audits and compliance checks should be mandated.

Regarding user privacy, implementing privacy by design principles can resolve concerns. Ensuring that only necessary information is shared, and user consent is obtained for each data transaction can build trust, and at the same time users must trust and adopt the digital identity system. Resistance to change and concerns about data security and privacy could hinder widespread adoption of digital identity solutions. To help build user trust, it is essential to develop a clear legal and regulatory framework for digital identity. The framework should deal with issues like liability, dispute resolution, and data protection.

The standard-related provisions illustrated above are presented in Table 3.3.

**Table 3.3: Issues Included in Digital Trade Agreements**

| Issue | USJDTA[a] | DEPA | ASDEA | UKSDEA | KSDPA |
|---|---|---|---|---|---|
| Logistics | - | Article 2.4 | - | Article 8.61-C | Article 14.9 |
| Electronic signature and electronic authentication | Article 10 | Article 16.9[b] | Article 9 | Article 8.61[c] | Article 14.8 |
| Electronic invoicing | - | Article 2.5 | Article 10 | Article 8.61-A | Article 14.10 |
| Express shipments | - | Article 2.6 | Article 13 | - | Article 14.13 |
| Electronic payments | - | Article 2.7 | Article 11 | - | Article 14.11 |
| Digital Identity | - | Article 7.1 | Article 29 | Article 8.61-S | Article 14.30 |
| FinTech | - | Article 8.1 | Article 32 | - | Article 14.29 |
| LawTech | - | - | - | Article 8.61-T | - |
| Artificial intelligence | - | Article 8.2 | Article 31 | Article 8.61-R | Article 14.28 |
| Paperless trading | - | Article 2.2 | Article 12 | Article 8.61-B | Article 14.12 |

ASDEA = Australia–Singapore Digital Economy Agreement, DEPA = digital economy partnership agreement, KSDPA = Korea–Singapore Digital Partnership Agreement, UKSDEA = United Kingdom–Singapore Digital Economy Agreement, USJDTA = US–Japan Digital Trade Agreement.

[a] Agreement between the United States of America and Japan Concerning Digital Trade.

[b] The DEPA has no article for electronic authentication.

[c] The UKSDEA has no independent article for electronic signature, however, the Article 8.61 specifies some parts of electronic signature.

Source: Compiled by authors from various agreements.

## 3.6. Digital Standards in Other Trade Agreements

### *G7 Ministry Digital Trade Principles*

The G7 has agreed on five principles for digital trade: Open digital market; data free flow with trust; safeguards for workers, consumers, and businesses; digital trading systems; and fair and inclusive global governance. Digital standards in digital trade agreements, whether national or international, can directly impact how these principles are put into practice. Some key implications for the G7 principles are as follows:

- **Interoperability.** G7 countries often emphasize the importance of digital systems being able to work seamlessly across borders. Digital standards that ensure interoperability between different systems, technologies, and platforms can help achieve this.
- **Security.** Digital trade principles often prioritize cybersecurity and data protection. Standards related to encryption, authentication, and secure communication are crucial in this regard. Adhering to recognized security standards helps ensure trust and compliance with these principles.
- **Data privacy.** Personal data protection is a recurring theme in digital trade principles. Compliance with standards is essential when managing cross-border data flows. Harmonizing these standards can simplify international data transfers.
- **Transparency.** Transparency and fairness are key principles in digital trade. Standards for transparent business practices, including e-commerce and online marketplaces, can help ensure fair competition and consumer protection. G7 countries may collaborate to develop or adopt such standards.
- **Consumer protection.** Digital standards can contribute to ensuring consumers are protected in online transactions. This includes standards for product information, online dispute resolution, and mechanisms for handling consumer complaints.
- **Emerging technologies.** As emerging technologies like AI and blockchain play an increasingly significant role in digital trade, G7 nations may work on setting standards and guidelines for their responsible and ethical use. This can align with principles related to innovation, ethics, and responsible AI.

In summary, digital standards can provide the technical foundation for implementing digital trade principles promoted by the G7. These standards help ensure that digital trade is conducted securely, fairly, and in a manner that protects the interests of all stakeholders, including consumers, businesses, and governments.

### *WTO Technical Barriers to Trade Principles*

Digital standards are increasingly important in the context of technical barriers to trade (TBT) principles as digital technologies take on bigger roles in international trade. Digital standards are related to the TBT principles in the following ways:

- **Nondiscrimination.** Digital standards should be applied without discrimination to both domestic and foreign digital products and services. Discriminatory technical barriers to trade can be challenged under the TBT Agreement.
- **Transparency.** The development and adoption of digital standards should be transparent, allowing all WTO members, including foreign stakeholders, to access information about these standards and provide comments, if necessary.
- **Proportionality.** When establishing digital standards, WTO members should ensure that they are proportionate and do not impose unnecessary restrictions on trade. Excessive or overly burdensome digital standards could be challenged under the TBT Agreement.
- **International standards.** The use of international digital standards, such as those developed by organizations like the ITU and the IEC, can promote interoperability and reduce trade barriers. WTO members are encouraged to consider these standards as a basis for their own regulations.

In summary, digital standards and the WTO's TBT principles are closely intertwined, as digital technologies continue to play a significant role in global trade. Ensuring that digital standards are developed and applied in a manner consistent with TBT principles helps facilitate international trade and promote a level playing field for businesses across borders. Box 3.1 introduces multilateral attempts to integrate digital standards into the trade norm.

**Box 3.1: Digital Trade and Indo-Pacific Economic Forum**

The Indo-Pacific Economic Forum (IPEF) has four core pillars: (1) achieving fair and flexible trade; (2) reconstructing diverse, secure, and predictable supply chains; (3) improving infrastructure disparities, achieving clean energy, and decarbonization; and (4) cooperation for taxation and anticorruption. Among the four pillars, Pillar 1 is dedicated to digital trade.

More specifically, Pillar 1 requires that countries need to discuss norms for the transition to a digital economy and the measures for trade facilitation, especially digital trade. Related standard issues presented so far include easing restrictions on cross-border data flows and requirements for data localization, abolishing tariffs on digitally traded goods, ending demands for the disclosure of source code and algorithms, cybersecurity, harmonization of intercountry personal data protection regulations, and the establishment of digital infrastructure.

In addition, considering that small and medium-sized enterprises have a relatively low share in the trade of countries located in the Indo-Pacific region, there is an argument that the IPEF should primarily contribute to streamlining trade procedures for these enterprises. Specific proposals include enhancing capacity-building programs and technical support for trade facilitation, and providing information to support the digitalization of small and medium-sized enterprises.

Source: Authors.

## 3.7. Compliance with Digital Standards in the Private Sector

Private sector cooperation and participation is essential to comply with digital standards in digital trade. Therefore, the issue of whether private standardization bodies are included in wider discussions on standardization and standards regulation is an important consideration.

The TBT Agreement encompasses central, local, and private standardization bodies, but the issue of regulating private standard-setters led to the introduction of best practice guidelines. The TBT committee focused on private standards as a core issue until recently, while the Services Trade Council has also been in long discussions over strengthening compliance with private standards since the General Agreement on Trade in Services (GATS) became effective in 1995.

Since private sector organizations cannot be excluded from discussions about standardization, finding effective ways to secure their involvement in government-level digital trade standard negotiations and, furthermore, to ensure compliance is an important task. In the example in Table 3.2, de facto SDOs and private consortiums are stakeholders with whom it is necessary to communicate closely when devising digital trade agreements. The technical fields suggested in Table 3.3 may be the promising areas for discussion on standards because they are already integrated into the contents of digital trade, which means that countries have recognized the importance of these technologies.

## 3.8. Recommendations for Development of Digital Standards

Standard provisions have been introduced in recent digital trade agreements. Compared to provisions and/or rules for trade in goods and services, these agreements include norms aimed at spreading international standards and promoting the development of domestic standards, rather than negotiations to remove trade barriers. From an institutional perspective, the challenge is that standards are needed to promote cooperation agreements, private sector compliance, and negotiations to reduce legal ambiguities.

Digital trade agreements differ fundamentally from trade agreements in goods and services, with key issues revolving around the free flow of data, network expansion, competition policies, and more. However, issues related to the basic types of standard-related provisions, concepts, and their scope of application are common institutional challenges stemming from key features of the digital trade system, regardless of specific cases. Coordination with the activities of international standardization organizations and regulation of the activities of private standardization bodies also demands concerted effort. Countries need to work together to find solutions to these issues, both to improve and implement digital standards principles and to put them into practice.

In addition, digital trade standards have recently been actively introduced into regional trade systems, with countries like the United States leading the way. These countries are using standard-related provisions and standard strategies as mechanisms to promote digital trade. Ultimately, countries establishing digital trade norms will also take the lead in digital trade standardization. Therefore, it is important that every nation participates in digital trade cooperation initiatives.

Capacity building in digital trade, including for digital standards for developing Asia, needs to be developed, and to be implemented. Gaps in participation in international standardization between developed and developing countries can widen if they are not addressed, leaving developing countries in a new type of vicious circle of dependency. As such, development partners—including multilateral development banks like ADB—need to pay attention to this as a possibility.

## References

Bergsen, P. et al. 2022. *Digital Trade and Digital Technical Standards: Opportunities for Strengthening US, EU and UK Cooperation on Digital Technology Governance*. Chatham House. https://www.chathamhouse.org/sites/default/files/2022-01/2022-01-24-digital-trade-digital-technical-standards-bergsen-et-al.pdf.

Kim, M. 2021. The GATT/WTO Rules for Standards and Regulatory Implications for Digital Trade Agreements. *Journal of International Trade and Industry Studies*. 26 (3). pp. 25–51.

Kwak, D. 2021. Formation of New International Rules regarding Digital Trade: Emergence of Dyadic Digital Trade Agreements and the Recent Discussions. Special Issue Brief. Lee & Ko Global Commerce Institute. https://www.leeko.com/newsl/gci/2105/specialissuebrief_may2021_internationaltradegroup.pdf.

Suominen, K. 2023. *Trust in Trade: Challenges to the Global Convergence on Digital Standards*. Hinrich Foundation. March.

### *Digital Economy and Trade Agreements*

Agreement between the United States of America and Japan Concerning Digital Trade.

Australia–Singapore Digital Economy Agreement.

Digital Economy Agreement between the United Kingdom of Great Britain and Northern Ireland and the Republic of Singapore.

Digital Economy Partnership Agreement.

Digital Partnership Agreement between the Government of the Republic of Korea and the Government of the Republic of Singapore.

# 4 Cross-Border Payments

Martin Chorzempa

## Introduction

Cross-border payments are a crucial building block for global commerce and the global financial system. When they work well, they allow migrants to send money home, merchants large and small to transact with a market of potential buyers and suppliers beyond home country borders, consumers to purchase a wider variety of goods, and the efficient allocation of capital among internationally active firms. However, cross-border payments can often be a stumbling block instead. Whereas digital finance has made domestic payments in many countries more efficient, competitive, and cheaper, the impact on cross-border payments has not been as consistent.

The Group of Twenty (G20) and other international authorities have put improving cross-border payments high on the agenda with a view to solving four main challenges: "high costs, low speed, limited access and insufficient transparency." However, improvements will require serious public–private sector partnership, innovation, and challenging regulatory harmonization (FSB 2020).

One important method is building out key financial and other infrastructure needed to engage in cross-border payments. Access to payment accounts for firms and individuals is crucial for connecting them with domestic and cross-border payment tools, which often requires other more basic infrastructure like digital identity verification systems. Domestic payments systems may need to be built out or reformed to connect domestic payment providers and customers effectively with infrastructures abroad. These improved infrastructures can facilitate more openness and interoperability between different payment systems domestically, across borders, and across currencies, and so raising competition.

Another promising avenue is inclusion of digital payments in trade agreements and harmonizing digital regulations. Cross-border payments are a great deal like cross-border trade, which can benefit from measures often found in trade agreements, including ensuring regulatory regimes can interoperate, expanded market access for participants from different countries, and digital issues like ensuring the ability to perform necessary cross-border data flows. The Digital Economy Partnership Agreement (DEPA) is one example of progress in this space involving multiple Asian countries, but others are advancing.

Finally, central banks and the international community are exploring whether central bank digital currencies (CBDCs) and the new payment systems and infrastructures built to handle them can improve cross-border payments in Asia. CBDCs are digital currencies that are issued by and the liabilities of central banks. Retail versions that resemble alternatives to physical cash are accessible to the broader public, while wholesale versions could rethink how payments between select institutions like central and commercial banks function. CBDCs differ from cryptocurrencies backed often by nothing but computer code and most digital money today, which is a liability of private entities like banks, payment companies, or even operators of stablecoins.

Policymakers around the world are exploring CBDC as a potential solution to leapfrog traditional patterns of financial development, jump-start financial inclusion domestically, and improve cross-border payments. Asian countries, notably the People's Republic of China (PRC), are among the leaders in developing CBDCs for both retail and wholesale cross-border uses, including pilots involving multiple central banks inside and outside the region. Yet, most central banks are not yet convinced of the need for a CBDC, as introducing a new form of currency is a risky endeavor with a host of unknowns, since no major economy has yet fully introduced a CBDC.

This chapter begins with an analysis of the current state of financial inclusion for payments in Asia, critical infrastructure needed to build out better payment systems, and cross-border payments. Financial inclusion is one of the most often cited justifications for CBDC exploration, and this chapter helps establish whether the data suggest a CBDC can help. It finds wide gaps between countries and within countries for account ownership and use, as well as patterns that show some trade-offs for digital financial inclusion policies. In terms of infrastructure, a major push has been made to build new digital payments systems aimed at interoperability through initiatives like standardized QR codes plugged into central bank payment systems, as well as build-outs of digital identity systems.

Cross-border payments in Asia today are largely denominated in US dollars, but few Asian countries have banks that participate directly in the key infrastructure for these payments. Therefore, they need to partner with another bank that is a direct participant, adding a step in what can become long chains of correspondent banks, with each step tacking on more fees. Despite this obvious inefficiency, transacting payments in dollars is generally preferred, due to advantages like abundant liquidity, and lower spreads to transact in dollars than today's systems for transacting in local currencies. CBDC advocates hope new technology could change that.

The chapter then gives an overview of the CBDC literature, including on the drivers of interest in CBDC and the difference between wholesale and retail forms, among other design choices that involve tough trade-offs. It also goes into the risks and macroeconomic implications of CBDCs. Finally, it covers the current landscape of CBDCs in Asia, where most central banks are at least exploring CBDCs, and many have begun pilot programs. There is a lot of commonality in the drivers of CBDC interest in Asia, though there seems to be more interest in CBDC for wholesale payments in most advanced economies. This section looks in most detail at the PRC, whose eCNY system is the most advanced retail CBDC pilot of any major economy and is also part of one of the most interesting cross-border CBDC pilots.

## 4.1. Why Cross-Border Payments Are Challenging

The simplest payments involve cash, in which physically handing over banknotes or coins completes the payment without needing to involve other parties in that transaction.[42] The need for physical proximity, however, makes cash unsuitable for transactions that occur at a distance or involving a gap in time between when goods are ordered and delivered, such as for e-commerce or cross-border transactions.

Many complex legal and technical systems need to work behind the scenes for a consumer to quickly tap a card or phone on checkout or click a button on a website to make payments. Consumers need protection from fraud, merchants need to know a payment has gone through before providing

[42] The central bank (typically) is in a sense involved as it issues the note, and a commercial bank may have distributed it.

or shipping goods, and the risk of payments failing needs to be mitigated. Therefore, payments tend to be made in a heavily regulated market, including consumer and data protection, financial stability, competition, and ensuring payment providers comply with anti-money laundering/combating the financing of terrorism (AML/CFT) laws. Payment providers often need to obtain a license and submit to regulatory supervision to ensure they are compliant with these laws.

Payments can be simplest when the payee and payer have accounts at the same bank or payment service domestically, an "on us" transaction requiring only that the provider raises one internal balance and lowers the other without any money flowing out or in from it. However, people and entities bank any pay with many different institutions, so those sending money usually need it to go from one financial institution to another. These payments require clearing networks that receive an order for payment, verify it, route it to the recipient institution with information about who is supposed to receive it, and accept or reject it (Federal Reserve 2023). Accepted payments then need to be settled with an actual transfer of value that fulfills the clearing obligation. Institutions handling settlement need to agree on the standards and systems for communicating payments.

Transactions can settle one by one, even nearly instantly, or many payments can be bundled together before settling later with a netted payment. For example, imagine that Bank of China (BOC) customers sent Industrial and Commercial Bank of China (ICBC) customers 50 payments totaling yuan (CNY)500 in 1 hour, during which ICBC customers sent 25 payments the other way to BOC customers totaling CNY400. Instant settlement would require the payment network to settle 75 individual payments, while a netted system could net them all together and end up with one payment of CNY100 from BOC to ICBC to settle all payments at the end of the hour. The former is faster for individual payments, but requires far more liquidity and many more small transfers, while the second carries the risk that institutions that end up with an obligation to pay later do not have the funds to cover it. Ensuring this risk does not interfere with payments is a key reason central banks are often involved in interbank settlement, either as a direct operator of the infrastructure or as a backstop to ensure participants are not afraid of losses from other participants in the system who owe them money (CPMI 2003).

Cross-border payments can be generally separated into retail payments and wholesale payments. Retail payments include remittances, peer-to-peer transfers, and those between either individuals and businesses or between two businesses. Wholesale payments, which tend to be much larger and between financial institutions, including transactions for the financial institution itself and for executing (possibly batched, as discussed) customer transactions (Bank of England 2023). For either one, cross-border payments navigate the already complex domestic payments landscape and can involve many more steps. First, the payment may require a foreign exchange transaction that converts one currency into another on the journey from payer to recipient. Second, the payment may need to comply with two or more regulatory regimes including consumer protection, many requirements and oversight rules that are part of financial supervision, as well as data privacy and AML/CFT in the sender's country, recipient's country, and stops along the way. Third, the payment may need to travel through multiple national payment systems, each with its own rules, before it reaches the recipient. This can complicate matters because many national payment systems operate only during their country's business hours in their time zone. A payment initiated in one location may be stranded until the payment system in the recipient's country, perhaps on the other side of the world, opens. Managing this complexity, risk, and compliance burden is a difficult task that can require large scale and significant cost. Therefore, challenges of cost, speed access, and transparency are unsurprising. Yet, there is much that public authorities and the private sector can do to make progress.

## 4.2. The State of Cross-Border Payments in Asia

The majority of cross-border payments worldwide and in Asia rely on the dollar and its accompanying financial infrastructure, despite long-standing efforts and commitments to increase the role of local currencies.

Direct trade between Asian currencies, especially the PRC's renminbi is on the rise, but it remains a minimal share of cross-border trade and investment activity across Asia. ADB (2023) shows that 78% of Asia and the Pacific's exports and 75% of total imports were invoiced in US dollars in recent years, much higher than the global average of 50% of trade invoiced in dollars about a decade earlier (Gopinath 2015). Most of this dollar-denominated Asian trade does not even involve the US as a trading partner, as the US made up only 13% of the region's exports and 9% of its imports. Therefore, Asia is particularly reliant on the US dollar for trade, leaving little share of trade finance left for the domestic currencies of most Asian countries. Consistent with this overall result, Ito and Kawai (2021) look at specific countries and surprisingly find low home currency shares, such as only 15% for Thailand's total trade. Despite the PRC's highly publicized efforts at internationalization of its currency, only 24.4% of its goods trade was settled in the renminbi in the first 9 months of 2023, an increase from 11% in 2017, but still far below the peak of nearly 30% in 2015 (DiPippo and Leonardo Palazzi 2023; and PBOC 2023). Japanese exports are a bit of an exception with US dollar denomination only at 50%, though around 75% of imports are denominated in US dollars.

Widespread use of the dollar throughout the world, not just Asia, for trade and investment flows leads to highly concentrated liquidity in the pair between each currency and the dollar. This creates what London Business School professor Hélène Rey calls a "thick market externality," which leads to low spreads and the availability of other services like hedging instruments to compensate for exchange rate risk (Rey 2001). Even with longer chains of intermediation—for example, the need to convert renminbi into US dollars, make a US-dollar payment, and then transfer that to Korean won—it is often cheaper and safer to transact with an extra step into the US dollar than to trade directly between two other currencies. That is because limited liquidity of the other currencies can lead to much larger spreads (higher cost to make the payment) and less ability to hedge risk.

### *Challenges: Access to Global Payment Systems*

Despite its advantages, widespread use of the dollar creates challenges for many Asian economies resulting from limited access to the infrastructure used when transacting in dollars. The Clearing House Interbank Payment System (CHIPS), one of the main ways to transact dollars globally, has 43 direct participant banks, including 10 in Asia (CHIPS 2021). However, most of those banks are in the PRC or Japan, with only one Thai bank and one Indian bank as direct participants. Another option for US dollar payment infrastructure is the Clearing House Automated Transfer System (CHATS), which is based in Hong Kong, China and includes a few more Southeast Asian banks (Greene 2022). Thus, coverage is scant for South and Southeast Asia. For the many ADB member economies lacking direct coverage, cross-border payments involving dollars must thus go through often long chains of correspondent banks before they can reach a direct correspondent in these systems. This adds cost, complexity, and delay.

Correspondent banking is when a bank holds deposits from another bank to provide them services, especially payment services (Rice, von Peter, and Boar 2020). For example, a large Chinese bank like Bank of China with direct access to CHIPS may provide dollar payment services for a smaller Chinese bank, allowing an importer in the United States to pay an exporter in the PRC or facilitating a remittance from family in New York—first in US dollars, and then in renminbi—to loved ones in Jiangsu. The large decline in correspondent banking relationships worldwide over the past decade thus poses a challenge for many payments (Boar 2019). The number of active correspondents has shrunk by around a quarter in Asia and Oceania while the volume of payments has increased, leading to more concentration. Some of the main factors driving increased isolation involve compliance costs and risks that have markedly increased in recent years, making it less attractive to maintain correspondent relationships with countries regarded as higher risk for money laundering or terrorist financing (Rice, von Peter, and Boar 2020).

### *Challenges: Time*

The Society for Worldwide Interbank Financial Telecommunications (SWIFT) and correspondent banking system, despite longer intermediation chains, have become remarkably fast after years of effort. In Asia and the Pacific, 90% of wholesale payments are processed from the originator to the beneficiary bank in less than 1 hour, and the other 10% are finished within 1 day—consistent with global averages (FSB 2023). There is a much larger delay, however, at beneficiaries receiving cross-border payments in their account. Only 31% of cross-border payments sent to Asia and the Pacific were credited to beneficiary accounts within an hour, much slower than 60% globally, and 14% of payments took longer than a day. One reason for the delay is that banks may receive payments when they are offline or when market infrastructures are not open. For example, if a payment was sent from New York mid-day, it may be many hours until working hours in an Asian financial institution or payment system, as well as capital controls (FSB 2023a). Issues with Know Your Customer (KYC) requirements may also require additional manual checks for compliance before the funds are transmitted to the recipient.

### *Challenges: Cost*

Another important case for cross-border payments are remittances. Asia is the largest recipient of remittances in the world, at $356 billion in 2022, and some countries rely on remittances for a substantial portion of their GDP (ADB 2024). The global average cost of remittances was quite high at 6.51%, more than double the Sustainable Development Goal (SDG) of 3%. Figure 4.1 shows a wide range of costs in Asia and the Pacific in the first quarter of 2024, from 12% to Papua New Guinea to under 4% for the Philippines, Nepal, and Pakistan.

**Figure 4.1: Remittance Prices Remain High Across Asia and the Pacific**

Average price of sending $200 to Asia in Q1 2024

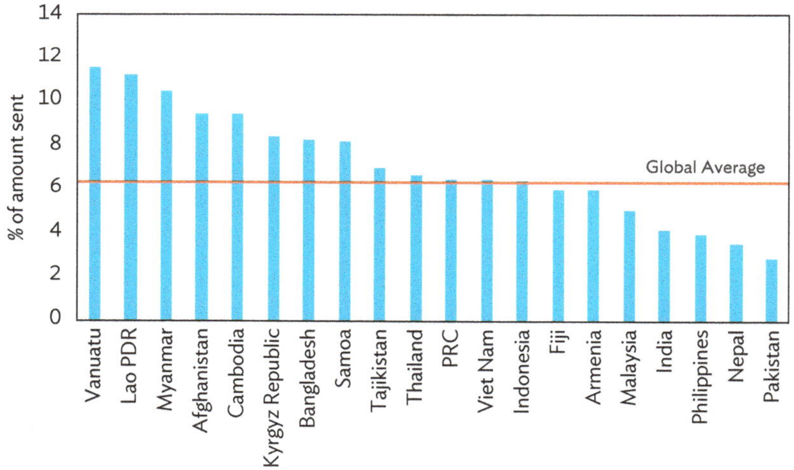


PRC = People's Republic of China, Lao PDR = Lao People's Democratic Republic, Q1 = first quarter.
Source: ADB, based on The World Bank, Remittance Prices Worldwide, available at http://remittanceprices.worldbank.org.

Increased competition for payment providers in any individual remittance corridor is associated with lower pricing, at least by money transfer operators (Beck, Janfils, and Wiegand 2022). Thus, new entrants like digital remittance providers are providing a beneficial effect that has contributed to lower costs. However, the same trend of de-risking that has driven a decline in correspondent banking relationships has affected remittance channels, both by reducing the number of banks competing for remittance service provision in given corridors and by cutting off banking services for money transfer operators (ADB 2021).

One way to reduce the cost of remittances is to reduce the need to convert payments into cash at either end, as cash contributes both to theft risks and to costs involved in maintaining a physical presence. The average cost of remittances sent between mobile money accounts was more than 3 percentage points lower than the overall average, close to the SDG goal, suggesting that increased digitization of payments can contribute to multiple goals like lower cost and increased access (Demirgüç-Kunt et al. 2022). Efforts to expand access to digital payments in individual countries should help lower the cost of cross-border payments by increasing competition and reducing the expenses required in the final domestic leg of the transaction, no matter what currency and payment system is used for the cross-border portion.

Some of the main barriers to increased payment digitization include large populations lacking mobile phones or which do not have the forms of identity required to open accounts. But there is also a chicken-and-egg situation in which countries with lower digital payments penetration require the population to also carry cash, and if operators do not have a sufficiently broad network of agents, the population fails to adopt digital payments over concern that cash will be tied up online when they need it to pay for something in physical cash. Successful cases like M-PESA in Kenya overcame this issue by leveraging networks and customer relationships, in this case, top-up agent networks for mobile phone customers to reach scale quickly and reduce the need for cash.

### *Efforts to Increase Use of Local Currency*

Policymakers across Asia have been working on initiatives that can link their currencies directly. Surprisingly, until recently there has been virtually no market for direct foreign exchange between many Asian currencies.

Sole reliance on the US dollar also increases exposure to financial conditions in the United States. In situations of the kind that led the United States Federal Reserve to tighten financial conditions to respond to domestic inflation as occurred in 2022 and 2023, the increased expense and difficulty of obtaining dollars internationally can create spillover effects and volatility (Ito and Kawai 2021). Many in the region are also concerned about the United States' use of sanctions power, which the dollar's international role helps it enforce extraterritorially. Even if countries do not anticipate being sanctioned and cut off from dollars themselves, they may fear a future inability to transact with trading partners like the Russian Federation that have been subject to sanctions if they do not have alternative payment channels (Greene 2023).

More liquid foreign exchange markets could help enable more trade, investment, and remittances to occur directly between involved countries. A recent survey of such efforts found that Indonesia, Japan, Malaysia, the Philippines, the PRC and Thailand have since 2016 been signing local currency settlement agreements that authorize designated banks to trade directly between currencies, deposit functions, and hedging instruments (Greene 2022). These are growing rapidly in volume, expanding the roster of participating banks, and receiving a lot of policy support. For example, from 2009 to 2023 Malaysia's share of trade with the PRC settled in local currencies increased from 1% to 24%; while with Thailand, the share rose from 6% to 19%; and with Indonesia, from 4% to 8% (Bank Negara Malaysia 2023). These figures show impressive growth, but from a small base with most transactions for intra-Asian trade still being settled in currencies like the US dollar due to remaining challenges like continued limited liquidity, limited hedging instruments, and high costs (Greene 2022). These arrangements are worth watching for their potential, but they are far from the kind of thick markets that can be a serious alternative to use of the US dollar and its infrastructure anytime soon.

The PRC is poised to play a larger role in international payments through the networks its state-owned banks have built across Asia and around the world, as well as its development of new financial infrastructure like CIPS, its Cross-Border Interbank Payment system (Greene 2022). Yet, much of the activity on CIPS still relies on the SWIFT system, the global financial messaging utility that effectively ensures that most banks speak the same "language" to direct payments using mutually intelligible messaging standards between each other. The renminbi also faces headwinds as a reserve currency compared to the US dollar as a result of the PRC's persistent capital controls, while the United States has an open capital account that allows investors to freely buy and sell dollars.[43]

[43] The United States does have some limitations—for example, entities targeted for economic sanctions—but does not restrict the movement of capital inside and outside the United States for residents and nonresidents making investments. In contrast, many countries, including the PRC, limit residents to a specific amount of foreign exchange per year and may require them to justify those flows, and they may also place restrictions on foreign exchange to prevent large outflows in moments of financial stress.

## 4.3. Harmonizing Standards, Regulations, and Digital Trade Agreements

The nature of cross-border payments requires interoperability of technical, regulatory, and other systems to ensure the linkages that allow payments to initiate in one jurisdiction and end in another quickly, cheaply, and reliably. Therefore, most building blocks to improve cross-border payments in the G20 initiative "relate to harmonizing, standardizing, and applying common features to payment systems" (Boar et al. 2021). The goal is less friction, which involves technical standards so that the technological and programming basis of payments systems work well together, regulatory coordination to avoid inconsistency or uncertainty in requirements for payment providers and systems, and removing barriers to the cross-border services trade that are hampering the expansion of banking and payment networks across borders. Digital trade agreements have the most promise for dismantling barriers to cross-border services trade.

### *Standards*

Common standards ensure that the "language" payment systems and operators speak in payment messages is mutually intelligible, even in different jurisdictions. The message, transmitted along the chain of payment, needs to hold enough data for each party involved to verify the sender, recipient, and possibly other information, and the messages need to be secure, such that, for example, only valid payment instructions should be processed. Incompatible message standards, or even different implementation of common standards, can result in misrouted payments, delays, added costs, and other challenges.

The previous standard, the 1970s SWIFT MT (Message Type), kept payment messages small, holding little data to avoid overloading the networks and computers of the time. Today, that trade-off manifests in "insufficient or poor quality data" (SWIFT 2019). If the payment message contains too little data, the payment may need to be held up to manually obtain more data from other parties to the transaction. Around 10% of international payments are delayed for this mostly unnecessary extra compliance verification as a result. Hence, the International Organization for Standardization (ISO) has developed the standard 20022 for payment messages, which is being used by 100 different jurisdictions and is aiming for complete adoption in 2025 (FSB 2023b). This process is ongoing for many key jurisdictions, including the CHIPS system for most international US dollar payments (CHIPS 2023). The new standard includes much more data, which should help more payments go through without issue.

Asian jurisdictions should do their best to adopt the ISO 20022 standard as soon as possible, as key networks like SWIFT will cease supporting old standards in 2025. Lack of adoption, whether designed as a quasi-protectionist measure or to avoid forcing domestic systems to make a change, would miss an important opportunity. International payments from non-adopting jurisdictions would need to be translated into separate domestic message standards, which makes payments more costly and slower for financial institutions and regular users alike (CPMI 2023). In addition, it is not only important to adopt the standard, but to engage in the process under way, especially at the Committee on Payments and Market Infrastructures (CPMI) and with SWIFT, to implement the standards consistently with other jurisdictions to reduce the odds of continued friction.

Jurisdictions should also work to ensure consistent implementation of the Financial Action Task Force (FATF) recommendations that constitute international AML/CFT laws and to evaluate the effectiveness of their implementation (FATF 2023). In particular, authorities can focus on improving the consistency of implementing FATF's recommendations on wire transfers, which are frequently cited as a major impediment to smooth cross-border payments (FSB 2023c). One important piece of the AML/CFT work recommended by FATF is ensuring those authorities coordinate with data privacy authorities to ensure that data rules do not interfere with information that needs to be transmitted abroad or shared with other parties to comply with AML/CFT regulations. That is one part of ensuring the regulatory environment in different jurisdictions can interact well to ensure that cross-border payment providers do not face incompatible regulatory demands.

Data rules are some of the most crucial for cross-border payments, as the value transferred is almost always digital data.

### *Digital Regulations and Digital Economy/Trade Agreements*

Finance is one of the most sensitive sectors of any economy, and financial data are some of the most sensitive data. Finance is also intimately tied with financial stability and macroeconomic policy. Thus, even trade agreements that generally commit signatories to more open electronic commerce and services trade tend to carve out financial services. Efforts to advance digital trade in financial services like payments will need to overcome political opposition to more openness to international competition.

The current barriers to cross-border payments that digital agreements can address include

- Data storage or processing localization requirements,
- Limits on market access for foreign payment providers, and
- Access to financial infrastructure like payment systems.

The rules of the World Trade Organization (WTO) most relevant to digital payments are in the General Agreement on Trade in Services (GATS) annex on financial services for market access and on telecommunications for data flows (Gallaher 2020). However, of the WTO's 164 members, as of 202, less than a third had liberalized cross-border supply of money transmission, either fully or partially (WEF 2020). This gives governments greater autonomy to put up barriers for a variety of reasons, including to limit foreign competitive pressures on domestic firms and to facilitate managing the ability of residents to transfer money abroad through capital controls.

Despite the barriers, there are good reasons to expand market access for financial service providers from other countries. New entrants allow local businesses and individuals to tap into that provider's global presence to make and receive payments more directly to members of their network all over the world. Reciprocal market access abroad then gives domestic payment providers the ability to expand to other countries, allowing their local clients to more easily make cross-border payments with fewer stops in the correspondent banking networks. Liberalization can extend to national treatment for foreign firms, which can include the ability to obtain a license to operate in the market, or even go further to allow cross-border provision of payment services without having to set up a presence in that jurisdiction.

However, rather than liberalize, more jurisdictions have been adding barriers, especially relating to data flows. Data localization and local processing requirements are on the rise. There are often legitimate privacy issues at play, ensuring, for example, that sensitive data are not exported to jurisdictions with weak privacy protections, but the effect can be protectionist and fall particularly hard on cross-border payments. Local processing and storage requirements can increase the cost of doing business for international players and new entrants who need to stand up separate IT infrastructure in the country involved. Financial data are sensitive, but cross-border payments require providers to transmit these data across at least two jurisdictions to track them, fulfill reporting requirements for KYC and anti-money laundering (AML) regulations, and check them for fraud and other risks (FSB 2023c).

Thus, some digital economy agreements include commitments to limit the scope of such requirements while ensuring legitimate concerns are dealt with. For example, from a financial supervisory perspective, it is essential that supervisors like financial intelligence units that investigate money laundering can quickly access information about payments that touch their jurisdiction. Some trade agreements have been tackling this issue. For example, the United States–Japan Digital Trade Agreement includes a commitment for both parties not to require data localization, if financial authorities have "immediate, direct, complete, and ongoing access" to information on transactions and operations for needed for supervisory purposes, even if it is stored abroad.[44]

The Comprehensive and Progressive Agreement for Trans-Pacific Partnership (CPTPP), to which many ADB members are signatories, includes useful commitments to accord national treatment to financial service providers of other signatories (Article 11.3), and some liberalized cross-border supply for specific areas of financial services.[45] Another section commits a signatory to allow "access to payment and clearing systems operated by public entities" to providers from other signatories "established in its territory" (Article 11.15). Its section on data flows, however, provide broad exemptions for financial services that allow more restrictions in this field than for other forms of electronic services (WEF 2020).

The 2020, the Digital Economy Partnership Agreement (DEPA) between New Zealand, Chile, and Singapore, to which the Republic of Korea has acceded,[46] includes a specific section on electronic payments. This commits signatories to "support the development of efficient, safe and secure cross-border electronic payments by fostering the adoption and use of internationally accepted standards, promoting interoperability" and even extends to "the interlinking of payment infrastructures..."[47]

[44] Agreement between the United States of America and Japan Concerning Digital Trade, Article 13.

[45] Consolidated TPP Text—Chapter 11—Financial Services. November 2016. https://www.international.gc.ca/trade-commerce/trade-agreements-accords-commerciaux/agr-acc/tpp-ptp/text-texte/11.aspx?lang=eng.

[46] Other jurisdictions that have requested to join DEPA include Canada, the People's Republic of China, Costa Rica, and Peru.

[47] DEPA's full signing text can be found at: https://www.mfat.govt.nz/assets/Trade-agreements/DEPA/DEPA-Signing-Text-11-June-2020-GMT-v3.pdf.

DEPA also included some of the underlying soft infrastructure required for digital payments, including digital identity and was the first trade agreement to call for open banking (Gallaher 2020). Open banking is designed to facilitate competition in finance by making it easier for customers to obtain and share data from their current accounts, including linking together different accounts that can be managed in one interface.[48] One part of open banking the DEPA will facilitate is advocating for the creation of application programming interfaces (APIs) that would facilitate competition from nonbanks in the payments space.

The Australia–Singapore Free Trade Agreement goes the furthest.[49] It repeats much of DEPA's language, but goes even further to commit parties to finish decisions on approvals for licensing payment providers on time, limit discrimination between financial and nonfinancial enterprises in access to payments infrastructure, and adopt standards like ISO 20022 (Article 11).

To realize the potential of such agreements, many more countries, including important global players like the United States, will need to join and aim, like the United States did with Japan, to set sensible guardrails around data localization requirements for financial services to ensure that data can flow under agreed upon safeguards that guarantee it can be properly protected and accessible by authorities for AML/CFT and other supervisory needs. Whether advanced through digital economy/trade agreements or through direct collaboration between central banks or multinational forum like the Financial Stability Board (FSB), FATF, or Committee on Payments and Market Infrastructures (CPMI), harmonization of digital regulations and ensuring reciprocal access to payments infrastructure can help improve cross-border payments in Asia.

## 4.4. Building Out Payments and Digital Economic Infrastructure

Access to cross-border payments requires key pieces of financial infrastructure, besides the basics of physical infrastructure like telecommunications networks that allow people to use phones (smart or not) to make payments. The first is identity: ensuring that the population

48 For more on open banking, see Babina, T. et al. Customer Data Access and Fintech Entry: Early Evidence from Open Banking. *Bank of England Staff Working Paper* 1,059, 2 February. https://www.bankofengland.co.uk/working-paper/2024/customer-data-access-and-fintech-entry-early-evidence-from-open-banking.

49 Full Text at https://www.dfat.gov.au/trade/agreements/in-force/safta/singapore-australia-fta.

has access to means to prove their identity digitally to perform digital transactions. The second is a retail payments infrastructure that ensures interoperability: e.g., that users of different banks and digital wallets can transact with each other and with merchants. That way, even if the direct account provider does not have international links, they may use a domestic link to another provider with international access.

### *Digital Identity*

In many countries inside and outside Asia, financial inclusion is hindered by the fact that a large share of the population lacks the requisite documents to prove their identity, which without financial firms aiming to serve them cannot comply with laws against facilitating money laundering, financing of terrorism, and tax evasion. Digital forms of identity can go further, allowing payment providers to "know your customer" without physical verification of documents. KYC processes can be expensive, especially for more remote populations, deterring financial intermediaries from serving them. For individuals with very low incomes who may make many low value transactions, the expected profit from serving them may be too low to justify incurring the cost if there is no way to conduct KYC procedures online.

In online identity, India has been a pioneer with its biometric-based Aadhar system, which is a base identity layer for not only payments, but a host of other services. In 2018, Aadhar provided identification for 1.2 billion people in India, and 84% of Indians opening a bank account used it as their form of identification or KYC (Abrahan et al. 2018). Identification is not only important for bank account ownership, but can also be required to obtain mobile phone service—a prerequisite for mobile money services (Demirgüç-Kunt et al. 2022). World Bank data shows that identity is not the main barrier in East Asia and the Pacific, where only 3% of the population lacked an official proof of identity in 2018, while South Asia faces more challenges. In Sri Lanka, for example, the government has identified the lack of a centralized digital ID database and lack of clarity on conducting KYC digitally as an underlying cause of its "modest" update for digital finance (Central Bank of Sri Lanka 2021). In countries without digital identification, it will be challenging for digital finance to take root. Even if governments try to jumpstart access through a CBDC that includes direct government provision of accounts to individuals, the system would be costly and error-prone if the population lacks identity documents or digital ways to prove identity, and the same would be true for private sector account or wallet providers for intermediated CBDC systems.

### *Financial Inclusion*

The most basic prerequisite to expanding access to cross-border payments is domestic financial inclusion. Without a digital financial account plugged into domestic digital payment systems, people trying to send or receive money across borders need to go through a costly and sometimes time-consuming process of bringing to send through a money transfer operator (MTOs) or retrieve a remittance received in cash as well. The leap to digital remittances has an outsized effect on the cost of payments compared to cash and MTOs, cutting costs in half on average for remittances (GSMA 2016).

Advanced economies tend to have well developed digital and other payment tools for retail use and significant uptake, while a look at account ownership and use of digital payments across Asia shows wide gaps in coverage for these essential tools to varying degrees across income levels, regions, and countries. Some countries also have wide gaps based on income and gender. The impacts are felt beyond cross-border payments, as an abundant literature in finance has demonstrated the link between finance sector development and inclusion on the one hand and economic growth on the other.[50]

Financial inclusion remains a global challenge despite rapid progress thanks in large part to expanded availability of digital payment tools. In 2011, barely over half of adults globally had an account at a provider like a bank or mobile money operator, meaning the other half lacked both a safe place to store money and an ability to make or receive digital payments. By 2021, to a large extent driven by progress in Asian countries like the PRC and India, the global average for account ownership reached around 76%.[51] In East Asia and the Pacific region over the past decade, the adult population share with a financial account has risen by a third, from 60% to 83% from 2011 to 2021, according to the World Bank's Global Findex data (Figure 4.2). South Asia's progress is even more impressive, more than doubling from only 32% of the population to 68%.

Room for improvement, however, remains large in many Asian countries. Just under half of the regional members of ADB included in the World Bank's Global Findex Database for 2021 (which does not include many

50 See Levine (2005) for a comprehensive review.

51 Demirgüç-Kunt et al. (2022) notes that "While account ownership and usage are similar in East Asia and the Pacific, only a third of South Asian adults reported making or receiving a digital payment in 2021, indicating that about half of the accounts there are dormant."

of the Pacific Island nations) are below the global average of 76% account ownership.

**Figure 4.2: Wide Divergence in Account Ownership Across Asia**

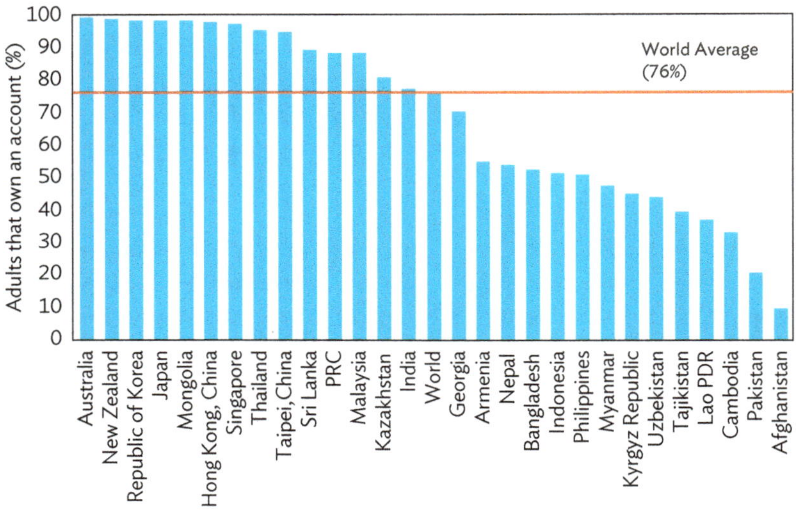


PRC = People's Republic of China, Lao PDR = Lao People's Democratic Republic.
Source: World Bank Global Findex Database.

At the high end of the income distribution, near universal access to financial accounts has been achieved, with no high-income Asian country below 95% account ownership. Success at financial inclusion varies widely, however, within regions and within lower income levels, which suggests that there are ways to boost inclusion in payments without waiting for overall economic development or income growth to bring financial deepening. For example, within South Asian lower middle-income countries, India has reached 78% account coverage and Sri Lanka 89%, while Pakistan is just over 20% and Bangladesh and Nepal around 53%. India's 42 percentage point increase over the past decade has been largely driven by a concerted policy effort to expand account ownership. There is a bit less variation in upper middle-income Asian countries, which range from 96% in Thailand to 55% in Armenia.

An interesting recent trend is the rise of mobile money accounts, digital first accounts that can store savings and make and receive payments using a mobile phone. These accounts have had limited penetration in Asia outside of Bangladesh and have been particularly important in Africa, where many users have seen them as replacement for bank accounts. More than half of unbanked adults in South Asia have mobile phones, so mobile money could be a sensible avenue to reach these 240 million people and onboard them right into a digital payment world (Demirgüç-Kunt et al. 2022). Mobile money is especially promising for more rural and/or remote populations in which it may not be economical to operate a bank branch, but which may already have reliable cell phone service and a telecommunications operator that could aim to provide payment services as well.

Yet, account ownership is only part of the picture for financial inclusion. A drive to open accounts, even if successful initially, provide little lasting benefit if those accounts are empty or unused for services like payments. Globally, digital payment use is ubiquitous in high income economies and rising rapidly in developing economies, from 35% of adults in 2014 to 57% in 2021, which as it advances will help reduce the need for expensive cash in and out points. Underscoring the importance of account ownership as an entry point to digital payments use, digital payments usage was much higher, 80%, for adults in developing economies with an account already (Demirgüç-Kunt et al. 2022). Figure 4.3 shows the share of adults in Asian economies sampled by the World Bank Global Findex 2021 who made or received a digital payment in the past year.

**Figure 4.3: Digital Payment Use is Ubiquitous in High-Income Economies but Has Room to Improve in Middle- and Lower-Income Economies**

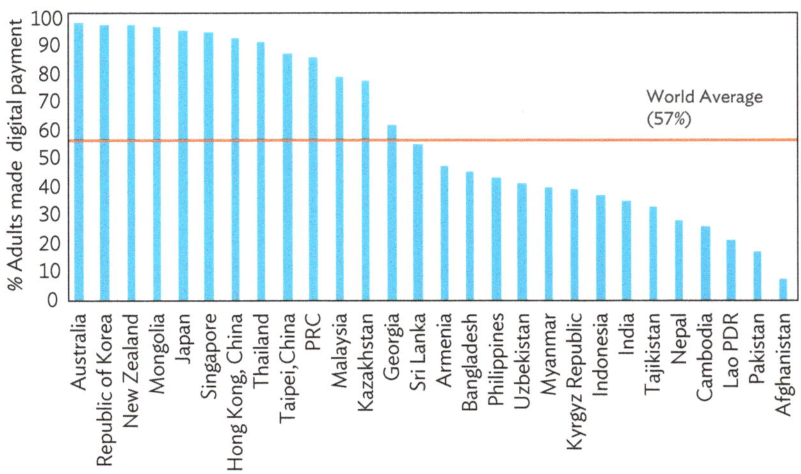


Lao PDR = Lao People's Democratic Republic, PRC = People's Republic of China.
Source: World Bank Global Findex.

Outside of high-income Asian economies, digital payment use is already very high in Mongolia, Thailand, the PRC, Malaysia, and Kazakhstan. They tend to be less used in South Asia, Cambodia, the Lao PDR, Tajikistan, and Indonesia. If the current trends continue, however, the next Global Findex will reflect continued digitization of payments post-pandemic as fintech companies compete to bring in new customers in places like Indonesia and India. Some of the paths to increase digital payment use include encouraging receipt of government transfers and private sector wages into digital accounts, expanding the use of online shopping that tends to be paid for online, online payment of utilities bills, and other expenses or sources of income shared by large portions of the population that could encourage new customers to try digital payments and find them more useful (Demirgüç-Kunt et al. 2022).

One of the most important elements of digital financial inclusion is creating an ecosystem that provides enough value for individuals to take what they perceive as a risk with their money and change long-ingrained habits of using cash. Open banking with APIs that allow different financial providers to interact is a promising avenue, allowing, for example, a customer's data from different accounts to more easily be managed in one aggregated app or service that can not only provide payment services, but enhance the value of payment services with payment data to unlock credit and other services that benefit users. In the PRC, for example, large technology platforms played the central role in becoming to some extent open platforms for financial services firms and nonfinancial firms to compete for customers on those platforms, creating an experience that led hundreds of millions of Chinese to adopt digital payments instead of cash for their daily lives (Chorzempa 2022). This was a major contributor to the PRC's high digital payments use compared to its income level.

Comparing the account ownership and usage figures can help diagnose economy-specific barriers to financial inclusion in Asia and identify potential in which many individuals have accounts, but are not yet using them. Overall, Asia does well; Figure 4.4 shows that 82% of Asian economies in the World Bank's Findex data outperform the world average of a 12% gap between account ownership and share of population making a digital payment.

**Figure 4.4: Examining Gap Between Account Ownership and Use of Accounts for Digital Payments Can Help Target Interventions**

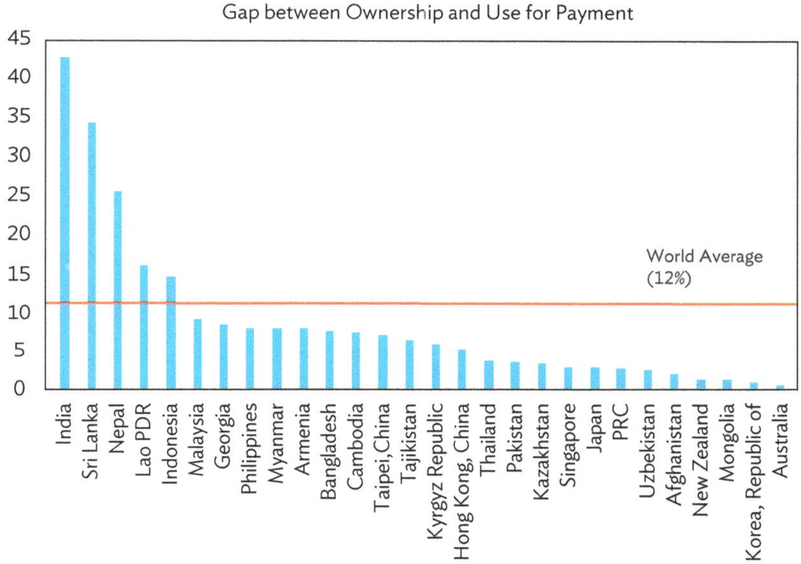


PRC = People's Republic of China, Lao PDR = Lao People's Democratic Republic.
Source: World Bank Global Findex Database.

The generally low incidence of dormant accounts, however, shows the issue of having accounts not seen as useful enough for their owners to make digital payments with them is concentrated in a few economies. Thus, financial inclusion strategy in India and Sri Lanka, which have high performance in account ownership but many dormant accounts, needs to focus on ways to expand uptake of existing accounts. Nepal, Indonesia, and the Lao PDR have a greater challenge of expanding both account ownership and use. One barrier to overcome is that many individuals who do not have an account feel they would need help to manage their account, keeping it safe and making sense of the fees, which could be a useful function for local agents (Chorzempa 2022).

### *Domestic Payment Infrastructure*

Once populations have ways to prove their identity digitally and an account, financial infrastructure is needed to facilitate their accounts to move and store money. Some systems are privately run, the central bank runs others, and in some cases privately run payments systems compete with publicly run ones (D'Silva et al. 2019). One such system is real-time payments infrastructures, which allow for nearly instant transfers of money and often include APIs that allow digital wallets to plug into these systems and facilitate payments. Figure 4.5 shows the economies in Asia that have real-time payment systems, either live or under development.

**Figure 4.5: Many Asian Economies Already Have Faster Payment Systems**

| Live | | Under Development |
|---|---|---|
| Australia | Singapore | |
| Hong Kong, China | Republic of Korea | |
| India | Sri Lanka | Indonesia |
| Japan | Taipei,China | New Zealand |
| Malaysia | Thailand | |
| Philippines | Viet Nam | |

Source: FIS Global Flavors of Fast Report 2020.

One key benefit of FPS systems is that they tend to operate 24/7 and, therefore, do not suffer from the issue of limited operating hours that other systems have (FSB 2023c). Only a few real-time gross settlement (RTGS) systems operate 24/7, though some are expanding their hours to increase overlap between jurisdictions. In the most recent progress report from the Financial Stability Board, many faster payment system operators plan to explore interlinking their system so that participants can send and receive payments from payment providers in other countries, which would be a positive step to shorten transaction chains (FSB 2023c).

There are many models for payments infrastructure, including for government involvement at different levels of services required to enable retail payments, from infrastructure to the generally private sector providers of digital wallets or accounts. Central banks themselves have different models for the extent to which they are public or private.[52]

[52] Typical central banks can be hybrid, neither fully public in that they are given a degree of independence from governments in their monetary policy and regulatory functions, nor are they fully private in that they exist to fulfill public functions and goals, rather than create returns for shareholders. Specifics of the institutional arrangements vary by country.

In India, building on Aadhar, the central bank spearheaded the creation of the Unified Payments Interface (UPI) in 2016, a real-time payments system that links together both bank accounts and digital wallets to allow fast, cheap payments for retail uses (D'Silva et al. 2019). Sri Lanka created LANKAQR in 2020, a national QR-code based payment system, that lets users pay merchants directly through their bank account through payment apps, with merchant fees capped at 0.5% of the transaction.[53] Cambodia's Bakong system, launched in 2020, goes beyond typical payment systems with a blockchain architecture underlying an app the central bank provides as a platform for financial service providers to serve individual users. It works not only for domestic payments, but has also added a cross-border service enabling Cambodians working in Malaysia to transfer money back home completely digitally. Around half of Cambodia's population had used it as of November 2021 (Jahan et al. 2022).

The PRC has had great success digitizing payments with private companies providing fintech wallets on top of existing and upgraded financial infrastructure. A look at the PRC shows some key elements that countries need to put in place, both for payments digitization to occur and for it to support the real economy. When the PRC's internet companies were small in the early 2000s, they struggled with missing or poorly functioning digital financial infrastructure for retail use, despite high bank account coverage in the country. An upgrade to the central bank's interbank payment system in 2010 was key to enabling "pull" payments in which a client links a digital wallet to their bank account and then can scan a QR code to pull money from their account—a key ingredient to making use of fintech services easy for consumers and thus spurring widespread adoption of digital payments (Chorzempa 2022). Bank accounts also served as a sort of digital identity and fund on-ramp that allowed individuals to have their identities verified and move money in and out of digital wallets all without expensive physical branches or agent networks. The government has also adapted the underlying infrastructure to move toward more interoperability and better government oversight, creating an institution called NetsUnion specifically to clear payments between banks and fintech wallets and between different fintech wallets.

[53] Central Bank of Sri Lanka. 2020. Launch of the National LANKAQR initiative. October. https://www.cbsl.gov.lk/en/news/Launch-of-the-National-LANKAQR-initiative.

### *Improving Global Interoperability*

Researchers at the BIS have developed a taxonomy of four ways payment systems can interoperate (Boar et al. 2021). The first model is a single access point. Many of the expanding cross-border payment initiatives are following this mode, which is the least ambitious and the least costly. In it, one or a few payment providers have accounts in each jurisdiction involved in a payment and serve as a "gateway" between the two. The BIS has flagged scalability issues, as that single institution can usually only handle a limited volume of business. In addition, only clients of that payment provider on each end would be able to transact directly. Others would need to first have their funds transferred to the gateway entity, then have it sent to the destination jurisdiction, which may then need to make another transfer to the payment provider of the payee if they are not a client of the gateway institution.

Bilateral links, for example, that between the Unified Payments Interface (UPI) and Singapore's PayNow launched in 2023, are more ambitious in that they allow any participant in one payment system to pay any participant in the other directly. To do so, this model requires significantly more work, and especially trust between the two payment systems and could require significant reforms to each system to ensure they can interoperate at scale. This system can handle more scale than the single access point model, but the effort to build a separate bilateral link for each payment channel is large and can lead to a proliferation of different arrangements. Hub and Spoke models are similar to bilateral links, but designate a settlement agent through which participants can access more than one country.

The most ambitious of all the ways to interoperate is the common platform model, where a new payment system with multilateral participation is created that many countries can plug into. The BIS Innovation Hub's M-CBDC Bridge project is an example, though still in experimental stage, using central bank digital currencies discussed in the next section.

One of the challenges for any of these models is how to handle the conversion of foreign exchange, as many cross-border payments require one currency to be converted to another, possibly also with a vehicle currency like the US dollar in between that could, therefore, require two foreign exchange transactions to complete. Common platforms and other forms of interlinking can either include foreign exchange inside the system or operate in one currency.

It is interesting that, of the 13 regional multilateral payment platforms found in a recent CPMI survey, none were in Asia (CPMI and Innovation Hub 2023). Many were created to serve common currency zones more common outside Asia. Global initiatives like CLS Bank and networks like Visa and Mastercard have significant presence in Asia, however, and many new initiatives involving experiments to use central bank digital currencies in cross-border payments with multilateral platforms are in Asia.

As Asian countries experiment with these platforms, they will have to grapple with major risks. The CPMI has flagged particular risks for multilateral platforms that could become a single point of failure if many parties rely on it to make payments (CPMI and Innovation Hub 2023). There are legal risks of connecting jurisdictions with very different legal systems for key payment concepts, operational risks like cyberattacks or IT system malfunctions, risks related to tracking flows for AML/CFT that can be hard to follow when operating across jurisdictions, and foreign exchange and liquidity risks that the platform might need to bear to convert currency. However, the potential benefits are significant if the challenges can be overcome. New platforms that can sidestep legacy risks and be open 24/7 like fast payment systems may help reduce costs to fund liquidity in multiple systems, shorten transaction chains compared to correspondent banking, and facilitate competition (CPMI and Innovation Hub 2023).

## Case Study: Central Bank Digital Currency (CBDC) for Cross-Border Payments

### *Literature Review*

Nearly all the world's central banks are exploring CBDC as a solution to many domestic and cross-border challenges. The Bank for International Settlements (BIS) found in 2022 that 93% of the central banks it surveyed were engaged in work related to CBDC, four had fully launched CBDCs, and many had advanced into the pilot stage (Kosse and Mattei 2023). There are many taxonomies and definitions of CBDC, but they generally refer to a new digital form of central bank money, with the same unit of account as currently available forms of currency (CPMI 2018). The first main type of CBDC currently being explored is a retail, or general purpose, CBDC which would be widely available to the public to hold and use for transactions. In contrast, a wholesale CBDC, like today's forms of digital central bank money in reserve and settlement accounts, would be available only to a select group of institutions, most likely financial intermediaries.

A key insight to understand CBDC is that it represents not only a new type of currency, but also a new type of payment system central banks design to transact CBDC. Digital forms of money are inextricably linked to the payments systems that transact them. Therefore, some of the most crucial design choices for CBDCs revolve around payment system design instead of the design of the currency portion. Of the three characteristics economists ascribe to money: a unit of account, a store of value, and a medium of exchange, ideas for CBDCs today mostly change the medium of exchange, through the new payment system. CBDCs have the same value as other forms of the same national currency (for example, in the PRC one "regular" digital or physical renminbi can always be converted to one unit of eCNY), so the unit of account does not change. CBDC held in a digital wallet are different than traditional bank accounts as a store of value in that they are a liability of the central bank, which should not be able to fail, unlike commercial banks. Whether this matters depends on the domestic financial market: where bank deposits are at risk this could matter a great deal, but in countries with well-regulated banks and government backstops for depositors, the distinction is of little importance.

### *The General Case for CBDCs*

Initial interest in CBDCs explored the use of distributed ledger technologies pioneered by cryptocurrencies for the back end of payment systems, seeing if they could improve safety and resilience of payment systems. Interest in CBDCs for retail use then surged in 2019 due to Facebook's Libra digital currency proposal, which would have created a new global currency and payment system with its own unit of account tied to a basket of currencies like the US dollar, the euro, and the yen. Central banks were concerned both about the increasing circulation of cryptocurrencies in their jurisdictions and that their position could be disrupted by private stablecoins like Libra or other central banks' digital currencies, a new form of "digital dollarization."

The Bank for International Settlements analyzed speeches from central bankers related to CBDC and found little interest before 2017 (Figure 4.6). Central bankers then began to give more speeches on CBDCs, but with strong negative sentiment focused on risks. The negativity, however, turned positive quickly in 2020 as CBDCs came to be seen as a way for central banks to avoid falling behind private sector currency innovations.

**Figure 4.6: Speeches on Central Bank Digital Currency Have Turned More Positive Since Late 2018**

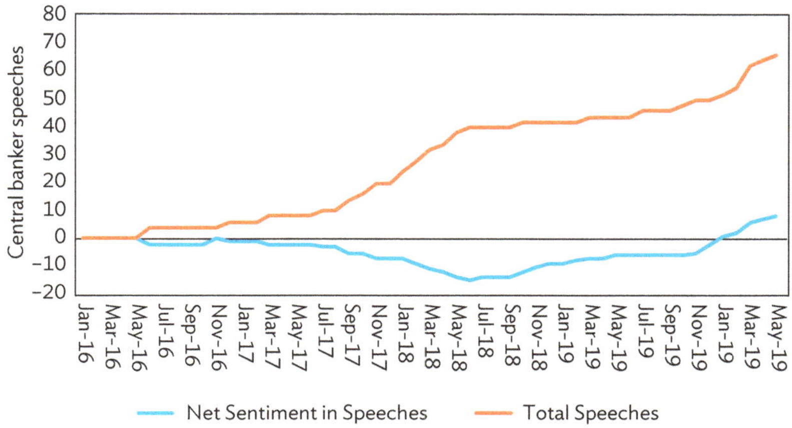


Source: Auer, R., G. Cornelli, and J. Frost. 2020. The Rise of Central Bank; Digital Currencies: Drivers, Approaches and Technologies. *BIS Working Paper* 880.

Another driver of interest in CBDC is the increasing digitization of economies. Central banks wanted to ensure they were not falling behind a new wave of monetary innovation. As digital commerce rises, digital payments do too, which has reduced the role of public money. Generally, only special institutions like banks have access to digital forms of central bank money, while the general population and most firms only have access to central bank money in the form of paper cash. Demand for cash in many countries remains robust, but in places like the PRC, it has all but disappeared in major cities as online payments have become dominant.

### *Wholesale and Retail*

Of the two types of CBCD, retail or general purpose have the most implications for the financial system and domestic payment systems, both in terms of benefits and risks. Frictions with cash, including having to physically retrieve banknotes from banks and transport them, the risk of loss with no recourse in the event of theft, and transacting in person, make using central bank money for large transactions or holding it in large quantities unpalatable. Therefore, adding a safe digital form of central bank money could create a product that competes more effectively with existing forms of money and payments, considering that central banks, unlike commercial banks, with few exceptions cannot fail. Central banks must worry about a wide variety of risks with CBDC, including effects on liquidity if many consumers and businesses shift savings out of commercial bank deposits into CBDC wallets. The risk of potentially destabilizing runs out of bank deposits into CBDC wallets in the event of financial instability is of concern to policymakers (Brainard 2022). A retail CBDC that could be used for transactions across borders could also facilitate capital flight. Though if properly regulated with safeguards, it could also help connect users to cross-border payment systems integrating CBDCs that could soon exist.

## 4.5. Central Bank Digital Currencies in Asia

### *Landscape of CBDC Interest in Asia*

Interest in CBDCs is strong throughout the world, with Asia no exception. Figure 4.7 shows a graphical representation of a recent International Monetary Fund survey that found 83% of central banks in Asia and the Pacific were working on a CBDC. A third have progressed to either pilot programs or proofs of concept, demonstrating more seriousness about CBDS than general research (Jahan et al. 2022).

**Figure 4.7: Most Asian Countries Are Exploring Central Bank Digital Currencies**

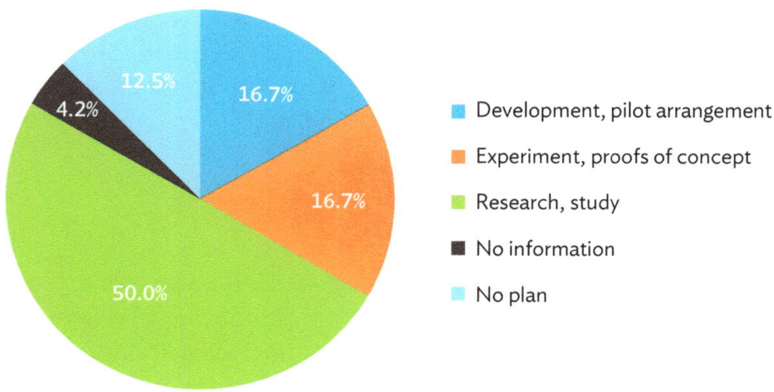


Source: Jahan, S. et al. 2022. Towards Central Bank Digital Currencies in Asia and the Pacific: Results of a Regional Survey. International Monetary Fund, *Fintech Notes* 2022(9). 28 September.

Table 4.1, based on the Atlantic Council's CBDC Tracker, shows the Asian economies and regions exploring CBDCs. The first category illustrates the stage of development. Since to date no CBDC has been officially issued in Asia, the farthest economies along are those that have progressed to the pilot stage. Others have CBDCs in development, and the earliest stage is simply research. Table 4.1 also shows whether the economy or region is exploring retail, wholesale, or both versions of CBDC and, if one has been chosen, the name of the CBDC or project name.

**Table 4.1: Status of Central Bank Digital Currency Projects in Asia and the Pacific**

| Economy/Region | Status | Type of CBDC | Project Name |
|---|---|---|---|
| People's Republic of China | Pilot | Both | eCNY |
| Hong Kong, China | Pilot | Both | e-HKD, Project mBridge |
| India | Pilot | Both | Digital Rupee |
| Kazakhstan | Pilot | Retail | Digital Tenge |
| Republic of Korea | Pilot | Retail | Undecided |
| Malaysia | Pilot | Wholesale | |
| Singapore | Pilot | Both | Project Orchid, Project Ubin |
| Thailand | Pilot | Both | Digital Baht, Project mBridge, Project Inthanon |
| Australia | Development | Both | eAUD |
| Bhutan | Development | Both | e-Ngultrum |
| Indonesia | Development | Both | Digital Rupiah |
| Japan | Development | Both | |
| Palau | Development | Both | |
| Bangladesh | Research | Undecided | |
| Fiji, Solomon Islands, Tonga, and Vanuatu | Research | Undecided | |
| Georgia | Research | Retail | Digital Gel |
| Lao PDR | Research | Both | |
| Nepal | Research | Undecided | |
| New Zealand | Research | Retail | |
| Pakistan | Research | Retail | |
| Philippines | Research | Wholesale | CBDCPh |
| Taipei,China | Research | Both | |
| Viet Nam | Research | Undecided | Digital Dong |
| Cambodia | N/A | Undecided | N/A |

CBDC = Central Bank Digital Currency, Lao PDR = Lao People's Democratic Republic, N/A = not applicable.
Source: Jahan, S. et al. 2022. Towards Central Bank Digital Currencies in Asia and the Pacific: Results of a Regional Survey. International Monetary Fund, *Fintech Notes* 2022(9). 28 September: Atlantic Council (2022).

The countries most seriously exploring CBDC tend to be at least middle-income, but are from all over Asia. One key takeaway from examining this data set is that almost all Asian countries considering CBDCs are exploring both retail and wholesale versions. This finding is broadly consistent with the BIS global survey results, which found two-thirds of respondent central banks were exploring both, a significant increase over previous years, while only about a third were considering retail only (Kosse and Mattei 2023). A 2022 ADB Survey of 13 Asia-Pacific Economic Cooperation (APEC) members found that of those economies that had determined which kind of CBDC to focus on, just over 40% were looking into both—though the perceived benefits they listed included both cross-border payments associated with wholesale and payments innovation (ADB 2022). However, the most recent data indicate an increase in pilots and intentions to launch wholesale rather than retail CBDCs, with the main drivers of interest in wholesale being cross-border use cases (Iorio, Kosse, and Mattei 2024).

### *Drivers of Interest and Case for CBDC in Asian Economies*

Asian authorities cite a wide variety of motivations for exploring CBDC, but there are patterns. Jurisdictions with already developed financial systems have greater interest in wholesale CBDCs. These may enhance functionality for cross-border payments without disrupting domestic financial arrangements and have infrastructure that generally functions well (Jahan et al. 2022). Potential risks and disruptions of CBDC introduction are thus more salient than potential improvements. That noted, the Bank of Korea's deputy governor has written, "there is a strong case for being prepared" if the need for a CBDC is recognized (BIS Monetary and Economic Department 2022). The lack of urgency may in part be because advanced economies may tend to have lower inflation and more trusted central banks, reducing the risk of domestic actors engaging in currency substitution through foreign or private currencies. This finding is consistent with BIS surveys that generally find advanced economies less advanced and more cautious in CBDC work than lower income and emerging market countries (Chorzempa 2021).

Motivations in emerging Asia are more focused on financial development and inclusion, like digitizing payments largely completed in cash today, lowering costs, and generating data for use in detecting money laundering and providing other financial services. The 2022 ADB survey found that all non-G20 economies listed spurring innovation for payments as high benefit for CBDC (ADB 2022). Pacific island nations and lower-income countries tend to be most focused on financial inclusion, but they are exploring alternatives to CBDC like mobile money that may be easier to introduce than CBDCs (Jahan et al. 2022).

Indonesia's central bank has identified three drivers of its interest in a CBDC. Firstly, it anticipates that a CBDC will help it retain monetary sovereignty as private and foreign digital currencies rise in popularity, updating its currency issuance and payments systems. It also wants to be on a footing to participate in the international development of CBDCs for cross-border payments. Finally, it anticipates that a CBDC could increase linkages between the digital economy and the financial system, expanding financial inclusion and innovation (BIS Monetary and Economic Department 2022).

Malaysia has no immediate plans to issue a CBDC, but its proof-of-concept exploratory work is divided into three phases that are revealing about its sense of the highest priority and greatest promise for CBDC. Cross-border wholesale payments are first, including Bank Negara's participation in Project Dunbar with other central banks in Australia, Singapore, and South Africa. Domestic wholesale follows, and finally domestic retail. Malaysia is not alone in assessing that cross-border payments "are typically more costly, slower, and less transparent compared to domestic payments," and thus may be a greater priority (BIS Monetary and Economic Department 2022).

The People's Bank of China (PBOC) was one of the earliest central banks to commit to launching a CBDC, in early 2016. After Bitcoin took off in the PRC in mid-2013, the PBOC created a special digital currency research institute, which now leads internal efforts to design and implement the eCNY. The eCNY is an intermediated "two-tier" CBDC to avoid disintermediating banks—users can exchange regular renminbi for the eCNY at designated banks and transact them with digital wallets, while the PBOC will provide the back-end infrastructure. The eCNY is not interest-bearing. The financial inclusion elements of the eCNY include enabling payments for people without bank accounts, as one can open a limited functionality wallet by only providing a phone number. Other elements include offline payments for those living in areas without consistent internet access and wearable devices for payments to include those without smartphones.

Its eCNY project remains at the pilot stage, but it is still the most advanced of any major economy, with 264 million individual wallets opened by the end of May 2022, CNY82 billon in transactions, and 4.57 million businesses participating. Nine banks are so far part of the pilot, as are digital wallets like Alipay and WeChat (Fan 2022). The PBOC describes the project as mainly domestic, but it is one of the most active central banks in pilot programs for new ways of doing cross-border payments based on central bank digital currencies, including a pilot with Hong Kong, China and the multilateral M-CBDC Bridge project described in this chapter.

### *Cross-Border CBDCs*

Central banks and other researchers are exploring many ways CBDCs could improve cross-border payments. Some are bilateral programs between two central banks exploring how CBDC could work for cross-border payments between their countries and currencies. Others are even more ambitious, bringing together multiple central banks to explore cross-border transactions. The Bank for International Settlements, based in Basel, Switzerland, and its multiple Innovation Hub locations have become key venues for both research and practical experimentation in CBDCs.

Many of the same type of models of interoperability, requirements for harmonization and standards, and challenges to be surmounted for non-CBDC payments interoperability apply for CBDCs (BIS CPMI and Innovation Hub, IMF, and World Bank 2021). CBDC as digital central bank money for cross-border transactions is far less unique for wholesale payments than for retailers, because central bank money is already being used throughout wholesale payment systems (CPMI 2003). Proponents, however, believe CBDCs may be able to find innovative ways around some of these challenges.

One of the ways CBDCs could improve cross-border payments is through smart contracts. These are not the same as a legal contract, but in a blockchain-based system can program functionality, for example, by automatically sending value from one account to another when certain conditions are met (Levi and Lipton 2018). Payment for goods could automatically be debited if, for example, a linked system registered that the shipping container with the goods arrived at port, instead of requiring someone to manually send a payment after being notified of the container's arrival.

One interesting proof of concept using smart contracts to solve existing payment issues is the joint New York Federal Reserve's New York Innovation Center (NYIC) and the Monetary Authority of Singapore (MAS) Project Cedar x Ubin+ which simulated wholesale CBDC systems that were interlinked to allow cross-border, cross-currency transactions. One of the issues it addressed was atomicity, using smart contracts to ensure that a complex transaction with multiple parts only executes if all the parts succeed at the same time (Federal Reserve Bank of New York 2023).

This could eliminate Herstatt risk: e.g., if a payment is initiated as a trade of US dollars for renminbi, the Herstatt risk is that the holder of renminbi receives the dollars, but fails to send the renminbi, or vice versa. The simulation showed promise to make payments faster, settle with less risk, and improve interoperability between payment systems, but such systems will rely on countries launching their own wholesale CBDC, which do not exist yet.

Project Dunbar involved the BIS Innovation Hub, the Reserve Bank of Australia, the Central Bank of Malaysia, the Monetary Authority of Singapore, and the South African Reserve Bank (BIS Innovation Hub 2022a). It developed multiple prototype that showed it was technically feasible to build a platform for multiple CBDCs for cross-border payments that could make payments simpler, require fewer intermediaries, and use smart contracts to increase automation.

One of the most promising projects is Project mBridge, also part of the BIS Innovation Hub. Project mBridge is a collaboration of the Bank of Thailand, Hong Kong Monetary Authority (HKMA), People's Bank of China (PBOC), and Central Bank of the United Arab Emirates, as well as other observer central banks. It aims to eventually become a "production ready" system for commercial and central banks to transact cross-border with CBDCs they issue and exchange (BIS Innovation Hub 2022b). Project mBridge completed a 6-week trial with its own blockchain in late 2022 with 160 transactions totaling $22 million across 20 commercial banks. Nearly half of the transactions involved the eCNY, in part because the PRC already had an operational eCNY system that could interact with the pilot more easily than countries without such extensive CBDC pilots.[54] The Project mBridge pilot was declared a success and is now advancing to further stages that could include more countries, use cases, currencies, and possibly adding a foreign exchange market.

The reports on Project Dunbar and Project mBridge both flagged issues that require further study needed to advance from pilots and proofs of concept to real financial infrastructure.

First, central banks need to consider the implications of extending access to central bank money to foreign participants in multiple CBDC platforms, including those that would not otherwise be able to transact in their

[54] Of the total 305 transactions, 142 were for the eCNY, making it the most used currency in the pilot. The eHKD was next with 86 transactions.

currency. Access to central bank payment infrastructure is a sensitive issue, and in countries like the United States is strictly controlled to include only specific types of participants under specific conditions. Expanded access through CBDC has some of the highest potential to increase competition and build larger networks, but the risks, especially across currencies, will need to be controlled. Risks include having less ability to supervise the flow of capital, which could jeopardize financial stability. Project mBridge excluded transactions using a CBDC foreign to both parties and domestic transactions in a foreign CBDC, for example, in part to avoid the possibility of facilitating displacement of local currency that could exacerbate volatile capital flows.

Conducting transactions on a shared ledger also creates legal questions around jurisdiction that could require changes to laws in participating countries for full certainty. Security and privacy protocols will need to resolve data privacy concerns. Governance challenges are some of the most complex, as central banks sharing the ledger would need to give up some of the control, they typically have in payment systems in their jurisdiction to govern such an arrangement together, including how to resolve disputes and responsibility for issues that may arise, how to fund the system, and procedures for accession of potential new member jurisdictions and participants.

**Table 4.2: Potential Benefits, Risks, and Challenges of Central Bank Digital Currencies for Cross-Border Payments**

| Potential Benefits | Risks | Challenges |
|---|---|---|
| • Nearly instant payments<br>• Shorter chains of intermediation<br>• Innovations based on smart contracts<br>• Lower cost due to streamlined processes<br>• Improved access<br>• Safe settlement asset<br>• Built from ground up with interoperability<br>• New tools to protect privacy | • Financial risks from expanded access<br>• Cybersecurity risk<br>• Legal risk<br>• Operational risk<br>• Currency substitution/displacement<br>• AML/CFT Risk<br>• Liquidity Risk<br>• Potential credit risk of participants | • Technical design<br>• Synchronizing legal regimes<br>• Coordinating supervisory and financial authorities in participant jurisdictions<br>• Platform Governance<br>• Delegation of monetary sovereignty<br>• Privacy for shared platforms |

AML/CFT = anti-money laundering/combating the financing of terrorism.
Source: Author's analysis, BIS, BIS Innovation Hub, Financial Stability Board.

Overall, CBDCs demonstrate promise based on the experiments to date and deserve further exploration. Yet, despite large-scale allocation of resources to the issue, there is not yet any fully operating wholesale CBDC, and there is no consensus on the technical architecture that best achieves objectives of different central banks. These initiatives are at an early stage, and the remaining barriers to be overcome are formidable. Payment infrastructure is so critical, with such a low tolerance for risk, that developing fully operational and scalable solutions will take time and collective effort.

As jurisdictions explore CBDCs, they should take them as an opportunity to build cross-border functionality in at the outset, starting with practical experimentation in CBDC that forces them to build new competencies and discover trade-offs, both domestic and cross-border, firsthand. However, in the near term, ways to improve interoperability without CBDCs covered earlier are more likely to bear fruit. In addition, many of those interventions would not only improve payments today and make future CBDC adoption and interoperability easier if that route is taken down the road. Payment dynamics are heavily related to networks, and without operational wholesale CBDCs in partner countries, those networks do not yet exist.

## Conclusion

Improving cross-border digital payments can unlock greater economic growth, cross-border commerce, more inclusive financial systems, more market access for entrepreneurs, and much more. Many of the gains would accrue to senders and recipients of remittances, who currently lose a sizable fee every time money is sent. Unfortunately, the barriers to improvement are challenging, and they go far beyond technology to thorny issues of governance, regulation, and infrastructure building in one of the most sensitive sectors of any economy.

Cross-border payments have improved, but in many use cases across Asia, they fall short of the goals for access, time, cost, and transparency that authorities are aiming to achieve with initiatives like the G20 program. Today, those payments largely go through the correspondent banking system through the dollar, a system with enormous advantages and efficiencies, but one for which authorities across Asia are exploring alternatives that rely more on local currencies. These have a variety of motivations, from experimenting with new technology to insulating themselves from sanctions or spillover effects from macrofinancial conditions elsewhere. Some are authorizing foreign banks to become gateways to their market, others are more ambitiously linking their payment infrastructures, and others are exploring the creation of entirely new infrastructures that envision directly trading new CBDCs with fewer steps in between.

Governments across Asia should ensure they have the key building blocks in place for their citizens to plug in to their domestic payment networks, including digital identity to facilitate obtaining an account with proper KYC/AML, and then, in turn, ensuring those domestic networks interoperate well with other networks abroad. That is true for existing systems, CBDCs, and new experiments that do not fit the definition of CBDC.

Much of the near-term promise for improving cross-border payments lies not with CBDCs that do not yet exist, but with harmonizing payment standards, digital regulations like those for KYC/AML, and ensuring their privacy frameworks are compatible with the needs of cross-border payments that require sending sensitive data across borders. Governments and private sector players should support the G20 initiatives under way, as well as those at the BIS and with SWIFT, that are aimed at the most pressing and often most addressable barriers to digital payments.

Digital trade and economy agreements can also help—if they break from tradition to include commitments to avoid nontariff barriers on cross-border payments and help to open up competition. More competition can make a payment corridor more liquid, easier to access, and cheaper, as well as open more opportunities for local payment providers to reach scale and build networks through presence in other markets. One of the most promising ways to improve cross-border payments, subject to security and financial stability safeguards, is expanding access to foreign and nonbank providers of payment services to key payment infrastructure, which can enhance competition.

## References


Abraham, R., E. Bennett, R. Bhusal, S. Dubey, Qian Li, A. Pattanayak, N. Shah. 2018. State of Aadhar Report. May. *ID Insight*. https://www.idinsight.org/wpcontent/uploads/2021/10/StateofAadhaarReport_2017-18.pdf.

Asian Development Bank (ADB). 2022. Asia-Pacific Financial Inclusion Forum: The Role of Central Bank Digital Currencies in Financial Inclusion. December. https://www.adb.org/publications/asia-pacific-financial-inclusion-forum-2022.

______. 2023. *Asian Economic Integration Report 2023: Trade, Investment, and Climate Change in Asia and the Pacific*. February. https://www.adb.org/sites/default/files/publication/859946/asian-economic-integration-report-2023.pdf.

______. 2024. Asian Economic Integration Report 2024: Decarbonizing Global Value Chains. February. https://www.adb.org/publications/asian-economic-integration-report-2024.

Awrey, D. 2022. Unbundling Banking, Money and Payments. *Georgetown Law Journal*. 110. https://www.law.georgetown.edu/georgetown-law-journal/wp-content/uploads/sites/26/2022/06/Awrey_Unbundling-Banking.pdf.

Bank of England. 2023. Cross-Border Payments. 31 January. https://www.bankofengland.co.uk/payment-and-settlement/cross-border-payments.

Bank for International Settlements Committee on Payment and Settlement Systems (CPMI). 2003. The Role of Central Bank Money in Payment Systems. August. https://www.bis.org/cpmi/publ/d55.pdf.

______. 2018. Central Bank Digital Currencies. March. https://www.bis.org/cpmi/publ/d174.pdf.

______. 2023. ISO 20022 Harmonisation Requirements for Enhancing Cross-border Payments. March. https://www.bis.org/cpmi/publ/d215.pdf.

Bank for International Settlements Committee on Payments and Market Infrastructures (CPMI) and Innovation Hub. 2023. Exploring Multilateral Platforms for Cross-border Payments. January. https://www.bis.org/cpmi/publ/d213.htm.

Bank for International Settlements Committee on Payments and Market Infrastructures (CPMI) and Innovation Hub, International Monetary Fund, and World Bank. 2021. Central Bank Digital Currencies for Cross-border Payments: Report to the G20. July. https://www.bis.org/publ/othp38.pdf.

Bank for International Settlements (BIS) Innovation Hub. 2022a. Project mBridge: Connecting Economies through CBDC. October. https://www.bis.org/publ/othp59.htm. And https://www.bis.org/press/p221026.htm.

_______. 2022b. Project Dunbar: International Settlements using Multi-CBDCs. March. https://www.bis.org/about/bisih/topics/cbdc/dunbar.htm/.

Bank for International Settlements (BIS), Monetary and Economic Department. 2022. CBDCS in Emerging Market Economies. *BIS Papers* 123. April. https://www.bis.org/publ/bppdf/bispap123.pdf.

Bank Negara Malaysia. 2023. *Annual Report*. https://www.bnm.gov.my/documents/20124/12142010/ar2023_en_box2.pdf.

Beck, T., M. Janfils, and J. Wiegand. 2022. "What Explains Remittance Fees? Panel Evidence" *International Monetary Fund Working Paper* 22/63. https://www.imf.org/-/media/Files/Publications/WP/2022/English/wpiea2022063-print-pdf.ashx.

Boar, C. 2019. New Correspondent Banking Data—The Decline Continues at a Slower Pace. Bank for International Settlements (BIS) Committee on Market Payments and Infrastructures.

Boar, C. et al. 2021. Interoperability between Payment Systems across Borders. *BIS Bulletin* 49. December 10.

Brainard, L. 2022. Digital Assets and the Future of Finance: Examining the Benefits and Risks of a US Central Bank Digital Currency. Testimony before the Committee on Financial Services, US House of Representatives, Washington, DC. 26 May. https://www.federalreserve.gov/newsevents/testimony/brainard20220526a.htm.

Central Bank of Sri Lanka. 2021. National Financial Inclusion Strategy for Sri Lanka (2021–2024). March. https://www.cbsl.gov.lk/sites/default/files/cbslweb_documents/NFIS%20Summary_%20English_2.pdf.

Chorzempa, M. 2021. China, the United States, and Central Bank Digital Currencies: How Important Is It to Be First? *China Economic Journal.* 14(1). https://www.tandfonline.com/doi/abs/10.1080/17538963.2020.1870278.

Chorzempa, M. 2022. *The Cashless Revolution: China's Reinvention of Money and the End of America's Domination of Finance and Technology.* Public Affairs.

Clearing House Interbank Payments System (CHIPS). 2021. CHIPS Participants. January. https://mc-e3a82812-8e7a-44d9-956f-8910-cdn-endpoint.azureedge.net/-/media/New/TCH/Documents/Payment-Systems/CHIPS_Participants_Revised_01-25-2021.pdf?rev=d222e47714a146369324dcd9450e7e4e.

Clearing House Interbank Payments System (CHIPS). 2023. TCH Reschedules CHIPS ISO 20022 Implementation to April 2024. February 9. https://www.theclearinghouse.org/payment-systems/Articles/2023/02/02-09-2023_TCH_Reschedules_CHIPS_ISO_20022_Implementation_April_2024.

Demirgüç-Kunt, A. et al. 2022. *Global Findex Database 2021: Financial Inclusion, Digital Payments, and Resilience in the Age of COVID-19.* World Bank Group.

DiPippo, G. and A. Leonardo Palazzi. 2023. It's All about Networking: The Limits of Renminbi Internationalization. Commentary, Center for Strategic and International Studies. 18 April 18. https://www.csis.org/analysis/its-all-about-networking-limits-renminbi-internationalization.

D'Silva, D. et al. 2019. The Design of Digital Financial Infrastructure: Lessons from India. *BIS Papers* 109. December.

Fan, Yifei. 2022. Speech at the Suzhou Conference on Finance Supporting Industry Innovation Cluster Development. 19 September. https://finance.caixin.com/2022-09-20/101942102.html.

Federal Reserve. 2023. Unpacking Clearing and Settlement. US Federal Reserve Board Services. https://www.frbservices.org/financial-services/fednow/instant-payments-education/unpacking-clearing-and-settlement.html.

Federal Reserve Bank of New York. 2023. Project Cedar Phase II x Ubin+: Improving Wholesale Cross-border Multi-currency Payments and Settlements. https://www.newyorkfed.org/medialibrary/media/nyic/project-cedar-phase-two-ubin-report.pdf.

Financial Action Task Force (FATF). 2023. Methodology for Assessing Technical Compliance with the FATF Recommendations and the Effectiveness of AML/CFT Systems. June. https://www.fatf-gafi.org/content/dam/fatf-gafi/methodology/FATF%20Methodology%2022%20Feb%202013.pdf.

Financial Stability Board (FSB). 2020. Enhancing Cross-border Payments: Stage 3 Roadmap. October 2020. https://www.fsb.org/2020/10/enhancing-cross-border-payments-stage-3-roadmap/.

_______. 2023a. Annual Progress Report on Meeting the Targets for Cross-border Payments: 2023 Report on Key Performance Indicators. 9 October. https://www.fsb.org/wp-content/uploads/P091023-1.pdf.

_______. 2023b. G20 Roadmap for Enhancing Cross-border Payments Consolidated Progress Report for 2023. 9 October. https://www.fsb.org/wp-content/uploads/P091023-2.pdf.

_______. 2023c. Stocktake of International Standards Relevant to Cross-Border Payments. September 25. https://www.fsb.org/wp-content/uploads/P250923.pdf.

Gallaher, M. 2020. *Trade Agreements to Move the Digital Economy*. Visa Economic Empowerment Institute. December. https://usa.visa.com/dam/VCOM/global/sites/visa-economic-empowerment-institute/documents/veei-trade-agreements-to-move-economy.pdf.

GSMA. 2016. GSMA Research Shows Mobile Money is Significantly Reducing the Cost of Sending International Remittances. November 2. https://www.gsma.com/newsroom/press-release/gsma-research-shows-mobile-money-significantly-reducing-cost-sending-international-remittances/.

Gopinath, G. 2015. *The International Price System*. Harvard University and National Bureau of Economic Research. 12 November 2015. https://scholar.harvard.edu/files/gopinath/files/paper_083115_01.pdf.

Greene, R. 2022. *Southeast Asia's Growing Interest in Non-dollar Financial Channels—and the Renminbi's Potential Role*. Carnegie Endowment for International Peace. 22 August. https://carnegieendowment.org/2022/08/22/southeast-asia-s-growing-interest-in-non-dollar-financial-channels-and-renminbi-s-potential-role-pub-87731.

______. 2023. The Difficult Realities of the BRICS' Dedollarization Efforts—and the RMB's Role. Carnegie Endowment for International Peace. 5 December. https://carnegieendowment.org/2023/12/05/difficult-realities-of-brics-dedollarization-efforts-and-renminbi-s-role-pub-91173.

Iorio, A., A. Kosse, and I. Mattei. 2024. Embracing Diversity, Advancing Together—Results of the 2023 BIS Survey on Central Bank Digital Currencies and Crypto. *BIS Papers* 147. June. https://www.bis.org/publ/bppdf/bispap147.pdf.

Ito, H. and M. Kawai. 2021. The Global Monetary System and Use of Regional Currencies in ASEAN+3. December. In *Redefining Strategic Routes to Financial Resilience in ASEAN+3*, Edited by D. Guinigundo, M. Kawai et al. Asian Development Bank.

Kosse, A. and I. Mattei. 2023. Making headway – Results of the 2022 BIS Survey on Central Bank Digital Currencies and Crypto. Bank for International Settlements. July. *BIS Papers* No. 36. https://www.bis.org/publ/bppdf/bispap136.pdf.

Levi, S D. and A B. Lipton. 2018. An Introduction to Smart Contracts and Their Potential and Inherent Limitations. Harvard Law School Forum on Corporate Governance. May 26. https://corpgov.law.harvard.edu/2018/05/26/an-introduction-to-smart-contracts-and-their-potential-and-inherent-limitations/#3.

Levine, R. 2005. Finance and Growth: Theory and Evidence. In *Handbook of Economic Growth* Vol. 1, edited by P. Aghion and S.N. Durlauf. Elsevier. pp. 865–934. https://www.sciencedirect.com/science/article/abs/pii/S1574068405010129.

People's Bank of China. 2023. *2023 RMB Internationalization Report.* 27 October. http://www.pbc.gov.cn/en/3688241/3688636/3828468/4756463/5163932/2023120819545781941.pdf.

Rey, H. 2001. International Trade and Currency Exchange. *The Review of Economic Studies.* 68(2). pp. 443–464.

Rice, T., G. von Peter, and C. Boar. 2020. On the Global Retreat of Correspondent Banks. *BIS Quarterly Review*. March. https://www.bis.org/publ/qtrpdf/r_qt2003g.htm.

Society for Worldwide Interbank Financial Telecommunications (SWIFT). 2019. ISO 20022: Better Data Means Better Payments. September. https://www.swift.com/sites/default/files/documents/swift_paper_iso20022.pdf.

World Economic Forum (WEF). 2020. *Connecting Digital Economies: Policy Recommendations for Cross-Border Payments*. June. https://www.weforum.org/publications/connecting-digital-economies-policy-recommendations-for-cross-border-payments/.

# 5 Taxing the Digital Economy: Cross-Border Data and Trade Policies in Asia

Julien Chaisse

## Introduction

Every element of an economy is impacted and transformed by technology, and the integration of data and technology is a defining feature of digital trade (Lim, Toh, and Xie 2022). The ability to gather, use, and analyze vast amounts of machine-readable information (digital data) about virtually anything propels the digital economy's rapid evolution (CLOUDSUFI 2024). Building strong economic ties has always been crucial for many major economies.[55] The growth of the digital economy brings up numerous new business prospects. As a result, it can influence innovation (Zhang et al. 2022) and productivity development and aid in enhancing economic and social results (Moulton 2000; Nathan Associates 2017).

New economic agreements, have been established to encourage firms to expand and protect users' interests in the digital age.[56] A Digital Economy Agreement (DEA) is a novel type of free trade agreement (FTA) that focuses exclusively on creating mutually acceptable standards for international digital trade among various countries (Table 5.1).[57] In Asia and the Pacific, a key example is provided by Singapore's determination to work with trading partners to expand the digital economy. The Association of Southeast

[55] For instance, Singapore, a global trading hub, must consistently build strong business ties with its partners, particularly in the current digital era (Lim, Toh, and Xie 2022).

[56] Specifically, DEAs aim to achieve three key objectives: (i) harmonising digital norms and standards and promoting communication between digital systems; (ii) enabling international data flows and protecting consumer rights and personal information; and (iii) promoting collaboration among business partners in developing regions (Lim, Toh, and Xie 2022).

[57] DEAs are considered a mechanism to bridge the gaps in international standards, particularly in developing technologies and policy sectors like artificial intelligence and digital identities, where the pandemic has been speeding the adoption of digital business models. See Xie, Chan, and Detros (2021).

Asian Nations (ASEAN) is also considering its own regional digital economy agreement, as outlined in the Bandar Seri Begawan Roadmap on ASEAN's Digital Transformation Agenda (Warren and Fan 2022).

Mapping the interaction between international tax and trade/investment regimes is a crucial regulatory issue because it affects the growth and development of the digital economy.[58] As the digital economy continues to expand, how it is taxed and regulated has become increasingly important. The absence of clear and consistent international tax rules for the digital economy can create uncertainty and obstacles for businesses operating in the global market. The implications of actual or potential international tax rules for the digital economy can vary. If the rules are too restrictive, they may hinder the growth of the digital economy and reduce the flow of investment and trade. If the rules are too lenient, they may result in a lack of revenue for governments and may enable multinational firms to avoid paying their fair share of taxes. This can lead to a decline in public trust in the digital economy and in the government's ability to provide essential services. Therefore, striking the right balance between promoting growth of the digital economy and ensuring adequate tax revenue is a major challenge for policymakers.

The development of international tax rules for the digital economy is complex and requires a thorough understanding of the interplay between tax, trade, and investment regimes, as well as the evolving nature of the digital economy.

This chapter explores the relationship between international tax and investment regimes and its effect on the digital economy. It also examines the connections between current frameworks for cross-border data flows and the taxation of digital products in various jurisdictions. It delves into the role of regional trade and investment agreements in implementing digital tax rules, providing real-world examples of best practices in tax provisions related to data flows and cybersecurity. The chapter also identifies emerging areas for digital taxation rules and standards and offers policy recommendations for Asian economies that align with existing trade and investment regimes.

58 DEAs seek to promote innovation in digital business models and enable cross-border data flows while safeguarding data and preserving public confidence in digital systems. Singapore, as the first to sign DEAs, has finalized four agreements, with Chile, New Zealand, Australia, the United Kingdom, and is negotiating a digital partnership with the Republic of Korea (Ministry of Trade and Industry 2022). A comparable formal treaty is being negotiated with Viet Nam (Tong 2021). Given the significance of establishing global benchmarks and standards for digital trade, it is anticipated that Singapore would continue to look for digital partnerships with important economies throughout the world.

**Table 5.1: List of Existing Digital Economy Agreements and Partnerships on Digital Economy**

| Agreement and Partnership | Signatories | Date of Signature | Date of Entry into Force | Status | Additional Remarks |
|---|---|---|---|---|---|
| ASEAN Agreement on Electronic Commerce | Brunei Darussalam, Cambodia, Indonesia, Lao PDR, Malaysia, Myanmar, Philippines, Singapore, Thailand, Viet Nam | 22 January 2019 | 3 December 2021 | Active | |
| EU-Singapore Digital Trade Agreement | European Union, Singapore | 25 July 2024 | Negotiations launched in 20 July 2023 | Active | |
| US–Japan Digital Trade Agreement | Japan, United States | 7 October 2019 | 1 January 2020 | Active | |
| Digital Economy Partnership Agreement (DEPA) | Chile, New Zealand, Singapore | 12 June 2020 | 7 January 2021 (New Zealand, Singapore)<br><br>23 November 2021 (Chile) | Active | The Republic of Korea submitted a formal application to join the agreement on 13 September 2021.<br><br>The People's Republic of China submitted a formal application to join the agreement on 1 November 2021. Its accession process began on 18 August 2022.<br><br>Canada submitted a formal application to join the agreement on 9 May 2022. Its accession process began on 25 August 2022. |

*Continued on next page*

**Table 5.1** *continued*

| Agreement and Partnership | Signatories | Date of Signature | Date of Entry into Force | Status | Additional Remarks |
|---|---|---|---|---|---|
| Australia–Singapore Digital Economy Agreement (ASDEA) | Australia, Singapore | 6 August 2020 | 8 December 2020 | Active | |
| United Kingdom–Singapore Digital Economy Agreement (UKSDEA) | Singapore, United Kingdom | 25 February 2022 | 14 June 2022 | Active | |
| EFTA–Singapore Digital Economy Agreement | EFTA states, Singapore | n/a | Ongoing | | |
| Korea– Singapore Digital Partnership Agreement (KSDPA) | Singapore, Republic of Korea | n/a | n/a | Negotiations concluded on 15 December 2021. | |
| US–Singapore Partnership for Growth and Innovation (PGI) | Singapore, United States | 7 October 2021 | | Active | |
| France– Singapore Digital and Green Partnership (DGP) | France, Singapore | 14 March 2022 | | Active | |

ASEAN = Association of Southeast Asian Nations, EFTA = European Free Trade Area, EU = European Union, Lao PDR = Lao People's Democratic Republic, n/a = not applicable, US = United States.
Note: Several free trade agreements (FTA) already include chapters or provisions regarding the digital economy and digital trade. See, for example, the Australia–United Kingdom FTA and the New Zealand–United Kingdom FTA, both pending ratification before entry into force, and the United States–Mexico–Canada Agreement. Steps are also taken to work toward the materialization of various agreements and partnerships, including a digital economy agreement (DEA) between Singapore and Viet Nam and an EU–Singapore Digital Partnership. Various countries also plan to upgrade their bilateral FTAs and/or work toward a DEA. For example, the United Kingdom is planning to conduct further negotiations with Switzerland to update its continuity trade agreement, to include provisions relating to services and digital trade. The country has also signaled its intention to work toward a DEA with Ukraine.
Source: Compiled by the author from publicly available sources.

## 5.1. Toward International Tax Rules for the Digital Economy

A favorable tax environment can attract foreign investment, signaling an investor-friendly regulatory regime. However, the issue of tax rules is more than just a simple conflict between states seeking to increase revenues and investors searching for lower tax burdens. Rather, it forms part of a broader, strategic intertemporal tax distribution challenge for states. States not only aim to expand their immediate revenue sources through taxation, but also strategically design tax policies to maximize long-term economic benefits. By creating an attractive tax environment, they encourage foreign investment, which can lead to positive externalities such as job creation, technological innovation, and overall economic growth.

The rise of the digital economy complicates this further by disrupting traditional tax systems. Digital multinational enterprises (MNEs) can now operate without a physical presence, allowing them to shift profit-generating activities to low-tax jurisdictions, thus reducing their overall tax liabilities and affecting indirect taxes, like value-added tax (VAT) (Avendano and Rosenkranz 2021; Juswanto and Abiyunus 2023). Although the digital transition presents challenges, it provides states with the opportunity to reform and digitalize their tax systems, capitalizing on the expanding digital economy as a new source of tax revenue. In addressing these changes, digitalization poses three significant challenges to the international tax system. First, digital MNEs can allocate profits to low-tax jurisdictions, minimizing their overall tax burden and threatening the fiscal stability of higher-tax countries. Second, the digital economy complicates the collection of indirect taxes such as VAT, as businesses can operate without physical presence in a country. Lastly, the growth of the digital economy prompts a reconsideration of international tax frameworks, raising questions about how these new business models should be taxed fairly across jurisdictions.

Thus, the interaction between international tax and international investment regimes must be analyzed not only for immediate conflicts, but also for their long-term strategic consequences on global economies.

### *Policy and Legal Interactions Between International Tax and Investment Regimes*

The nature of the taxation regime in a state is inarguably one of the most crucial regulatory factors that any multinational corporation considers when deciding where it wishes to invest (Burgstaller and Zarowna 2018; Vasudev

2020). Countries that provide a more favorable tax climate for investors are more likely to attract more foreign investment (Chaisse 2016).[59] This is because such a regulatory regime is friendly to potential investors and gains their confidence more easily. However, a favorable tax climate alone may not be sufficient to attract investment. Other key elements, such as the predictability of the business environment, transparency in regulatory practices, and overall legal stability, must also be present.

These factors collectively contribute to an investor's confidence in the long-term viability of their investments, ensuring that the fiscal environment is not only attractive, but also reliable and clear.

In doing so, they are undeniably more prone to using fiscal tools, such as taxation, to achieve their objective. The opposite interests for a state's taxation system induce a conflict between states and investors.

Developed and developing states often impose a suite of measures to increase their taxation revenue from large firms and relocate these resources to small and medium-sized enterprises (SMEs) in the same sector. For example, France introduced the Taskforce on taxation of the digital economy, which explicitly aimed to collect taxation from big tech firms and create a favorable tax climate for new firms (Collin and Colin 2013).[60] Industrial SMEs can deduct up to 40% of the cost price of goods and software that contribute to their digital transformation from their taxable income.[61] Kenya also adopted a similar policy structure. Kenya introduced a 1.5% tax on digital services in 2019 and published its digital economy blueprint in the same year (Mpofu and Moloi 2022). In the blueprint, Kenya explicitly promised to offer tax and other incentives (including subsidies and waivers) to innovation-oriented firms including those involved in the production of digital products (Kenya Ministry of ICT 2024). Multiple critiques indicate that the Kenyan digital service tax would result in a drop in investment (Latif 2021; US State Department 2022). However, the Central Bank of Kenya published a survey of foreign investors in which 94.4% of the respondents indicated they would invest in digital technology (Central Bank of Kenya 2021). Therefore, it is important to avoid the oversimplification and mischaracterization of the relationship between a state's taxation system and investors' business strategies.

[59] The consensus within economic literature has also been that the elasticity of foreign direct investment (FDI) toward the tax rate is negative—i.e., a rise in the tax rate would lead to a decrease in FDI. See, for example, De Mooij and Ederveen (2003) and Egger, Merlo, and Wamser (2014).

[60] Hereinafter""Taskforce on Taxation of the Digital Economy."

[61] Government of France (2020).

Academics such as Walde and Kolo (2007) have argued that the potential for unfavorable changes in the host country's fiscal regulatory environment has replaced the political risk of confiscation or nationalization of assets as the greatest threat to the interests of foreign investors. Therefore, several investment treaty disputes on taxation measures have occurred because the host state's fiscal regulatory framework was insensitive to the business interests of foreign investors.[62] That foreign investors have the option of using International Investment Agreements (IIAs) to have an impartial international tribunal adjudicate their tax-related complaints, rather than going through local courts and tax authorities who might be more favorable to the host's interests, has led to an increase in the number of tax-related investment claims (Chaisse 2015; Vasudev 2018, footnote 15).

### *Implications of the Adoption of International Tax Rules for the Digital Economy*

Significant changes from the recent, quick, and widespread digital transition have had profound effects on the economy and society.[63] The shift has exposed gaps in traditional tax frameworks, particularly concerning profit allocation and the avoidance of direct taxation, such as corporate income tax. MNEs can attribute minimal value to data generated in market jurisdictions and allocate profit-generating activities to low-tax regions (Estevão 2024; Hodžić 2022). The digital economy allows businesses to operate without a physical presence (Ismail 2020; Ndulu, Joseph, and Tryphone 2021), while the tax obligation of MNEs situates at the production site—as opposed to where the consumers are (Mpofu 2022). Digital MNEs often avoid income tax by operating without a taxable presence and shifting profit-generating activities to low-tax jurisdictions, while assigning minimal value to data from market countries (Li 2015).

Digital MNEs also disrupt indirect taxations, such as VAT, through their virtual operation and aggressive taxation structuring. Take the European system of VAT as an example. A European VAT system was developed in the 1950s (Kollmann 2019). The European Commission first defined e-commerce

[62] See, for example, Cairn v. India and Vodafone v. India (I) and (II) (a retrospective modification of income tax legislation and application of capital gains tax), The PV Investors v. Spain, Charanne and Construction Investments v. Spain (a change in the feed-in tariff program to incentivize investors to invest in the host country's renewable energy sector), and Greentech and NovEnergia v. Italy (an elimination of the adoption of a windfall profits tax, an elimination of incentive tariffs and a change of the existing taxation regime and minimum guaranteed prices). See Ranjan (2022) and Tandon (2022).

[63] Organisation for Economic Co-operation and Development. Action 1 Tax Challenges Arising from Digitalization (Action 1—OECD BEPS). https://www.oecd.org/tax/beps/beps-actions/action1/ (accessed 15 September 2024). (hereinafter "OECD Action 1").

in 1997 and clearly identified the application of VAT as an e-commerce issue (Trenta 2019). In 2013, the Commission established the High Level Expert Group on Digital Economy Taxation and introduced VAT, which had previously disadvantaged European suppliers compared to US digital service providers exempt from VAT (de Mello and Ter-Minassian, 2024).

The digital economy offers states a new source of tax revenue and the opportunity to digitize their taxation systems, improving tax tracking, collection, and reducing administrative costs (de Mello and Ter-Minassian (2020). The question of whether foreign income tax regulations, created in a "brick-and-mortar" economy more than a century ago, are still useful today is at the heart of the discussion. However, three significant phenomena have been made possible by digitalization in recent years—scale without mass,[64] reliance on intangible assets, and the centrality of data[65]—and pose substantial threats to the fundamentals of the international tax system (Walker 2020).

New intangible value drivers have transformed industries and reduced the need for proximity to customers, while new technologies have enabled MNEs to shift profits to low-tax countries, avoiding taxes. This is the core of the base erosion and profit shifting (BEPS) initiative, which continues to be a high priority for the members of the OECD/G20 Inclusive Framework (Adshead 2024). To ensure that multinational corporations pay a fair share of tax wherever they operate, more than 140 nations and jurisdictions have endorsed the Two-Pillar Solution (OECD 2022a).

In relation to the major MNEs, particularly digital enterprises, Pillar One will enable a more equitable division of profits and taxing rights across nations.[66] Regardless of whether firms have a physical presence, Pillar One would transfer some taxing authority over MNEs from their home nations to the regions where they conduct business operations and generate revenues. Pillar One calls for the annual reallocation of taxing authority over more than $125 billion in earnings to market jurisdictions (footnote 35).

---

[64] Scale without mass refers to the phenomenon where corporations can grow in "scale," i.e., to have businesses, without having its "mass" increased— i.e., without being physically present in the particular country. See Ramírez Ocampo (2019).

[65] Reliance on intangible assets refers to the growing importance of intellectual property, computer software and licensing, brand equity and other intangible assets. Centrality of data refers to the growing prominence of data and its usage. See (Adshead 2024).

[66] OECD Action 1 (footnote 28).

Pillar Two introduces a global minimum corporation tax rate that nations might use to safeguard their tax bases in an effort to put a floor under competition over corporate income tax (footnote 35). It is predicted that the worldwide minimum corporate income tax under Pillar Two, with a rate of 15% (OECD 2022b), will increase global tax receipts by about $150 billion every year (TUAC 2021). Stabilization of the international tax system and the improved tax certainty for taxpayers and tax administrations will also have other advantages. The Pillar Two Model Rules, also known as the Global Anti-Base Erosion (GloBE) Model Rules, were published/released on 20 December 2021 and outline the rules' definitions and operative sections (Chaisse and Mosquera 2022; OECD 2022b).[67] These regulations were supposed to be put into domestic law starting in 2022 as a part of a single strategy.

Multilateral initiatives, such as the OECD Inclusive Framework, can support developing countries in enhancing their capabilities to ensure that new regulations are applied properly and efficiently (footnote 35). In collaboration with regional organizations and development banks, this effort will be reinforced through substantial technical support programs (footnote 40). To assist developing countries in implementing the Two-Pillar Solutions, OECD has already started this in 2022 through regional consultations (OECD 2022c) and by developing training seminars and virtual resources (OECD 2022d). The OECD is also preparing detailed assistance on how developing countries should analyze the impact of the global minimum tax on their domestic tax incentives and the implementation of the international standard for VAT on e-commerce.[68]

## 5.2. Cross-Border Data Flows and Taxation of Digital Products in Asia and the Pacific

Data has become a valuable resource for businesses and societies with the rise of big data, cloud computing, and information technology. It is used for commercial purposes and to defend human rights, create social consensus, and uphold national security. However, there is no comprehensive international framework for regulating cross-border data flows. Many countries have their own data protection laws, leading to legal uncertainty and conflicts between different legal systems. Trade agreements play a dominant role in the governance of cross-border data flows, but

[67] OECD Pillar Two (footnote 47).

[68] OECD Action 1 (footnote 28).

the World Trade Organization (WTO) has not adequately adapted to the growth of digital trade. Countries have resorted to unilateral regulations, bilateral trade agreements, or regional trade agreements to regulate cross-border data flows. The digital economy has also made it challenging for governments to tax business income generated from foreign activities.

The growth of electronic commerce has led to the rise of intangible assets, making it harder to regulate and enforce taxation regimes. The growing presence of cross-border data flows pushes further the need for developing frameworks to regulate the same (Figure 5.1). Questions as to the universality and harmonization of such frameworks naturally arise. Moreover, such flows demand an effective response to the needs of the digital economy. However, digitalization has undoubtedly weakened the traditional tax structure and now requires us to envision newer solutions (Strauss, Schutte, and Fawcett 2020). With this in mind, this section first broadly discusses the open-ended question of cross-border data flows, and then addresses the more specific issue of taxation of digital products in Asia and the Pacific.

**Figure 5.1: Expansion of Global Internet Traffic in the Past 3 Decades**

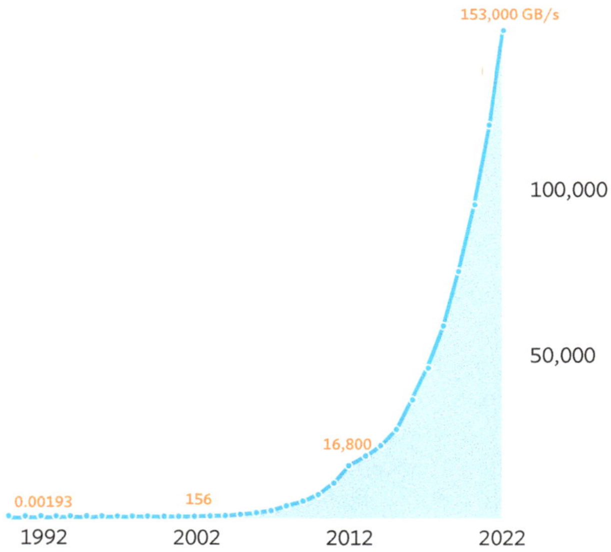


Source: World Bank. "Crossing Border" (*World Bank | World Development Report 2021*) https://wdr2021.worldbank.org/stories/crossing-borders (accessed 15 September 2024).

### *The Issue of Cross-Border Data Flows*

In the context of cross-border data flows, data have evolved into vital strategic assets for both businesses and society, particularly with the advent of big data, cloud computing, and other advanced information technologies (Figure 5.2).[69] Businesses leverage data as a critical resource for gaining a competitive edge in the global market, while data are also essential for advancing both individual and societal values (Chaisse 2023a; UNCTAD 2021).

**Figure 5.2: Growth of Global Trade in Data-Driven Services**

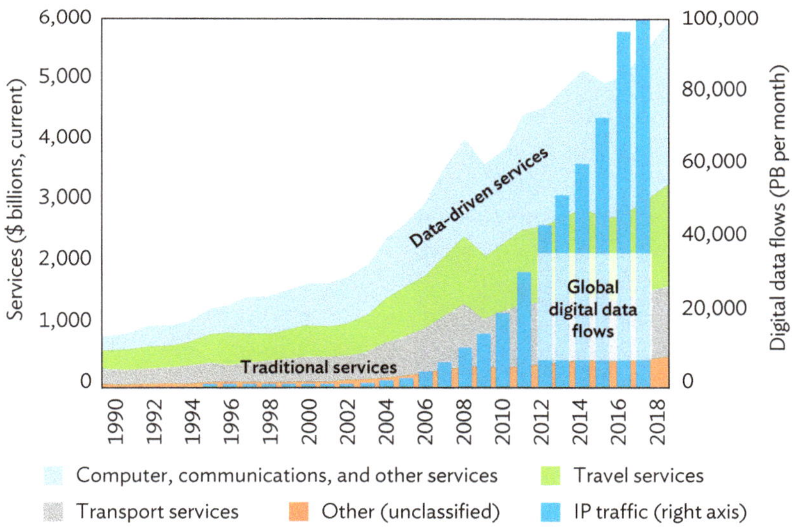


IP = internet protocol.
Source: World Bank, "Overview" in *World Development Report 2021: Data for Better Lives* (World Bank 2021).

Beyond commercial importance, data are pivotal for safeguarding human rights and privacy, fostering social consensus in decision making, and supporting critical national security objectives (Chin and Zhao 2022). Given the multifaceted significance of data, various countries have adopted distinct regulatory and policy approaches to data collection, storage, and transmission.

[69] The growth of global trade in data-driven services has been significant in recent years, driven by increasing adoption of technology and the widespread availability of high-speed internet. Figure 5.2 shows this growth is expected to continue as businesses and individuals increasingly rely on data-driven services such as cloud computing, artificial intelligence, and the Internet of Things. The growth of e-commerce and online marketplaces has also contributed. In addition, the development of 5G networks is expected to further drive growth in this sector by enabling faster and more efficient data transmission.

The lack of a comprehensive international framework addressing the fragmented rules governing cross-border data flows presents significant challenges (Chaisse 2023a; Chin and Zhao 2022). Governments are increasingly engaging in regional and international dialogues on digital trade to regulate these flows in a manner that maximizes the economic potential of big data. For example, most African countries have implemented their own data protection laws, contributing to this fragmentation (Hennemann, Lienemann, and Spirkl 2022). This divergence in regulations can lead to legal uncertainty and conflicts between different legal systems, as each country maintains its own data protection standards—some more stringent than others. Nations with higher standards may pressure those with weaker regulations to elevate their protections. Consequently, there is a pressing need to harmonize regional data protection laws and to develop a cohesive international framework (Salami 2022).

The governance of cross-border data flows made possible through trade agreements has emerged as the dominant trend when one reviews the major trade agreements that have been signed in recent years. Undoubtedly, cross-border data flows are one of the main concerns of such international digital trade agreements in the context of the digital economy, regardless of whether they are the Regional Comprehensive Economic Partnership (RCEP), the United States–Mexico–Canada Agreement (USMCA), or the Comprehensive and Progressive Agreement for Trans-Pacific Partnership (CPTPP). The governance of cross-border data flows is undoubtedly one of the negotiation priorities for recent trade agreements. Its prominence is not surprising when considering the massive developmental potential of the free flow of data (Drake-Brockman et al. 2021). The massive potential of cross-border data transfer is not without controversies.

Nearly all trade-related matters are under the purview of the WTO treaty system, which has been institutionalized, and related trade disputes may be brought before WTO panels and the Appellate Body for the purposes of resolution and enforcement. The WTO rule system differs from conventional international law and is, to some extent, “hard law” in its nature. In addition, the WTO serves as a forum for global trade negotiations, which ought to make it the best place to settle disputes involving cross-border data flows and digital trade. In fact, the WTO established a working group on electronic commerce in 1998 after realizing the significance of the development of digital technology. This group’s mandate included trade in services, trade in goods, trade-related intellectual property rights, and trade and development issues (Chin and Zhao 2022; WTO 1998). Its goal was to encourage responsive changes in trade regulations. The 2 decades of work that went into this, however, did not provide the desired outcomes. More importantly, the WTO has not adequately adapted to the expansion of digital trade since it has not been able to handle many of the controversial problems that stymie digital trade negotiations because of the inherent and unavoidable cultural and policy differences between nations.

The fragmented legal framework for cross-border data flows is partially remedied by countries through unilateral regulations, bilateral trade agreements, or regional trade agreements, when the multilateral WTO mechanism governing cross-border data flows is unable to respond to the real needs of digital trade or the digital economy in a timely and effective manner. These mechanisms provide some divergent solutions to the protection of personal information, the promotion of free trade, and the maintenance of national security. In greater detail, international cross-border data flows digital trade agreements can be roughly categorized into three groups: the People's Republic of China's "balancing security, personal data protection, and free flows of data model"; the EU's "balancing human rights and digital trade model"; and the United States' "trade-first free flow model" (Chin and Zhao 2022, pp. 3–4). The key feature of the first two models is that trade agreements are designed to strike a balance between the free flow of data and mentioned values. In contrast, the last model prioritizes trade interest over other values by guaranteeing the free flow of data.

### *Changing Taxation and Issues of Digital Products in Asia and the Pacific*

The digital economy has paralyzed the ability of governments to tax the business income generated from foreign activities in their jurisdictions. Digitalization has challenged the existing traditional structure, which assumes the physical presence of businesses in any given jurisdiction that gave the taxation authorities a tangible basis to secure tax compliance. The rise of electronic commerce now allows businesses to sell products to customers across the world without fulfilling the previous necessity of having a local physical establishment. Consequently, the revenue generated by these businesses may not fall within the scope of the financial system of a particular jurisdiction where their products are digitally sold (Figure 5.3). This eliminates the traditional connection that usually facilitates the regulation and supervision of transactions and the enforcement of taxation regimes (Chin and Zhao 2022, pp. 3–4).

**Figure 5.3: Tax Revenue as a Percentage of Gross Domestic Product**

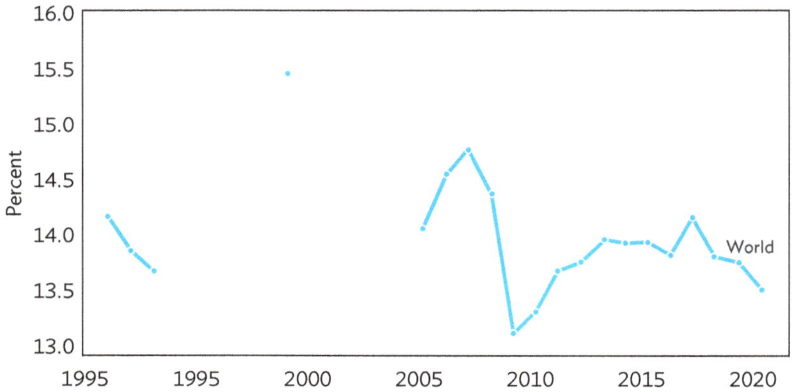


Source: World Bank. "Tax Revenue (% of GDP)" (*World Bank|Data*) https://data.worldbank.org/indicator/GC.TAX.TOTL.GD.ZS?view=chart (accessed 15 September 2024).

The rising importance of intangible assets is a by-product of the growth of electronic commerce. Intangible assets are "*identifiable non-monetary assets without physical substance. They can be acquired through development, purchase, or legal rights and include things like intellectual property, software, and brand value.*"[70] Such intangible input has allowed businesses to use accounting techniques in a way that manages their tax liabilities in a manner that is against the interests of the local tax collecting authorities (Shanda 1992).

These challenges are having an impact across the world, and economies in Asia and the Pacific are no exception. What is unique in this region is that developing countries therein still lack effective tax options for tapping into the digital economy revenue base, despite the existence of growing fiscal pressure that could support a strong economic recovery in the short-term and the effective achievement of the UN's Sustainable Development Goals in the long term.[71]

[70] IAS 38 Intangible assets, IFRS. https://www.ifrs.org/issued-standards/list-of-standards/ias-38-intangible-assets/.

[71] United Nations Economic and Social Commission for Asia and the Pacific (UNESCAP) Taxation (footnote 60).

## 5.3. Global Multilateral Instrument Rules and Digital Taxation in Asia and the Pacific

The many challenges in tax systems of various nations essentially result from globalization and the consequences of discrepancies in tax systems on international trade and investment. Double-tax treaties were created to prevent double taxation, but these can also result in untaxed income and open the door to legal repercussions. The Global Rules set out in the Multilateral Instrument (MLI) for Bilateral Tax Treaties play an important role in addressing base erosion and profit shifting (BEPS) by multinational enterprises. The MLI is a treaty that amends existing bilateral tax treaties between participating countries to include measures to prevent tax avoidance. In the context of digital taxation, the MLI provides a framework for implementing the provisions of the BEPS Action Plan relating to the taxation of the digital economy. This includes provisions on the modification of the permanent establishment definition, the taxation of cross-border digital services, and the allocation of taxing rights between countries.

The MLI and its Global Rules have three different implications for digital taxation in the economies of Asia and the Pacific. First, the MLI provides a way for countries to work together to prevent MNEs from exploiting the gaps and mismatches in the international tax system. Second, the MLI provides a framework for implementing measures to tax the digital economy, which is becoming increasingly important as more businesses shift to digital models. Third, the MLI allows countries to adopt a consistent approach to addressing the taxation of digital services, reducing the risk of double taxation and helping to prevent disputes between countries.

This chapter first outlines the role that global rules play in the MLI for bilateral tax treaties, then discusses the specific implications that digital taxation can have for the economies in Asia and the Pacific. This discussion is all the more important in light of the developing circumstances that have been outlined so far.

### *From Bilateral Tax Treaties to Base Erosion and Profit Shifting*

The economic impact of discrepancies in tax systems has intensified with globalization (Shukla and Shukla 2013). International trade and investment have been double-taxed because of the discrepancies between national tax systems, even if unilateral tax relief was in place (Friedlander and Wilkie

2006). Double-tax treaties were created to address this issue (Blonigen and Davies 2009; Neumayer 2007), delimiting tax rights between states and offering predictable frameworks for taxation or exemptions (Holmes 2007). However, these treaties may lead to untaxed income and facilitate treaty shopping, a risk for both developed and developing countries (De Broe and Luts 2015; Elliffe 2016).

A key focus of the OECD's BEPS project is the right to treaty benefits (EY Global 2020). The project aims to reduce double taxation risks by incorporating more subjectivity into profit attribution (the "arm's length standard"), making cross-border profit shifting less viable. Improved dispute resolution is crucial to lowering double taxation risks. Modifying the global network of bilateral tax treaties to reflect these changes is made complex by the number of treaties. Even widespread support for modifications to the OECD Model Tax Convention takes significant time and resources to implement across many bilateral agreements.

To streamline this, the OECD proposed a Multilateral Instrument (MLI) in its 2015 BEPS Action Plan (EY Global 2020). The MLI, signed by 102 jurisdictions in 2024, allows for simultaneous renegotiation of tax treaties to prevent base erosion and profit shifting. Key BEPS Actions, including Action 6 (preventing treaty shopping) and Action 14 (enhancing dispute resolution), set minimum standards for addressing these issues (EY Global 2020).[72] Members also will include an express statement on non-taxation and one of three methods tackling treaty shopping in their tax agreements (OECD 2015b). Action 14 represents a commitment for members to implement a minimum standard on dispute resolution to ensure that treaty-related disputes are resolved in a timely, effective, and efficient manner. Members also agree to go through a peer-review process to evaluate the implementation of this standard (OECD 2015c). The MLI was designed with flexibility to accommodate various jurisdictions, allowing minimum requirements to be met in multiple ways, reflecting the diverse perspectives involved in the discussions.

The MLI also gives flexibility to clauses that do not adhere to the basic requirements by

- Providing the jurisdictions with the option to designate which tax treaties the MLI applies to.

[72] Organisation for Economic Co-operation and Development. Action 14 Mutual Agreement Procedure. Action 14— OECD BEPS. https://www.oecd.org/tax/beps/beps-actions/action14/ (accessed 15 September 2024).

- Adding flexibility to the clauses relating to a minimum standard so that nations can select the choice that best suits them.
- Including the choice to accept or reject provisions if they do not adhere to a minimal standard.
- Including the option for a nation to reject any existing clauses in treaties that have characteristics that are clearly and precisely specified.
- Offering the possibility to apply optional or substitute clauses, such as the optional clause on mandatory and binding arbitration (EY Global 2020).

With the execution of the BEPS basic standards relating to the treaty, another significant milestone was reached. The signatories provided a list of the current tax treaties they wished to identify as covered tax agreements (CTAs), which are agreements that can be changed through the MLI (EY Global 2020). After matching the precise terms that jurisdictions seek to add to or amend within the CTAs specified by the signatories, it was anticipated that over 1,100 tax treaties would be updated (Frelich 2018). Signatories submitted preliminary reservations and notifications (MLI stances) with their list of CTAs. Each jurisdiction's final MLI positions were made available after ratification or approval.

The MLI became effective on 22 March 2018. That this happened just a year after the signing ceremony highlighted the strong political support for a multilateral approach to addressing BEPS. The MLI already covered 102 jurisdictions as of 17 January 2024, and more were expected to join after (OECD 2022e). Ratification of the current signatories is moving along, with 79 jurisdictions having deposited their instruments of ratification.[73]

The "MLI Matching Database," a tool created by the OECD as a depositary of the MLI, can be used to simply examine how the provisions of the MLI affect a particular bilateral tax agreement.[74] It enhances transparency, aids in decision-making, and helps reduce double taxation. However, its effectiveness is limited by the accuracy of the entered data and the timeliness of updates, necessitating supplementary research for comprehensive analysis.

[73] For examples, see OECD (2022f).

[74] The "MLI Matching Database" refers to the database created to match provisions in the Multilateral Instrument (MLI) to specific provisions in existing bilateral tax treaties between the signatory countries available at https://www.oecd.org/tax/treaties/mli-matching-database.htm. The MLI Matching Database serves as a tool to assist tax administrators in determining which provisions of the MLI apply to specific bilateral tax treaties, and to keep track of the status of each treaty covered by the MLI.

Finally, the MLI also includes provisions related to hybrid mismatch arrangements, treaty misuse, and permanent establishment.[75] These tackle tax avoidance by targeting mismatches in tax laws between countries. The hybrid mismatch rules prevent entities from exploiting differences to reduce tax liability, while treaty misuse rules stop taxpayers from misusing them for tax reductions. The permanent establishment provisions ensure businesses cannot use treaties to avoid taxation. BEPS Action 6 sets a minimum standard to prevent treaty abuse by stopping profit shifting to low or no-tax jurisdictions. Its implementation, which includes anti-abuse rules and limiting benefits, is expected to have the greatest impact on international tax treaties.

## *The Way Forward*

The evolving role of global rules within the Multilateral Instrument (MLI) for Bilateral Tax Treaties, particularly concerning digital taxation in the economies of Asia and the Pacific, is a key focus as the international community seeks to modernize tax systems in response to the digitalization of the economy. One such initiative is the BEPS project, which aims to tackle tax avoidance by multinational corporations. The implementation of the MLI, which allows countries to modify their bilateral tax treaties in a consistent manner, can also play a role in addressing digital taxation in Asia and the Pacific. However, more comprehensive solutions and regulatory changes may be needed to fully address the implications of digital taxation in this region.

Members of the OECD/G20 inclusive framework are required to incorporate the following in their tax treaties to comply with Action 6's minimal standard:

- A revised preamble stating that the parties' shared goal is to end double taxation while preventing opportunities for tax avoidance or evasion, including the use of treaty shopping arrangements, to avoid paying taxes at all.
- A clause in a contract against abuse. The principal purposes test (PPT), the PPT and a simple limitation on benefits (LOB) provision, or a detailed LOB and anti-conduit rules, are all examples of anti-abuse provisions.

[75] The MLI improves provisions for resolving treaty disagreements, such as the adoption of mandatory binding arbitration by 31 signatories.

All CTAs from the lodged MLI positions will, at the very least, contain the new preamble wording and the PPT requirements, bringing the 4,735 agreements up to Action 6's minimum level.[76] To update the remaining agreements, jurisdictions are renegotiating treaties on a bilateral basis. As a result, when the bilateral agreements and the MLI enter into force and effect in respect of all signatories, the majority of the bilateral tax treaties in force and listed by the MLI signatories in their country positions will have been updated to implement the Action 6 minimum standard.

Bilateral tax treaties have already seen their initial changes. More treaty amendments are projected to take effect in the upcoming months, given the estimated time required for ratification. An unprecedented change in international taxes is anticipated as a result of 89 governments signing the MLI, which is expected to result in the modification of more than 4, 735 tax treaties. The PPT effectively replaces the existing global standard that bases treaty entitlements primarily on legal relationships between countries by limiting treaty benefits by reference to commercial nexus, except for those countries (most importantly, the United States) that have already incorporated limitations on benefits clauses in their tax treaties. Even while a PPT differs from a comprehensive LOB, it frequently has the same effect of limiting treaty advantages in comparable situations. The effects of these changes on multinational corporations' business structures, particularly with regard to dividends, interest, royalties, and capital gains, will need to be properly monitored.

Comprehensive solutions and regulatory changes are needed to fully address the implications of digital taxation in Asia and the Pacific. These can take the form of proposals aimed at achieving consistency, fairness, and efficiency in the tax treatment of digital firms. The proposals are divided into short-term and long-term objectives. One such proposal is the introduction of a unified digital tax framework across the region to ensure consistent and fair tax treatment of digital firms. Another is the implementation of a destination-based tax system for digital services, aligning the tax liability with the place of consumption. To enhance transparency and cooperation, a cross-border information sharing mechanism among tax authorities could be established. In addition, the development and promotion of technology-based solutions, such as blockchain, could improve the accuracy and efficiency of tax administration.

[76] Tax Notes, "MLI Covered Tax Agreements Tracker" (MLI Covered Tax Agreement Tracker, OECD MLI Tracker—Tax Notes). https://www.taxnotes.com/worldwide-tax-treaties/mli-covered-tax-agreements-tracker (accessed 15 September 2024).

investment in digital infrastructure and research and development in digital technologies. Moreover, international tax cooperation and coordination could be strengthened through forums such as the OECD and the Asia-Pacific Economic Cooperation (APEC). To deal with cross-border tax disputes in a timely and effective manner, a digital tax dispute resolution mechanism could be created. The region could also engage in dialogue with the global community to deal with the challenges posed by digitalization and the implications for tax policy. Finally, capacity building programs for tax authorities in Asia and the Pacific could be developed to improve their technical expertise and regulatory enforcement capabilities.

## 5.4. Trade Policy Role for Implementing Digital Tax Rules, Improving Coordination

Several agreements have been concluded to facilitate cooperation in the area of regional trade and investment. These include the RCEP among nations in Asia and the Pacific, the CPTPP among the Trans-Pacific nations and the Digital Economy Partnership Agreement (DEPA) between Chile, New Zealand, and Singapore. The CPTPP and RCEP agreements are considered important for Asia and the Pacific for several legal and economic reasons. First, both agreements aim to promote regional trade and investment by reducing barriers to trade, such as tariffs and nontariff measures. This liberalization of trade and investment is expected to enhance economic growth and competitiveness in the region. Second, both include provisions on intellectual property protection, which is critical for the growth of innovation and technological development in the region. They also promote cross-border data flows, which are crucial for the growth of the digital economy in the region. Third, the agreements contain provisions on labor and environmental standards, which can help to promote sustainable and inclusive economic growth in the region. These provisions aim to ensure that economic integration is not achieved at the cost of workers or the environment. Fourth, the agreements aim to enhance regional cooperation and integration through the creation of institutions and forums for dialogue and cooperation. This is expected to enhance the stability and predictability of the business environment in the region and to encourage further economic integration and growth.

This section first provides insights into perhaps the two most significant of these agreements—the RCEP and CPTPP. It then explores the role that these agreements play when it comes to implementing digital tax rules and promoting coordination among different tax administrations.

### *Asia and the Pacific's Mega Trade Deals: RCEP and CPTPP*

The Regional Comprehensive Economic Partnership (RCEP) and the Comprehensive and Progressive Agreement for Trans-Pacific Partnership (CPTPP) are both pivotal trade agreements for Asia and the Pacific, each offering unique benefits and addressing different aspects of economic integration.

The RCEP, often seen as a milestone of ASEAN's diplomatic efforts, brings together 15 nations, including major economies like the People's Republic of China (PRC) and Japan, as well as Australia and New Zealand. As the largest free trade agreement (FTA) in history, RECEP covers about 30% of the world's population and output. The partnership is expected to significantly boost global trade and income by fostering regional supply chains and increasing market access, particularly enhancing Southeast Asia's connectivity with the PRC's Belt and Road Initiative. However, RCEP is less comprehensive than CPTPP, as it does not include stringent provisions on labor, the environment, or state-owned enterprises, and focuses primarily on economic integration while accommodating political sensitivities.

On the other hand, the CPTPP, finalized in 2018, represents a high-standard trade agreement that includes 11 countries, many of which overlap with RCEP, such as Japan, Australia, and several ASEAN members. The CPTPP goes beyond traditional trade deals by incorporating robust rules on labor rights, environmental protections, and intellectual property, setting a high benchmark for trade agreements. While RCEP is broader in scope, CPTPP is seen as a model for future trade agreements due to its comprehensive standards. Together, these agreements are expected to enhance regional economic integration, partially mitigating global trade tensions, particularly between the US and the PRC, while strengthening economic resilience in Asia and the Pacific.

### *Improving Coordination of Tax Administrations on Digital Tax Rules*

Arguably, the role that RCEP, CPTPP, and the DEPA will play in implementing digital tax rules and improving the coordination of tax administrations can be significant, even though indirect.

The gradual elimination of tariffs on goods will stimulate cross-border activities and attract firms to invest and enter into business with the member states of these FTAs. However, this increase in activities will further the administrative burden on tax administrations, particularly because of the complications arising from the principle of taxing profits, which is based on the destination to which the profits are generated (Hebous, Vernon, and Prihardini 2022). For example, as more firms seek to do business in RCEP member states, domestic tax administrations will have to distinguish the place-of-origin of corporate profits before they can be taxed accordingly. It should also be noted that an increasing number of firms operating their businesses in multiple countries presents challenges to "Function, Assess and Risk" analysis in the context of transfer pricing, with implications when the results of such an analysis are used to perform a comparability analysis[77] to determine whether the BEPS' "arm's length standard" has been complied with.

Correspondingly, as discussed earlier in the section on the interactions between international tax and Investment regimes, decisions relating to investment and entry into business into a foreign country will, among other factors, depend on the nature of the particular state's taxation regime. The difference in the taxation regime among member states of RCEP and CPTPP, whether it be the tax rate, tax base, or transfer pricing rules, means that those with higher taxes will be unable to fully take advantage of these FTAs. Another form of inequality can also be seen for certain taxes, such as withholding taxes, where many countries apply the tax differently to domestic and foreign investors. Such an application is permissible under Article 10.3 of RCEP, so long as it is justifiable and not discriminatory.[78]

RCEP and CPTPP contain provisions that address tax: chapters 2, 3, 4, 7, 8, and 17 for the former agreement and chapters 2, 3, 5, 14, 15, 26, and 29 and Annex 2-C in CPTPP. However, customs duties are exempted from the relevant tax rules[79] and in both FTAs, international tax treaties would

[77] Transfer pricing is the price determined when two or more associated firms (for example, one is the parent company and the other is its subsidiary) conduct transactions with each other. In the context of transfer pricing, a Function, Assets, and Risk (FAR) analysis entails identification and assessment of: (i) the functions that associated parties to a transaction perform; (ii) the assets used to conclude the transaction; and (iii) the risks that are assumed. This analysis gives an overview of the role that each party plays in the transaction, and forms the first step toward calculating the arm's length price and whether the arm's length standard had been complied with (see footnote 59 for an explanation of the arm's length price/standard). In this regard, the results of a FAR analysis on the controlled transaction will be used in the performance of a comparability analysis. As such, having an accurate FAR analytical result will be important to ensure that the results of the comparability analysis are as accurate as possible. A comparability analysis seeks to assess the comparability between a controlled transaction (which is concluded by parties associated with each other) and an uncontrolled transaction (which is concluded by parties independent of each other). This analysis is conducted to determine which transfer pricing method is used to calculate the arm's length price.

[78] RCEP (footnote 104) art 17.12(2).

[79] RCEP (footnote 104) art 17.14(1); CPTPP (footnote 106) art 29.4(1).

also take precedence over the RCEP where there are inconsistencies.[80] However, RCEP also goes beyond that since member states are not required to "extend benefits provided in tax treaties" under the Most-Favored Nation principle, and domestic tax does not fall within the scope of the rules, as stipulated in RCEP. Such "carve-outs" thus indicate that RCEP and CPTPP tax provisions are not apt to overcome problems that inevitably will arise once the agreement is implemented.

One may, therefore, suggest that perhaps international tax treaties could be used to overcome the RCEP and CPTPP tax-related challenges. The various bilateral and multilateral tax agreements in existence are severely outdated (Moller 2016) and relying on them to resolve tax challenges stemming from RCEP and CPTPP would require that they be updated before doing so. In light of the increased taxation challenges that stem from these agreements, coordination between tax administrations is an important solution. For example, from a practical point of view, given challenges that tax administrations will encounter as a result of a rise in cross-border activities, coordination between tax administrations, whether by sharing information or creating a more efficient way of collecting tax, will help ease the administration's burden.

In the context of the implementation of digital tax, the RCEP, while permitting countries to impose taxes so long as they are consistent with the agreement,[81] disallows parties from imposing customs duties on cross-border electronic transmissions.[82] In doing so, the FTA explicitly mentions that this negative obligation is in line with the WTO Ministerial Decision of 13 December 2017 (2017 WTO Ministerial Decision) in relation to the Work Programme on Electronic Commerce (which also prohibits member states from doing the same). If parties want to make any changes regarding this RCEP obligation, the changes will also have to be made relative to the work program's ministerial decisions in future.[83] This is significant: should the ban in the 2017 WTO Ministerial Decision not be renewed in further ministerial meetings, it could open the door for states to introduce a digital tax (Kelsey 2022). In contrast, the CPTPP only prohibits the imposition of customs duties on electronic transmissions;[84] any other forms of charges levied against electronically transmitted content would have to comply

[80] RCEP (footnote 104) Article 17.14(4); CPTPP (footnote 106) Article 29.4.

[81] RCEP (footnote 104) Article 12.11(5).

[82] RCEP (footnote 104) Article 12.11(1).

[83] RCEP (footnote 104) Article 12.11(3).

[84] CPTPP (footnote 106) Article 14.3(1).

with the rules as stated in the agreement.[85] Subsequently, in circumstances where RCEP and CPTPP members do introduce digital taxes through mutual coordination, tax administrations would be able to enforce digital tax rules while also reducing the tax losses that come from a lack of coordination.[86]

To sum up, the implementation of the FTAs will cause tax-related challenges stemming from the FTAs. Solving them will require a concerted effort from tax administrations. This will encourage tax administrations to coordinate with each other. In turn, in the area of digital tax, this will also facilitate effective collection and thus an efficient implementation of digital tax rules.

## 5.5. Best Tax Provision Practices for Digital Policy in Asia and the Pacific

It is important for ADB's developing member economies to receive policy recommendations regarding the policies on digital taxation as they face various challenges in data flows, cybersecurity, data protection and data privacy. The need for policy recommendations for taxation of digital policy in these realms stems from several considerations. First, with the rapid growth of the digital economy in developing member economies, there is a pressing requirement for a regulatory framework to manage digital activities, including for data flows, cybersecurity, data protection, and data privacy. Second, taxation of digital activities can offer a substantial revenue source for these countries, contributing to their economic development. Third, these policy recommendations can safeguard the privacy and security of citizens' personal data in digital activities. Fourth, the recommendations can foster fair competition in the digital economy, avoiding the concentration of power in the hands of a few large corporations. And finally, by aligning with international standards and best practices in digital taxation, these countries can become more appealing to international businesses and investors.

In sum, the digitalization of business and trade practices has resulted in increased demand for regulations and measures to safeguard sensitive information, secure critical infrastructure and provide privacy to individuals. In light of these developments, policy recommendations for digital taxation in developing member economies are essential to ensure their tax systems

[85] CPTPP (footnote 106) Article 14.3(2).

[86] The OECD estimates that around $100 billion to $240 billion of global corporate income tax revenue is lost to BEPS, with one of the factors being a lack of coordination between tax administrations. (See OECD 2015a).

are equipped to handle the evolving digital landscape and address the related issues effectively.

The final section of this chapter consists of four parts that focus on policy recommendations for developing member economies. Their aim is to provide a comprehensive examination of the best practices in tax provisions for digital policy, including data flows, cybersecurity, data protection, and data privacy. Insights and recommendations are intended to help develop effective and efficient regulations and policies to support digital economies while protecting the privacy and security of personal data.

### *Digital Service Taxes as Double-Edged Swords*

Digital Service Taxes (DSTs) are domestic taxes imposed on technology firms offering digital services, such as online retail, streaming, and social media, within a country. These taxes provide governments with a potential source of revenue for public programs and services, even if the firms do not have a physical presence in the country. This can help address the issue of firms engaging in tax avoidance to reduce their liabilities. However, DSTs can also have significant implications for the growing digital world, including the imposition of additional costs on technology firms and the potential barriers to trade. In addition, they do not address the pressing issues related to digital policy, such as data security and privacy protection. To address these concerns, best practices in tax provisions for digital policy, such as data flows, cybersecurity, data protection and data privacy, are important to achieve.

Following these best practices can lead to a more effective tax administration and increase public legitimacy for the introduction of DSTs. The importance of best practices in tax provisions for digital policy, including for data flows, cybersecurity, data protection, and data privacy, lies in the fact that they can provide a framework to ensure that digital businesses operate within guidelines that promote efficiency, security, and privacy. By developing and adopting some best practices, countries in Asia and the Pacific can reduce risks associated with digital transactions, protect the privacy and security of personal data, and promote the free flow of data and information, which is essential for the growth and development of the digital economy. These best practices also provide some certainty for digital businesses and consumers, thereby promoting greater confidence in the digital economy and reducing the potential for disputes. As such, it is important for countries to adopt these best practices in tax provisions for digital policy as a means of promoting the growth and stability of the digital economy and ensuring that digital transactions are conducted in a fair, secure, and efficient manner.

For governments, DSTs are a useful tool for raising significant revenues to fund public programs and services (Table 5.2).[87] Regardless of whether they have a physical presence in the economy, these technology firms are benefiting from and making potentially substantial profits by providing their services in the particular country. Governments would be eager to be able to levy taxes against these profits (Morris and Brown 2021). In addition, to reduce their tax liabilities, many firms will engage in BEPS. Consequently, despite making substantial revenue, these firms can pay very little income and corporate tax. As such, the implementation of DSTs will enable economies to capture the tax revenues that had been lost to tax avoidance strategies.

Despite the benefits that come with the implementation of DSTs (Table 5.2), in reality, their implementation also has huge implications for a growing digitalized world—and, therefore, for digital policy. DSTs have been accused of disrupting the status quo in several ways, which could have far-reaching consequences on digital policy. The implementation of DSTs can impose potentially substantial additional operating costs on technology firms, considering how significant their revenues are (Bulusu and Ali 2020). This might act as a barrier to trade (Bunn 2020) and could result in firms ceasing to provide their digital service in the economies which are implementing DSTs. Contrastingly, digital service firms may also decide to pass the burden of the additional operating costs to their customers (Kundaliya 2020), which will have knock-on effects on access to information and the internet.[88] Alternatively, to reduce operating costs that increased as a result of DSTs, digital service firms could decide to cut costs in other areas, such as measures to safeguard data and enhance cybersecurity.

It should also be noted that the fiscal nature of DSTs also means they do not necessarily address the more-pressing issues relating to digital policy, including data security, data privacy, and data protection. Consequently, having best practices will be desirable. Also, the World Bank-conducted Enterprises Survey shows that tax administration to be one of the most

[87] Table 5.2 shows the diversity of approaches and attitudes to DST across the world, which can help to inform debates and discussions on its purpose, design, and impact. See also Chaisse (2023b).

[88] The role that accesses to information and the internet play has been recognized in the UN Human Rights Council Resolution on The Promotion, Protection and Enjoyment of Human Rights on the Internet. See UN Human Rights Council (2016).

significant hindrances to operating a business.[89] As such, following best practices in taxation will allow for a more effective tax administration practice. This could be an incentive for firms to do business in a specific country. Finally, best practices can help address public concerns about certain categories of taxation. This will be important given the novel nature of DSTs, and that a digital tax is not one that arose from the status quo and existing taxation model. Following best practices will aid in legitimizing the introduction of such a tax and facilitate its implementation.

**Table 5.2: Tax Revenue as a Percentage of Gross Domestic Product**

| Economy | Status on DST Implementation |
|---|---|
| Australia | Awaiting a worldwide solution as introduced by the OECD |
| Austria | Implemented |
| Belgium | Has proposed the implementation of DST |
| Brazil | Has proposed the implementation of DST |
| Cambodia | Implemented |
| Canada | Has proposed the implementation of DST |
| Chile | Decision as to whether to introduce DST is under consideration |
| People's Republic of China | Decision as to whether to introduce DST is under consideration |
| Costa Rica | Implemented |
| Czech Republic | Awaiting a worldwide solution as introduced by the OECD |
| Denmark | Awaiting a worldwide solution as introduced by the OECD |
| Egypt | Decision as to whether to introduce DST is under consideration |
| European Union | Decision as to whether to introduce DST is under consideration |
| Finland | Awaiting a worldwide solution as introduced by the OECD |
| France | Implemented |
| Germany | Awaiting a worldwide solution as introduced by the OECD |
| Greece | Implemented |
| Hungary | Implemented |
| India | Implemented |
| Indonesia | Implemented |
| Ireland | Awaiting a worldwide solution as introduced by the OECD |
| Israel | Implemented |
| Italy | Implemented |
| Japan | Decision as to whether to introduce DST is under consideration |
| Kenya | Implemented |

*Continued on next page*

[89] World Bank. Regulations and Taxes' (*Enterprises Surveys—What Businesses Experience*). https://www.enterprisesurveys.org/en/data/exploretopics/regulations-and-taxes (accessed 15 September 2024); World Bank. Why It Matters in Paying Taxes (*Subnational Studies—Measuring Business Regulations*) https://subnational.doingbusiness.org/en/data/exploretopics/paying-taxes/why-matters (accessed 15 September 2024).

**Table 5.2** *continued*

| Economy | Status on DST Implementation |
|---|---|
| Republic of Korea | Decision as to whether to introduce DST is under consideration |
| Latvia | Decision as to whether to introduce DST is under consideration |
| Malaysia | Implemented |
| Mexico | Awaiting a worldwide solution as introduced by the OECD |
| New Zealand | Decision as to whether to introduce DST is under consideration |
| Nigeria | Has proposed the implementation of DST |
| Norway | Decision as to whether to introduce DST is under consideration |
| Pakistan | Implemented |
| Paraguay | Implemented |
| Philippines | Has proposed the implementation of DST |
| Poland | Implemented |
| Romania | Decision as to whether to introduce DST is under consideration |
| Russian Federation | Decision as to whether to introduce DST is under consideration |
| Singapore | Awaiting a worldwide solution as introduced by the OECD |
| Slovakia | Implemented |
| Slovenia | Decision as to whether to introduce DST is under consideration |
| South Africa | Decision as to whether to introduce DST is under consideration |
| Spain | Implemented |
| Sweden | Awaiting a worldwide solution as introduced by the OECD |
| Switzerland | Awaiting a worldwide solution as introduced by the OECD |
| Taipei,China | Implemented |
| Thailand | Has proposed the implementation of DST |
| Tunisia | Implemented |
| Türkiye | Implemented |
| Ukraine | Implemented |
| United Kingdom | Implemented |
| United States | Opposed |
| United States - Louisiana | Has proposed the implementation of DST |
| United States - Maryland | Implemented |
| United States - Massachusetts | Has proposed the implementation of DST |
| United States - New York | Has proposed the implementation of DST |
| Uruguay | Implemented |
| Viet Nam | Implemented |
| Zimbabwe | Implemented |

DST = digital service tax.
Note: The United Nations and the Organisation for Economic Co-operation and Development (OECD) have also proposed the implementation of a DST.
Source: Eversheds Sutherland, "Digital Taxation Map" (Mapme). https://viewer.mapme.com/eversheds-sutherland-digital-tax (accessed 15 September 2024).

### *The OECD Guidelines on the Protection of Privacy and Transborder Flows of Personal Data*

The OECD Guidelines on the Protection of Privacy and Transborder Flows of Personal Data (the OECD Guidelines)[90] result from a collaboration between the OECD member states and other relevant stakeholders.[91] Since first publication in 1980, the OECD Guidelines have undergone multiple revisions, with the latest being in 2013.[92] Although not legally binding, the OECD Guidelines have influenced and transformed the way that domestic privacy laws are drafted. The OECD Guidelines recognize eight principles on data collection that relate to the extent, purpose, and nature of the collection of information, usage of collected data, security safeguards, and individuals' right to know if their information has been collected.[93] These have formed the foundation for data protection legislation from OECD countries and beyond.[94] In addition, notwithstanding other guidelines on how cooperation between countries can be promoted, the OECD recommends nations adopt measures that would aid the implementation to protect data flows. These include the adoption of legislation designed to safeguard data privacy and the establishment of impartial and well-qualified enforcement agencies.[95]

These recommendations can be mirrored toward taxation. For example, the OECD suggests that national strategies on privacy laws that account for cross-government agency coordination should be developed and adopted. In the context of taxation, that does not necessarily nor automatically mean that these policies have to or should solely be aimed at this area. Rather, the development and adoption of domestic strategies and legislation could tackle a combination of taxation and technology-related issues to strike a balance between raising tax revenues and promoting the digital economy.

---

[90] Organisation for Economic Co-operation and Development (OECD). Recommendation of the Council Concerning Guidelines Governing the Protection of Privacy and Transborder Flows of Personal Data, (adopted 23 September 1980) OECD/LEGAL/0188 (hereinafter "The OECD Guidelines").

[91] UNCTAD Data Protection Regulations (footnote 145) 26.

[92] Organisation for Economic Co-operation and Development. OECD Guidelines on the Protection of Privacy and Transborder Flows of Personal Data. https://www.oecd.org/sti/ieconomy/oecdguidelinesontheprotectionofprivacyandtransborderflowsofpersonaldata.htm (accessed 15 September 2024).

[93] The OECD Guidelines (footnote 148) Articles 7–14.

[94] UNCTAD Data Protection Regulations (footnote 145) 26.

[95] The OECD Guidelines (footnote 148) Article 19(c).

Likewise, adherence to the OECD Guidelines' eight principles in taxation will enhance public confidence in the tax administration system. In particular, preventative measures, such as restrictions regarding personal information collection, limits in terms of how they can and are to be used and data safeguards to ensure that they do not fall prey to unauthorized or illegal activities, can be set up in the tax administration and collection systems. These will allow taxpayers to know that only personal data that is required and relevant are collected and that they are adequately protected. In addition, giving individuals the right to seek confirmation as to whether the tax administration and collection system has personal data on them and raising public awareness about the types of data being collected and the purpose for doing so will promote transparency. These are important, given that the focus toward data privacy has continued to grow and gain importance.

### *The International Data Protection Commissioner's Initiatives*

Similar to the OECD Guidelines, the International Data Protection Commissioner's Initiatives are not legally binding, but their influence is far-reaching. These initiatives are introduced by the International Data Protection authorities, whose responsibilities include the supervision of domestic data protection legislation. The initiatives call for the organization of a conference to be held each year, as well as for the establishment of a system that will enable the coordination of complaints that arise transnationally and internationally.[96] Moreover, the initiatives issued the "Montreux Declaration" in 2005,[97] which relates to personal data protection and privacy. Although they have been criticized for a lack (of formal organization or monitoring), these initiatives remain relevant and authoritative, given the reputation of the International Data Protection authorities have in this field.[98]

There is a possibility that International Data Protection Commissioner's Initiatives can be applied to taxation. In the context of DSTs, given how fast-paced technological changes and developments can be, it will be important for the policymakers in charge of introducing digital taxation to at least have a basic understanding of the workings of technology and stay up to

[96] UNCTAD Data Protection Regulations (footnote 145); See also Arner, Castellano, and Selga (2022).

[97] International Conference of Data Protection and Privacy Commissioners. The Protection of Personal Data and Privacy in a Globalised World: A Universal Right Respecting Diversities (adopted on 16 September 2005, and hereinafter the "Montreux Declaration").

[98] Montreux Declaration.

date with digital policy. This can be done so through the organization of an annual tax conference; and since this is not a novel and radical concept,[99] countries would be more receptive to it. Such a tax meeting would also be beneficial for policymakers to gain insights into the relationship between taxation and technology and the impact that DSTs will have on digital policy. These lessons will be crucial when attempts are made to strike a balance between these two areas during the introduction and implementation of DSTs. Moreover, a system for cooperating in taxation complaints will ensure that the integrity and credibility of the taxation system are being upheld; this will also foster transparency and public confidence toward it.

More significantly, compliance with the Montreux Declaration will allow for greater transparency and public confidence in the taxation system. For example, the declaration recognizes the right to data protection and privacy, its contributions to human rights, data flow, and a free market economy, as well as the need to strengthen it when it comes to data procession.[100] Correspondingly, it urges countries to ratify and implement data privacy and protection legislation and mentions the various principles that are relevant to data protection and privacy, including transparency, purpose-specification and limitation, and data security (footnote 111); many of which are specified in the OECD Guidelines. Currently, there is an increasing number of electronic taxation payment systems. Thus, a recognition of a right to data privacy and protection, on top of actions to consolidate and reinforce it, be it an implementation of legislation and compliance toward data privacy principles, will be important. This is because people using these electronic payment systems will be concerned that their personal data could be exploited and whether any measures will be put in place to prevent this from happening.

## *Promoting Corporate Governance*

The digital economy has brought significant changes to the way businesses operate, with significant implications for taxation and corporate governance. In terms of taxation, the digital economy poses challenges to traditional methods of taxation, as the cross-border nature of digital transactions makes it difficult to accurately tax them.

---

[99] For example, the United Nations Climate Change Conferences and the International Energy Agency's Global Conference on Energy Efficiency are both held annually.

[100] Montreux Declaration (footnote 155).

The value of good corporate governance has become increasingly recognized in Asian economies, which has forced many business leaders and controlling shareholders in the region to reevaluate their interactions with their organizations and with minority shareholders who vie for partial ownership in them. However, participants in the Asian Roundtable on Corporate Governance indicate that many businesses are still happy to follow the letter of the law rather than going above and beyond to implement good practices and national codes: this is known as a "box-ticking compliance approach" (OECD 2013). The authorities, professional organizations, investors, and institutes of directors continue to play a significant role in advancing the case for excellent corporate governance. Better corporate governance procedures should also be encouraged by other professional organizations (such as the institutes of accountants, company secretaries, directors, and so on).

The recommendation (OECD Principle I.A) that "the corporate governance framework should be developed with a view to its impact on overall economic performance, market integrity and the incentives it creates for market participants and the promotion of transparent and efficient markets" (footnote 14) is particularly pertinent in the Asian context given the risks of a "box-ticking compliance approach" (footnote 15). The recommendation makes it clear that promoting the advantages of sound corporate governance is, in this context, a crucial aspect of the policy-making environment, with comprehensive and ongoing public engagement a crucial component largely acknowledged as good practice. A few nations have chosen a "champion" organization to guide market-wide corporate governance efforts and changes. With tight collaboration from institutions of directors, professional bodies, and investors, these institutions have enough power to potentially influence the culture and behavior of the industry actors.

Sound corporate governance practices are crucial for doing businesses successfully in the digital economy. Three key practices should be given greater attention: transparent reporting, effective risk management, and responsible use of data. Transparent reporting is critical for ensuring that businesses are accountable to their stakeholders, including investors, employees, customers, and the wider community. This helps to build trust and confidence in the firm and its operations, which is essential in attracting investment, retaining employees, and maintaining customer loyalty. By being transparent in reporting, firms are also better able to manage risk, as they can identify potential issues before they become major problems.

Effective risk management is important in the digital economy as new risks are constantly emerging, such as cyberattacks, data breaches, and technology failures. With strong risk management processes in place, firms are better equipped to mitigate risks and prevent them from hurting their business. This helps to ensure the long-term stability and success of the firm, as well as the protection of its stakeholders. Responsible use of data is also critical in the digital economy, as firms are constantly collecting and using large amounts of personal and sensitive information. Firms must ensure that they use this data ethically and responsibly, and that they protect the privacy and security of their customers' information. This helps to build trust and confidence in the firm and prevents reputational damage and potential legal action.

In sum, sound corporate governance practices are crucial in the digital economy. They help firms to operate effectively, manage risk, and protect their stakeholders. By promoting these practices, businesses can reap the benefits of the digital revolution and avoid its negative consequences.

Transparent reporting, effective risk management, and responsible use of data are especially important in Asia and the Pacific, for several reasons. First, the region is experiencing rapid economic growth, which has led to an increase in the number of businesses in operation. This growth has brought with it new challenges, including increased competition, changing consumer preferences, and new risks, such as cyberattacks and data breaches. By promoting transparent reporting, effective risk management, and responsible use of data, firms in the region can better manage these challenges and ensure their long-term success.

Second, the regulatory environment is rapidly evolving, with many countries in Asia and the Pacific implementing new laws and regulations to address the challenges posed by the digital economy. By having sound corporate governance practices in place, firms in the region can ensure that they comply with these regulations and minimize the risk of legal action.

Third, in the region, reputation is especially important, as consumers are highly influenced by the reputation of a firm. By promoting transparent reporting, effective risk management, and responsible use of data, firms can build trust and gain the confidence of their stakeholders, which is essential in attracting investment, retaining employees, and maintaining customer loyalty. And finally, as a culturally diverse region, Asia and the Pacific has a range of attitudes and values toward business practices. Cultural diversity can sometimes lead to misunderstandings and conflicts, especially when it comes to the use of personal data. By promoting responsible use of data, firms in the region can ensure that they are respecting the cultural attitudes and values of their customers, which again is essential for building trust and confidence.

In sum, the Asia and Pacific region is facing unique challenges and opportunities, and by promoting transparent reporting, effective risk management, and responsible use of data, firms in the region can better manage the digital economy and regulatory challenges and take advantage of these opportunities.

## Conclusion

The digital economy's rapid expansion has profoundly influenced global trade and investment, creating new challenges at the intersection of taxation, trade policies, and data governance. This chapter addresses these challenges and presents strategic recommendations, particularly focusing on Asia and the Pacific.

1. The digital economy has outpaced traditional bilateral tax treaties, which were crafted for a predominantly physical economy. These treaties often fail to adequately address the complexities of taxing digital services and cross-border data flows. To ensure their continued relevance, it is crucial to update these treaties by incorporating provisions tailored to the digital landscape. A significant step in this direction is the adoption of global standards, particularly those outlined in the OECD's Base Erosion and Profit Shifting (BEPS) framework, including the Two-Pillar Solution. Pillar One advocates for reallocating taxing rights to market jurisdictions, enabling countries where substantial digital revenue is generated to tax these profits. Pillar Two proposes a global minimum tax, which is vital in curbing profit shifting to low-tax jurisdictions. The implementation of these measures would bring much-needed clarity and fairness to international tax systems.
2. In the digital economy, data is an invaluable asset, and its protection is paramount, especially within tax systems. Governments must establish robust data privacy frameworks that secure personal data while enabling its legitimate use for tax purposes. Effective data protection laws, aligned with international standards, such as the OECD Guidelines on the Protection of Privacy and Transborder Flows of Personal Data, are

essential. These laws should enforce transparency in data collection and usage, mandate safeguards against unauthorized access, and ensure that taxpayers are fully informed about the handling of their data. Integrating these principles into tax administration is not only crucial for protecting individual privacy, but also for maintaining public trust in digital taxation systems.

3. The digital economy blurs the boundaries between trade and taxation, necessitating a more coordinated policy approach. Regional trade agreements like the Regional Comprehensive Economic Partnership (RCEP) and the Comprehensive and Progressive Agreement for Trans-Pacific Partnership (CPTPP) provide platforms for harmonizing tax policies and enhancing cooperation among tax administrations. However, these agreements should extend beyond reducing trade barriers to include provisions for taxing digital services and frameworks for information exchange between tax authorities. Such coordination is critical in preventing double taxation, curbing tax evasion, and reducing legal disputes, thereby fostering a more predictable and stable business environment. Aligning trade and tax policies is essential for supporting the digital economy's growth while ensuring fair competition and revenue generation.

The evolution of bilateral tax treaties in the digital era will hinge on their ability to adapt to a rapidly changing economic landscape. As multilateral efforts like the OECD's BEPS initiative gain momentum, bilateral treaties must remain flexible to integrate these global standards. The relevance and effectiveness of these treaties in a digitalized world depend on their capacity to evolve alongside global economic trends.

In summary, while the digital economy presents complex challenges for taxation, trade, and data governance, it also offers significant opportunities. Adopting international tax rules that reflect digital realities, enhancing data protection within tax regimes, and fostering greater alignment between trade and tax policies will enable countries—especially in Asia and the Pacific—to effectively navigate this evolving environment, ensuring sustainable economic development.

## References

Adshead, A. 2021. What Digital Transformation Means for Data Storage. *Computer Weekly*. 20. https://www.computerweekly.com/feature/What-digital-transformation-means-for-data-storage (accessed 15 September 2024).

Arner, D W., G G. Castellano, and E K. Selga. 2022. The Transnational Data Governance Problem. *Berkley Tech Law Journal.* 37. p. 623.

Avendano, R. and P. Rosenkranz. 2021. *Digital Platforms and International Taxation in Asia*. Asian Development Bank. https://aric.adb.org/pubs/digitalmarket/managing-development-digital-marketplaces-asia_CH9.pdf.

Blonigen, B A. and R B. Davies. 2009. Do Bilateral Tax Treaties Promote Foreign Direct Investment? In *The Effect of Treaties on Foreign Direct Investment: Bilateral Investment Treaties, Double Taxation Treaties, and Investment Flows*, edited by K P. Sauvant and L E. Sachs. Oxford University Press. https://doi.org/10.1093/acprof:oso/9780195388534.003.0017 (accessed 5 December 2022).

Bulusu, S. and H. Ali. 2020.Global Value-Added Tax Crackdown Costing Firms Millions. *Bloomberg Tax*. 28 January. https://news.bloombergtax.com/daily-labor-report/global-value-added-tax-crackdown-costing-firms-millions?context=article-related (accessed 15 September 2024).

Bunn, D. 2020. US Launches Trade Probe into Digital Taxes. Tax Foundation. 2 June. https://taxfoundation.org/us-trade-representative-ustr-digital-services-tax-investigations/ (accessed 15 September 2024).

Burgstaller, M. and A. Zarowna. 2018. The Growing Importance of Investment Arbitration in Relation to Tax Measures in the Energy and Natural Resources Sectors. *Turkish Commercial Law Review.* 4. p. 81.

Chaisse, J. 2015. Investor-State Arbitration in International Tax Dispute Resolution: A Cut Above Dedicated Tax Dispute Resolution. *Virginia Law Review.* 35. pp. 149–221.

______. 2016. International Investment Law and Taxation: From Coexistence to Cooperation. *The E15 Initiative*, International Centre for Trade and Sustainable Development (ICTSD) and World Economic Forum. https://www.unescap.org/sites/default/files/5b.%202016%20final%20International%20Investment%20Law%20and%20Taxation-%20From%20Coexistence%20to%20Cooperation.pdf (accessed 15 September 2024).

______. 2023a. The Black Pit: Power and Pitfalls of Digital FDI and Cross-Border Data Flows. *World Trade Review*. 22 (1). pp. 73–89. doi:10.1017/S1474745622000337.

______. 2023b. Toward a Big Bang for the Taxation of the Digitalized Economy: A Business Retrospective, Perspective, and Prospective. *Virginia Tax Review*. 41 (3). pp. 345–389.

Chaisse, J. and I. Mosquera. 2022. Public International Law, International Taxation and Tax Dispute Resolution. *Asia Pacific Law Review*. 31 (1). pp. 192–203. doi: 10.1080/10192557.2022.2102585.

Chin, Y C. and J. Zhao. 2022. Governing Cross-Border Data Flows: International Trade Agreements and Their Limits. *Laws*. 11 (4). p. 63.

CLOUDSUFI. 2021. Why is Data the Backbone of the Digital Economy? CLOUDSUFI. https://www.cloudsufi.com/why-is-data-the-backbone-of-the-digital-economy/ (accessed 15 September 2024).

Collin, P. and N. Colin. 2013. *Report to the Minister for the Economy and Finance, the Minister for Industrial Recovery, the Minister Delegate for the Budget and the Minister Delegate for Small and Medium-Sized Enterprises, Innovation and the Digital Economy*. Task Force on Taxation of the Digital Economy, Government of France. https://convention-s.fr/wp-content/uploads/2014/06/Taxation_Digital_Economy_Jan2013_France.pdf.

De Broe, L. and J. Luts. 2015. BEPS Action 6: Tax Treaty Abuse. *Intertax*. 43. p. 122.

De Mello, L. and T. Ter-Minassian. 2020. *Digitalization Challenges and Opportunities for Subnational Governments*. OECD, 2020. https://www.oecd-ilibrary.org/taxation/digitalization-challenges-and-opportunities-for-subnational-governments_9582594a-en (accessed 15 September 2024).

De Mooij, R A. and S. Ederveen. 2003. Taxation and Foreign Direct Investment: A Synthesis of Empirical Research. *International Tax and Public Finance*. 10. pp. 673–693.

Drake-Brockman, J. et al. 2021. Digital Trade and the WTO: Top Trade Negotiation Priorities for Cross-Border Data Flows and Online Trade in Services. *Jean Monnet TIISA Network Working Paper* 2. https://www.t20italy.org/wp-content/uploads/2021/09/TF3_PB04_LM04.pdf (accessed 15 September 2024).

Egger, P H., V. Merlo, and G. Wamser. 2014. Unobserved Tax Avoidance and the Tax Elasticity of FDI. *Journal of Economic Behavior and Organization*. 108. pp. 1–18.

Elliffe, C. 2016. The Lesser of Two Evils: Double Tax Treaty Override or Treaty Abuse. *British Tax Review*. pp. 62–68.

Estevão, M. 2020. Why Digital Transformation Matters for Taxation. *World Bank Blogs*. 12 June. https://blogs.worldbank.org/en/voices/why-digital-transformation-matters-taxation (accessed 15 September 2024).

Frelich, R. 2018. Czech Republic: How and When will Double Tax Treaties be Modified? The Multilateral Instrument Will Amend More than a Thousand Treaties. *Mondaq*. 18 January. https://www.mondaq.com/tax-treaties/665074/how-and-when-will-double-tax-treaties-be-modified-the-multilateral-instrument-will-amend-more-than-a-thousand-treaties.

Friedlander, L. and S. Wilkie. 2006. The History of Tax Treaty Provisions—And Why It Is Important to Know about It. *Canadian Tax Journal*. 54 (4). p. 907.

Government of France. 2020. *Tax Incentives*. March. https://www.impots.gouv.fr (accessed 15 September 2024).

Hebous, S., N. Vernon, and D. Prihardini. 2022. Excess Profit Taxes: Historical Perspective and Contemporary Relevance. *IMF Working Papers*. 2022/187. International Monetary Fund (accessed 15 September 2024).

Hennemann, M., G. Lienemann, and C. Spirkl. 2022. Mapping Global Data Law. Part I: Data Protection Legislation. *University of Passau Institute for Law of the Digital Society Research Paper Series* 22–15. August.

Hodžić, S. 2022. Tax Challenges in the Digital Economy: EU Perspective. In *The New Digital Era: Digitalization, Emerging Risks and Opportunities*. 109A, edited by S. Grima, E. Özen, and H. Boz. Emerald Publishing Limited.

Holmes, K. 2007. *International Tax Policy and Double Tax Treaties: An Introduction to Principles and Application*. IBFD.

Ismail, Y. 2020. *Digital Economy: State of Play and Implications for Developing Countries*. CUTS International.

Juswanto, W. and Y F. Abiyunus. 2023. Taxing the Digitalized Economy: An Emerging Markets Perspective. In *Taxation in the Digital Economy*, edited by N. Hendriyetty et al. Routledge Studies in Developmental Economics.

Kelsey, J. 2020. Important Differences between the Final RCEP Electronic Commerce Chapter and the TPPA and Lessons for e-Commerce in the WTO. *Bilaterals*. 10 February. https://www.bilaterals.org/?important-differences-between-the (accessed 15 September 2024).

Kenya, Central Bank of Kenya and National Bureau of Statistics. 2021. *Foreign Investment Survey 2020*. https://www.centralbank.go.ke/wp-content/uploads/2021/08/Foreign-Investment-Survey-2020-Report.pdf (accessed 15 September 2024).

Kenya, Ministry of ICT. 2019. Digital Economy Blueprint. https://ca.go.ke/wp-content/uploads/2019/05/Kenyas-Digital-Economy-Blueprint.pdf (accessed 15 September 2024).

Kollmann, J. 2019. Taxable Supplies and Their Consideration in European VAT: With Selected Examples of the Digital Economy. *IBFD Doctoral Series* 46. International Bureau of Fiscal Documentation.

Kundaliya, D. 2020. Google and Amazon will Pass Digital Service Tax on to Advertisers. *Computing*. 2 September. https://www.computing.co.uk/news/4019604/google-amazon-digital-service-tax (accessed 15 September 2024).

Latif, L. 2019. The Challenges in Imposing the Digital Tax in Developing African Countries. 9 June. https://papers.ssrn.com/abstract=3901955 (accessed 15 September 2024).

Li, J. 2015. Protecting the Tax Base in a Digital Economy. In *United Nations Handbook on Selected Issues in Protecting the Tax Base of Developing Countries*, edited by A. Trepelkov, H. Tonino, and D. Halka. United Nations Digital Library. https://digitallibrary.un.org/record/1319276?v=pdf (accessed 30 September 2024).

Ludovici, P. and A. Gallizioli. 2022. A Landmark Decision of the Italian Supreme Court Might Finally Lead to a Better Tax Environment for Foreign Investment Funds. International Bar Association. 5 October. https://www.ibanet.org/landmark-decision-might-lead-to-better-tax-environment-for-foreign-investment-funds (accessed 15 September 2024).

Moller, L. 2016. Why Unfair Tax Treaties Hold Back Developing Countries. *The Guardian*. 15 June. https://www.theguardian.com/global-development-professionals-network/2016/jun/15/why-unfair-tax-treaties-hold-back-developing-countries (accessed 15 September 2024).

Morris, W. and P. Brown. 2021. Digital Service Taxes: Are They Here to Stay? PwC. March 4. https://www.pwc.com/us/en/services/tax/library/digital-service-taxes.html (accessed 15 September 2024).

Morton, P. 2012. The EU VAT System in a Digital Age. *International Tax Review*. 1 December. https://www.internationaltaxreview.com/article/2a69ixqe8r3jlfuwdvvuo/the-eu-vat-system-in-a-digital-age (accessed 15 September 2024).

Moulton, B R. 2000. GDP and the Digital Economy: Keeping Up with The Changes. In *Understanding the Digital Economy: Data, Tools, and Research*, edited by Erik Brynjolfsson and Brian Kahin. MIT Press. 1, 34. https://www.bea.gov/sites/default/files/2018-05/gdp-and-the-digital-economy.pdf.

Mpofu, F Y. 2022. Taxation of the Digital Economy and Direct Digital Service Taxes: Opportunities, Challenges, and Implications for African Countries. *Economies*. 10 (9). p. 219.

Mpofu, F. Y. and T. Moloi. 2022. Direct Digital Services Taxes in Africa and the Canons of Taxation. *Laws*. 11 (4). p. 57.

Nathan Associates Inc. 2017. *Promoting the Digital Economy in the ASEAN And APEC Regions*. United States Agency for International Development.

Ndulu, B., C. Joseph, and K. Tryphone. 2021. Fiscal Regimes and Digital Transformation in Sub-Saharan Africa. *Digital Pathways at Oxford*, Blavatnik School of Government and University of Oxford.

Neumayer, E. 2007. Do Double Taxation Treaties Increase Foreign Direct Investment to Developing Countries? *Journal of Development Studies*. 43 (8). pp. 1501–1519.

Organisation for Economic Co-operation and Development (OECD). 2022a. *Progress Report on Amount A of Pillar One, Two-Pillar Solution to the Tax Challenges of the Digitalization of the Economy*. OECD/G20 Base Erosion and Profit Shifting Project. 1 July. https://www.oecd.org/tax/beps/progress-report-on-amount-a-of-pillar-one-july-2022.pdf (accessed 15 September 2024).

_______. 2022b. *Tax Challenges Arising from the Digitalization of the Economy—Global Anti-Base Erosion Model Rules (Pillar Two): Inclusive Framework on BEPS*. OECD/G20 Base Erosion and Profit Shifting Project. https://www.oecd.org/tax/beps/tax-challenges-arising-from-the-digitalization-of-the-economy-global-anti-base-erosion-model-rules-pillar-two.htm.

_______. 2022c. OECD Launches Public Consultation on the Tax Challenges of Digitalization with the Release of a First Building Block under Pillar One. OECD. April 2. https://www.oecd.org/tax/beps/oecd-launches-public-consultation-on-the-tax-challenges-of-digitalization-with-the-release-of-a-first-building-block-under-pillar-one.htm (accessed 15 September 2024).

_______. 2022d. OECD Tax and Development Days 2022. February 17. https://www.oecd.org/tax/tax-and-development-days.htm (accessed 15 September 2024).

_______. 2022e. Signatories and Parties to the Multilateral Convention to Implement Tax Treaty Related Measures to Prevent Base Erosion and Profit Shifting. https://www.oecd.org/tax/beps/beps-mli-signatories-and-parties.pdf (accessed 15 September 2024).

_______. 2022f. Mongolia Signs Landmark Agreement to Strengthen Its Tax Treaties and South Africa Deposits an Instrument for the Ratification of the Multilateral BEPS Convention. 6 October. https://www.oecd.org/tax/beps/mongolia-signs-landmark-agreement-to-strengthen-its-tax-treaties-and-south-africa-deposits-an-instrument-for-the-ratification-of-the-multilateral--beps-convention.htm.

_______. 2015a. Explanatory Statement. OECD/G20 Base Erosion and Profit Shifting Project. https://www.oecd.org/ctp/beps-explanatory-statement-2015.pdf (accessed 15 September 2024).

_______. 2015b. Preventing the Granting of Treaty Benefits in Inappropriate Circumstances, Action 6—2015 Final Report.

_______. 2015c. Making Dispute Resolution Mechanisms More Effective, Action 14—2015 Final Report.

_______. 2013. Reform Priorities in Asia: Taking Corporate Governance to a Higher Level. https://read.oecd-ilibrary.org/governance/reform-priorities-in-asia_9789264204416-en#page1 (accessed 15 September 2024).

_______. 1980. Recommendation of the Council Concerning Guidelines Governing the Protection of Privacy and Transborder Flows of Personal Data. Adopted September 23. OECD LEGAL/0188.

_______. Action 1 Tax Challenges Arising from Digitalization. Action 1—OECD BEPS. https://www.oecd.org/tax/beps/beps-actions/action1/ (accessed 15 September 2024).

_______. Action 14 Mutual Agreement Procedure. Action 14—OECD BEPS. https://www.oecd.org/tax/beps/beps-actions/action14/.

_______. Action 15 Multilateral Instrument. Action 15—OECD BEPS. https://www.oecd.org/tax/beps/beps-actions/action15/.

_______. OECD Guidelines on the Protection of Privacy and Transborder Flows of Personal Data. https://www.oecd.org/sti/ieconomy/oecdguidelinesontheprotectionofprivacyandtransborderflowsofpersonaldata.htm (accessed 15 September 2024).

Ramírez Ocampo, A F. 2019. Scale without Mass: Permanent Establishments in the Digital Economy. *Revista de Direito Tributário Internacional Atual.* 5 (5). p. 13.

Ranjan, P. 2022. Investor-State Dispute Settlement and Tax Matters: Limitations on State's Sovereign Right to Tax. *Asia Pacific Law Review.* 31 (1). pp. 219–234.

Salami, E. 2022. Implementing the AfCFTA Agreement: A Case for the Harmonization of Data Protection Law in Africa. *Journal of African Law.* 66 (2). pp. 281–291.

Samios, Z. Netflix Australian Tax Bill was $868,000 Last Year. *Sydney Morning Herald.* 15 May. https://www.smh.com.au/business/firms/netflix-s-australian-tax-bill-was-868-000-last-year-20220515-p5algf.html (accessed 15 September 2024).

Shukla, V. and S K. Shukla. 2019. Globalization and Tax Jurisdiction. *ZENITH International Journal of Multidisciplinary Research.* 9 (2). pp. 58–64.

Singapore, Ministry of Trade and Industry. 2022. Digital Economy Agreements. Digital Economy Agreements. https://www.mti.gov.sg/Trade/Digital-Economy-Agreements (accessed 15 September 2024).

Strauss, H., D. Schutte, and T. Fawcett. 2020. An Evaluation of the Legislative and Policy Response of Tax Authorities to the Digitalization of the Economy. *South African Journal of Accounting Research.* 35 (3). pp. 239–243.

Tandon, S. 2022. Issues and Challenges with Applying Investment Agreements to Tax Matters in the Context of India's Experience. *Asia Pacific Law Review.* 31 (1). pp. 235–252.

Tong, L. 2021. Vietnam, Singapore Begin Negotiations on Digital Trade Agreement. *The Diplomat*. 30 June. https://thediplomat.com/2021/06/vietnam-singapore-begin-negotiations-on-digital-trade-agreement/.

Trade Union Advisory Committee to the OECD (TUAC). 2021. Global Tax Reform Process Kept Alive. https://tuac.org/wp-content/uploads/2021/07/2107t_beps.pdf (accessed 15 September 2024).

Trenta, C. 2019. European VAT and the Digital Economy: Recent Developments. *eJournal of Tax Research.* 17 (1). pp. 118–133.

United Nations Conference of Trade and Development (UNCTAD). 2021. *Digital Economy Report 2021*. UNCTAD. https://unctad.org/webflyer/digital-economy-report-2021 (accessed 15 September 2024).

______. 2021. Data Protection Regulations. UNCTAD. https://unctad.org/page/data-protection-and-privacy-legislation-worldwide.

United Nations Human Rights Council. 2016. Resolution 32/13: The Promotion, Protection and Enjoyment of Human Rights on the Internet. United Nations, A/HRC/RES/32/13.

United States Department of State. 2022. *2021 Investment Climate Statements*. Government of the United States of America. https://www.state.gov/reports/2021-investment-climate-statements.

Vasudev, V. 2020. Interactions between Taxation Measures and International Investment Agreements. In *Handbook of International Investment Law and Policy* 1, edited by J. Chaisse, L. Choukroune, and S. Jusoh. Springer.

Walde, T. and A. Kolo. 2007. Investor-State Disputes: The Interface between Treaty-Based International Investment Protection and Fiscal Sovereignty. *Intertax*. 35. pp. 424–425.

Walker, K. 2020. A New Global Taxing Right: Report on the Statement by the OECD/G20 Inclusive Framework on BEPS on the Two-Pillar Approach to Address the Tax Challenges Arising from the Digitalization of the Economy. *Fasken Tax Blog*. 29 June. https://taxedinternational.com/a-new-global-taxing-right-report-on-the-statement-by-the-oecd-g20-inclusive-framework-on-beps-on-the-two-pillar-approach-to-address-the-tax-challenges-arising-from-the-digitalisation-of-the/ (accessed 15 September 2024).

Warren, M. and Z. Fa. 2022. Digital Economy Agreements Are a New Frontier for Trade—Here's Why. World Economic Forum, *Agenda*. 24 August. https://www.weforum.org/agenda/2022/08/digital-economy-agreements-trade/. Accessed 15 September 2022.

World Bank. Regulations and Taxes. Enterprises Surveys—What Businesses Experience. https://www.enterprisesurveys.org/en/data/exploretopics/regulations-and-taxes (accessed 15 September 2022).

_______. Why It Matters in Paying Taxes. Subnational Studies—Measuring Business Regulations. https://subnational.doingbusiness.org/en/data/exploretopics/paying-taxes/why-matters (accessed 15 September 2024).

World Trade Organization. 1998. *Work Programme on Electronic Commerce of 30 September 1998. Adopted September 25*. WTO Doc, WT/L274.

Xie, T., M. Chan, and F. Detros. 2021. Gauging Readiness for Digital Economy Agreements. *Asia Competitiveness Institute Research Paper* 18-2021. https://lkyspp.nus.edu.sg/docs/default-source/aci/gauging-readiness-for-digital-economy-agreements.pdf (accessed 15 September 2024).

Zhang, J. et al. 2022. Digital Economy: An Innovation Driving Factor for Low-Carbon Development. *Environmental Impact Assessment Review*. 96. 106821.

www.ingramcontent.com/pod-product-compliance
Lightning Source LLC
Chambersburg PA
CBHW041302210926
51847CB00010B/110
*9789292772932*